# Upon the Elysian Stream

 *Rowing is anything but a natural set of movements. It is not natural to pull sitting down; it is not natural to open and close like a concertina whilst trying to breathe fast; it is not natural to jump with one's feet anchored and one's rump on a moving seat. Nor does it come naturally to co-ordinate all these strange antics with seven other men.*

*Swing Together* by R. D. Burnell, 1952.

Hugh Benjamin Cotton, by Spy, for Vanity Fair 15th March 1894

# Upon the Elysian Stream

## 150 YEARS OF MAGDALEN COLLEGE BOAT CLUB, OXFORD

MARK BLANDFORD-BAKER

The production of this book would not have been possible
without the very generous support provided by the P. F. Trust.
Philip Fleming (below) was stroke of Magdalen's highly successful 1910 and 1911 crews,
and the winning Olympic Eight of 1912. The author is indebted to his son, Robin Fleming,
Chairman of the Trustees, and the other Trustees, for enabling the Boat Club
to copy and digitise many pictures in its archive.

Text © 2008 Mark Blandford-Baker
Layout © 2008 Magdalen College, Oxford
Published in 2008 by Magdalen College, Oxford

Cataloguing in data is available from the British Library

ISBN 978-0-9536435-5-4

Typeset in Baskerville MT,
titles in Edwardian Script and Baskerville MT Bd

Designed by Justin Hunt
Archive photography by John Gibbons
Printed and bound by Butler Tanner & Dennis

# Subscribers

Joseph Abdalla
Lauren Adair
Michael Allingham
A. Kader Allouni
J.M.G. Andrews
Iain Anstess
Dr Arzhang Ardavan
Professor Barry Baker
John P.P. Baker
Lord Balfour of Inchrye
Peter Bancalari
Michael G. Barratt
Dr Viva Bartkus
Michael Barton
Professor Sir John Bell
Alan Naismith Binder, O.B.E.
Michael Bithell
Mr & Mrs Howard Blandford-Baker
Mr Gerald F. Bowden
Alice Brennan
S.J. Brickell, Esq.
J.W. Browne
James Buckley
Clare Bucknell
Nick Burch
Emma Burgham
Captain G.P. Burke
P.C.D. Burnell
Patrick Carroll
Dr Ian Cartmill
Heather Amy Chapman
Kenneth Chapman
Owen J. Clarke
The President and Mrs Clary
Hugh Clay
John Clay
Colin Cooke
Corpus Christi College, Oxford
Mr Jeremy Cotton
Charles Cozens
Dr Andrew Crowther
Peter Cusack
Dr Robin Darwall-Smith
Caroline Dixon
Samuel Dixon
Professor L. Dreyfus
N.S.R. Duffin
Air Commodore Brian Easton
P.S.A. Edwards
Eton College Library and Archives
Kenneth Boothby Everard
Exeter College, Oxford
Robert Fleming
The Revd Walter John Fletcher-Campbell

Daren Forward
Richard A.D. Freeman
Peter Fullerton
Sashikesh Ganeshalingham
Susan George née Carpenter
Elliot F. Gerson
Hugh Gillespie
Gathorne Girdlestone
Sir James Gobbo
Kevin T.L. Gooding
Mr R.A. Greatorex
John Gregg
Neil Guthrie
Philip Halford-MacLeod
J.F. Hall-Craggs
Benjamin Harrop-Griffiths
Robert Allen Hastie
Richard Orbell Havery
Rachael Hawes
Mr & Mrs V.N. Hawes
Antony Hichens
Frank Hodgson
S.E.K. Hulme
Martin Humphrys
Dr Imre Hunyor
Farid A. Husain
Dr & Mrs Bill Ives
Arend Janssen
Marcus Jones
Chris Juckes
A.D. Karenowska
Lucas Kello
Graham Kent
Max B. Kirby
Stefan Knapik
Eric R.W. Knight
Philip and Claudia Krinks
Jon Krohn
Megan Langham
Francis Lascelles-Hadwen
Donald Legget
Ian Le Guillou
Janny M.Y. Leung
Stuart Lever
Hon. Robin W. Lewis
Joshua Lin
Andrew Lodder
Magdalen College Archives
Magdalen College Library
Magdalen College Senior Common Room
Duncan Matthews, Q.C.
Rich Mawdsley
Elizabeth Mayhew
Jonathan McDonagh
Michael McGowan
David Michael Melamed
Donald Menzies
E.G.H. Moody
Dr John Moon

Dr Alfonso Moreno
Mark Mussared
New College Library
Henry Northern
Rosemary N. Nyabadza
Richard Oake
Dr Simon Oakes
Oxford Studies, Oxford Central Library
Judith and Richard Packer
Andrew Porter
Robert Posarsek
John H. Richards
John Rippington
Angus Ritchie
Giles Robbins
Angus Robertson
Louis Rooney
Francis Rose
David Rutherford
St John's College, Oxford
Mrs Sue Salmon
Gordon Sargood
Norman Scarfe
Markus Schwarzlander
Eloise Scotford
Alex Shutter
K.L. Silver
Paul Simpson
Reesha Sodha
Jonathan James Solly
Anthony Smith
David Staton
Alastair Stewart
Ian Stokes
Sarah Strasser and Ben Kremer
Chlöe Strevens
Andrew Tayler
Andy and Nic Thomas
Ian M. Thompson
Brett Tully
A.J. Turberfield
James Turner
G. van Boxel
Richard van Oss
Mrs Venita Vicary
Roger Vickers
T.R. Waterfall
Richard Way
Robin Webster
Kenneth Wells
Tom Westerling
Sir Michael Wheeler-Booth
M.D. Williams
Dr Peter Wothers
Elizabeth Wray
T.E. Wright
Christopher J.S. Young
Gavin Young
H.A. Zarach

Magdalen College Eight. 1859.

H.B. Middleton. 7       P.J.S. Stanhope. Cox.    T.H.T. Hopkins. Stroke.    W.G.G. Austin. 5.

W.D. Mackenzie. 2    E.V. Westmacott. Bow.   G. Norsworthy. 6.    T.S. Tuckwell. 4.    H.R. Marres. 3.

# Foreword

Magdalen College Boat Club is a remarkable institution with a magnificent history. There is something about going out on the river in those icy early mornings in the middle of winter that creates lifelong friendships and deep loyalty. If you row for the College, whether it is in the first boat going Head of the River or the fourth boat getting bumped on the first day of Eights Week, you are a member of the Boat Club for life.

In this superbly illustrated book Mark Blandford-Baker catches the special spirit of the Magdalen Boat Club. He traces the origins of Magdalen rowing back to 1836 when Tom Harris rowed for Oxford in the second Boat Race and shows how increased participation in the sport led to the formation of the Boat Club in 1859. He goes on to tell the stories of the characters who built the fine traditions of rowing in the College such as the legendary Benjie Cotton, the Nickalls brothers and Harcourt Gold. He describes the highly successful years of the late 1800s and early 1900s when the majority of the Oxford Boat Race crew were from Magdalen. The magnificent 1912 Olympics, when we had seven oarsmen and the cox in the Eight who won gold medals, features prominently. Women were first admitted to the College in 1979 and their enthusiastic participation in the Boat Club is fully described. The book finishes with a proud description of the return to excellence in the early 2000s with four consecutive Heads of the River.

The fascinating and extensive illustrations vividly portray the colourful paraphernalia associated with the Boat Club such as scarlet ties, jackets, scarves, caps and flags which invariably display the lily of William Waynflete who founded the College 550 years ago. The spectacular range of oars, medals and trophies which have been won by so many Magdalen rowers and crews also feature prominently. Pride of place goes to the Head of the River Trophy which has the names of all winning crews on its base. It is not just races on the Isis that are described but many successes at Henley and on rivers further away are documented also. Those who like statistics will be pleased to find full details of races and rowers in the years for which records are available.

Mark Blandford-Baker describes how college crews in 1841 entered the Henley Regatta with pseudonyms so as not to receive the displeasure of their Heads of House who perhaps were worried about the influence of this new sport in Oxford. I am pleased to say that this has all changed and the President of Magdalen is now delighted to join the throng of vociferous students and supporters who gather to cheer on our boats in Torpids or Eights.

## Professor David Clary
President of Magdalen, October 2008

# Contents

# Acknowledgements

The author is grateful to the many who have contributed to the preparation of this book and enabled it to become more than an idea. Magdalen's Archivist, Dr Robin Darwall-Smith has been principal among those who have helped – tirelessly assisting with queries and searches, a great source of wisdom and guidance. Roger Hutchins generously allowed me to use his work on *Well Rowed Magdalen!*, without let or hindrance; it was, of course, invaluable. Emma Burgham's recataloguing of the Boat Club archive, during her year as graduate trainee archivist, made the whole task much easier. Angus Robertson has read every page with the same care he has been applying over many years to Henley records, always very speedy and thorough; his suggestions have been a great help.

My Secretary, Marilyn Evans, endures much but kindly agreed to handle the subscription forms. The great support that she unflinchingly provides is much appreciated. Dr Christine Ferdinand, Magdalen's Fellow Librarian, has given guidance and allowed the book to be published in the College's name. Of my other colleagues on the Fellowship, I have benefitted from the wisdom and patience of Dr Robert Douglas-Fairhurst and the Vice-President, Dr Ralph Walker. I am also grateful to the College Accountant, Heather Rossotti, and her team for their care of the Boat Club's accounts.

Particular thanks are due to the Rt. Hon. Christopher Geidt, Private Secretary to H.M. The Queen, for guidance over the use of the letters of Edward, Prince of Wales. I have known Mark Nelson-Griffiths since I was 11 years old, we remain close friends, and, though one of the world's leading fencing coaches, he has never been involved in rowing but acquired R.S.C. Lucas's entire medal collection and kindly allowed them to be photographed. Candida Lycett Green's support, in allowing me to reproduce two of her late father's poems, is generous. During his time at Magdalen Sir John Betjeman did not row but his works on Henley show perfectly how he had grasped the essence of the sport and life on the river.

John Gibbons has made a marvellous job of photographing innumerable items in the Boat Club collection, thereby enabling them to appear here but also preserving them for the archive. Justin Hunt caught my attention with his work on *Water Boiling Aft*, Chris Dodd's history of London Rowing Club, and I was delighted when he agreed to design this book. He has given great care and attention to its feel and prepared it for printing. Without these two, this book would be no more than pages of plain text. Quite sizeable amounts of this book were written during intensive periods away from Oxford and that would not have been possible but for the use of cottages in Kirkby Lonsdale and Castle Acre; for which I am indebted to Reuben and Willow Johnson, and to Bob Greatorex and Carol Mahoney respectively. The team at the Summer Isles Hotel, Achiltibuie, run one of the very best hotels in the country and provide an atmosphere conducive to writing. Had Duncan and Christine McKie not introduced me to the hotel years ago, I might not have discovered the glorious and rugged country of Assynt Coigach.

Much of the material comes from the Boat Club archive but many have assisted with information, anecdotes, pictures and help, including: Sarah Boada-Momtahan, Peter Burnell, Diana Cook, Charles Cozens, Chris Dodd, Professor Robin Dunbar, The Rev Jock Fletcher-Campbell, John Friend, Peter Fullerton, Gathorne Girdlestone, Daniel Grist, Dr Tim Hands, Eric Houston, Richard Hunt, Donald Legget, Hon. Robin Lewis, David Lloyd, Andrew Lodder, Kate Longworth, Peter Nordberg, Hart Perry, Sophie Petersen, Angus Ritchie, Dan Robson, Michael Rowe, David Rutherford, Mark Simon, Chlöe Strevens, Alastair Stewart, Mike Sweeney, Peter Treloar: Hon. Secretary of St John's Barge Ltd., Andy Trotman, Richard Van Oss.

The following bodies have given gracious permission for items to be quoted or photographed: Henley Royal Regatta (quote from the Committee of Management Minute Book, the Record of Nickalls and Lucas race of 1924, and photograph of the Silver Goblets and Nickalls' Challenge Cup), Imperial War Museum (picture of J.R. Somers-Smith), Leander Club (cartoons of R.D. Burnell, J.L. Garton and G.O. Nickalls, and the 1907 Henley Tribute), Magdalen College School (photographs of School oarsmen who joined the College), The *Oxford Mail* (reproduction of the article on the glassfibre boat), River and Rowing Museum (photographs of a number of items in the collection), *The Times* (reproduction of the articles of 1859 and 1911), Vincent's Club (photographs of the club's Magdalen Presidents).

# Introduction

Team spirit and the friendships formed in sport are as much a part of why the competitive streak bonds a person to that activity just as much as the physical and mental skills they can bring to it gives them satisfaction in taking part and in enjoying success. Rowing, perhaps above all other sports, engenders the team spirit. For without it an eight or a four cannot work; the common purpose is reached by the same task being achieved together. All have to do the same thing at the same time; not for the boat is there the divergence of skills seen on a rugby pitch. The aim is common and a crew works together in a quite different way to the players on a pitch. The role of the coxswain is unlike that of any other sport – a competitor, but with an entirely different job to the rest of the crew, and yet also having to act as motivator, and sometimes coach, whilst steering and working to a plan. The single sculler is perhaps more like the track athlete, alone with their wits to drive them, yet on the water the ability to cope on their own with the elements often marks out the very best from the rest.

When rowing developed from being either purely recreational, or from a means of earning a living, into a competitive sport, the Universities and Colleges of Oxford and Cambridge were among the first to form clubs and challenge each other to race. Magdalen College, Oxford was a late-comer to this diversion, probably mainly because it was a very small body until the later part of the nineteenth century. Life has changed since, and whilst the Oxford Colleges are generally smaller than their Cambridge counterparts, Magdalen has grown more than many of its neighbours. The arrival of women and the increase in graduate students have both had their influence not only on the life of a college but also of its Boat Club. Magdalen is no exception.

What does mark out Magdalen College Boat Club from the rest is it place in the history of the sport not only on the Isis, but at University and national level. There is no satisfactory algorithm for determining an absolute position in the rowing firmament but a soup of achievements in Torpids and Eights combined with Henley Royal Regatta, international representation and the contributions of some notable individuals must put M.C.B.C. in the top four or five of the Oxbridge College Boat Clubs, indeed the upper echelons of rowing clubs generally.

However, this history is about much more than pure success. I have tried to paint a picture that gives some insight to the characters that have made up the Boat Club, and sometimes what they have gone on to achieve after Oxford. In trying to write for those who know of the sport but not the College and vice versa, I hope I have provided some context of both elements that explains to some extent what was going on and why. The quantity and quality of material available for the research varies enormously over the 150 years. This is partly due to the degree of diligence applied by some Club Officers but also to how well things have been preserved. In the electronic age in which we now live it is more important than ever to ensure writings and images are stored for their historical value. I urge the future generations of Magdalen oarsmen and women to commit their records to paper, as well as to disk, and to add to the archive so carefully stored in the College towers. In selecting the items to be photographed for this book, I have sought to digitise as much material as possible so that as originals deteriorate we have a record of them for the future.

While the Boat Club has been marking its 150th year, the College has been celebrating its foundation 550 years ago. Both have a fascinating and distinguished history; I trust the reader will get as much out of this small contribution to recording our past as I have out writing it. Perhaps most importantly, I hope it will inspire future generations of Magdalen members to go down to the river and join a very special club that will bring the enjoyment and satisfaction of time spent in boats but also form lasting friendships from that common purpose.

Magdalen College, Oxford
Michaelmas Day 2008

The 2008 Eights

# 1 pre 1859

## Early Beginnings

The earliest record of Magdalen and rowing begins in 1836 with the second University Boat Race on a course from Westminster to Putney. In that year Tom Harris rowed in the losing Oxford crew. He was in the middle of the boat, in the number 4 seat. Harris, then 25 years old, had been elected a Fellow of the College the previous autumn. There was a lot of debate between the Universities over the arrangements for the race: the length and location of the course, whether with or against the tide, and the use of professional watermen as steerers. Eventually it was settled that the course would be from Westminster to Putney, with student coxes, and the race took place on 17th June. The Oxford crew wore white jerseys with dark blue stripes, Cambridge were wearing plain white; just before the boats went out it was noted that the Fenland crew had no colours and a Cambridge supporter ran over to a haberdasher's shop and bought a piece of Eton blue ribbon and then affixed it to the bows of the boat. There is no detailed account of the race but Cambridge won easily, nearly a minute ahead of Oxford, in 36 minutes. This second race between the two Universities was the first on London waters and their rowing was criticised by watermen and amateurs alike. Amateur talent had not yet sufficiently developed to be effective in a coaching capacity and the crews had apparently had little professional coaching until they reached the Tideway. Harris's crew mates included three undergraduates from Christ Church (two of whom were Baronets), two from Jesus College and one each from St John's, Balliol and Exeter. At 12 stone 4 pounds, Harris was the second heaviest man in a crew which averaged 11 stone $7^{3}/_{4}$ pounds.[1]

Rugby was not a rowing school and Harris had been there just after William Webb Ellis invented the great game that bears its name; it is likely he played as games were a compulsory activity. When he came to Oxford in 1828 he spent his first undergraduate year at Exeter College, whose first records of a structured and established Boat Club date from 1831, and he went down to the river for the first time. A year later Harris was elected to a Demyship at Magdalen though it seems he may have continued to row with friends at Exeter for there is no record of any racing boats at Magdalen then or for a long while after. He took a 2nd in Lit. Hum. in 1833; during his time as a Fellow he held many of the College Officerships.

Rowing at Oxford seems to have begun soon after the beginning of the 19*th* century, but the accounts of that time are merely traditionary. A variety of boats were used, much wider recreational craft than the fine racing shells that were to follow. One of the earliest descriptions is of a crew 'which consisted of four rowers, a steersman, and two trimmers, seven in all.' The first accounts of eight-oared boat racing in Oxford are from 1815 when Brasenose College were Head with Jesus College possibly the only other competitor. The Oxford University Boat Club was founded in 1839.

# Rowing at Oxford seems to have begun soon after the beginning of the 19th century, but the accounts of that time are merely traditionary

The same year Magdalen College School founded its Boat Club, called the Lily Boat Club, the records referring to 'boating' rather than 'rowing'. In that first year they joined the end of the Procession of Boats, held a few days after Eights Week, the rowed with 'an elegant little flag, blue with white lilies, at the stern….. The dress of the crew consisted of blue striped jerseys, straw hats and blue ribbons.'[2] This was precisely the colours of clothing adopted by the College Boat Club at its foundation. Indeed, it used these colours prior to that as the book *Oxford Aquatic Dresses*, published in 1856 shows, but the flag shown is red (the lilies were added later). It is not clear why red was chosen; it was soon to become the adopted colour of sports at both College and School, alongside the black and white of the arms.

Though the foundation of Magdalen's Boat Club was not to occur until 1859, as with other colleges, there was much activity on the river well before that mainly on a social and pleasure basis. Early on six-oared boats were rented rather than owned and early beginnings grew out of friendships translated into casual afternoon expeditions, sometimes with picnics. Crews customarily rowed down to Sandford or Nuneham and back. It is probable that on leaving Iffley Lock on the return journey some chasing and racing home developed. These early rowing men dashing for home would have had little thought that they were making history and revolutionising sport; such trips, and the organised races which followed, were unnoticed and unrecorded. Though Oxford records are incomplete, Cambridge racing, which had begun some twelve years earlier, has been chronicled from the start and gives some insight to the process taking place on the Isis. Eight-oared boats probably found their way to Oxford from Eton as they became the racing boat of choice over the ten-oared and the six, though the latter continued to be used in inter-university contests in the United States of America until the mid 1870s.[3] Accounts of collegiate racing in 1824 explain that racing began from Iffley Lock where the boats would be held in the pound until the start was given. At that moment the lock gates were opened and the boats scrambled out as best they could. The usual method was for stroke to stand in the bows with a boat hook and, as the gate swung open, to run down the middle of the boat on a plank or 'gangway' which separated the oarsmen on one side from the other, jump into his seat and begin to row. Alternatively, the stroke would push the boat out with his hands, going down the side of the boat just inside the gunwale, in which case the crew sat with their oars tossed (held vertical). The lock could hold only four boats and so in 1825 when a larger number of colleges put on boats, a new system was started, and they took their stations 100 feet apart – the arrangement which remains in place today. Little change took place in the design of the boats until 1837 when it is recorded that Balliol rowed without a gang-board for the first time. [4]

After Cricket, which was much earlier, Rowing was among the first recreations to become a competitive sport. Indeed as single sculling racing its roots go back to 1715 when Thomas Doggett, the famous comedian, created the wager for newly-qualified watermen from London Bridge to the White Swan Inn near Chelsea Bridge, raced against the tide; a race which has continued annually unbroken to the present day. The first Oxford and Cambridge Boat Race was in 1829, the Wingfield Sculls were instituted in 1831 (to become the Amateur Championship of the Thames in 1849), and the first regatta at Henley followed in 1839. This time before the foundation of the College Boat Club was a period when the question of what constituted amateurism raged; essentially a social issue of gentlemen and the working classes. This went through a variety of debates and attempts at definition but did not settle until the twentieth century. Collegiate and university rowing was largely unaffected by such matters though in the early 1820s there had been a dis-

Leaving Iffley Lock. Note the
stroke man pushing off.
(see page 17)

pute over watermen rowing in some college boats; such was the argument that no Eights were held in 1823 and the practice was ceased.

Virtually nothing is known of rowing at Magdalen during these early years of development elsewhere. Tom Harris may have opened the book for the College, and for the Senior Common Room, but further recorded activity is patchy through the following two decades. Much of the early Oxford records and accounts were written by the Revd. W.E. Sherwood, who had been at Christ Church, was a Fellow of Magdalen, Master of Magdalen College School from 1888 to 1900 and sometime Mayor of Oxford; and by Sir Courtenay Knollys who was an undergraduate of the College in the 1870s and a highly successful oarsman. Sherwood was Treasurer of the O.U.B.C. from 1874 to 77 and again from 1890 for many years. The O.U.B.C. records show that Magdalen 'put on' a boat for the last two nights of the 1837 Eights then a gap followed until a combined crew of Magdalen and Corpus Christi was entered in 1845. This eight first appeared on the third evening of the races, in an outrigger boat built by Venables. They named themselves *Caudlen* and made a bump, rose two more places through boats above them taking off. They withdrew for the last two nights' racing. A year later Magdalen found nine of its own men for the first time and starting fifteenth at the bottom of the order, rowed on the second evening. However they finished in fourteenth position as Oriel had withdrawn. The College, with its tiny undergraduate population during this period, did not enter Eights again until the Boat Club was founded in 1859.

In 1842 a crew competed in a four-oared boat at Reading Amateur Regatta, racing St John's and Wadham Colleges. 150 years on, Magdalen was invited back to mark that anniversary and sent a scratch crew which beat the same pair of opponents.

During this period the Eights races were held in early May, from 1852 the second boats, or Torpids, raced separately in June; the Procession of Boats followed a few days later. Magdalen sometimes rented a boat from a waterman but were not always able to put a crew together even for the June racing. This problem was shared by New College; both they and Magdalen had only around 40 undergraduates each in the period 1842-61 and were therefore weaker than some of the private Halls. This question of size has much to do with why Magdalen was so late among the colleges in founding a boat club. Nonetheless individual men of talent competed; in 1846 Edward Graham Moon (later to become a knighted cleric on succeeding to a baronetcy and becoming vicar of Fetcham in Surrey) won both the recently instituted O.U.B.C. Sculls, and Diamond Challenge Sculls at Henley; the end of his first year at the College. It is thought his use of a mahogany outrigger, built by Clasper of Derwenthaugh, was a first for the university races; however it was eyed with suspicion by his rivals who objected to the Proctors on grounds of safety. The Proctor was Tom Harris, Magdalen's first Blue and now a Fellow of 21 years' standing: the decision went in Moon's favour. His opponent in the final was W. Wilberforce of St Mary's Hall. Moon's success at Henley was the first time the College's name appeared in the Henley programme; a year later, and despite not having won a Blue, he was in the bow seat of the University boat that won the Grand Challenge Cup. The 1849 races for the O.U.B.C. Sculls were conducted in the form of bumping races (as they, and the pairs challenge, had been for a few years); C.H. Cholmeley and J.E. Henderson competed for Magdalen. In the third round no bumps occurred so the scullers raced again and still no bumps were made so a draw was held for side by side racing, neither Magdalen man made it to the final. In 1858 W.G.G. Austin became Magdalen's second Blue rowing in the 4 seat of the losing Oxford crew.

It is not quite accurate to say that Moon's appearance at Henley was the first time the College's name had been in the programme. At the 1841 regatta various Oxford colleges entered under pseudonyms to appease their Head of House. In the preceding couple of years crews had entered, not unreasonably, in the name of their respective colleges. However this was an era when inter-collegiate competitive sport was somewhat new and though natural to use the name to reflect the crew, permissions had not been sought. Trinity entered The Grand Challenge Cup as 'The Pope', Brasenose as 'The Childe of Hale Club', these being the names of their boats. Another entry was 'The John Cross Club' and this consisted of four men from University College, in whose colours of blue and yellow they rowed. The rest of the crew was made up of two from Oriel, and one each from Worcester, St John's and Magdalen. The Regatta Records list the person from Magdalen as being called Macdie, with no initials shown, occupying the bow seat. There was no one in the University at that time bearing this surname but a closer look at the other members of the crew shows that they were nearly all Scottish. The Magdalen lists of the period give no clue as to who this oarsman might have been and so the College's first appearance at Henley is a mystery. This crew lost in the first heat.[5]

# a 'critical enquiry into the after health of the men who rowed in the Oxford and Cambridge Boat Race from 1829 to 1869'

Before leaving the era prior to the Club's foundation it is interesting to note that in this period of the rise of competitive sport there was some concern about the impact of strenuous exercise on the health of participants. Dr John Morgan, a member of the university, conducted a 'critical enquiry into the after health of the men who rowed in the Oxford and Cambridge Boat Race from 1829 to 1869' and published his findings in 1873 under the title *University Oars*. Tom Harris was one of the oarsmen to whom he wrote over thirty years after he had made the College's debut rowing for Oxford. Morgan asked these men 'whether the training and exertions demanded of men who row in the Oxford and Cambridge Race are of so trying a character that in numerous instances the constitution is liable to be permanently injured?' Harris replied:

'For my own part I can safely say that I am not aware that my health has suffered in any way either now or in the past. I would observe, however, that in those early days the training was neither so strict nor so protracted as it has become since. Indeed, little was ordinarily done in that respect at that time, beyond an extra beefsteak occasionally, abstinence from pastry &., and moderation in the use of wine, cigars &., not, I fear, always very strictly observed. Whether the health would be more likely to suffer from this loose training than from a stricter system, prolonged for an excessive length of time, you will be better able to judge than myself. I am sorry that I cannot give you more information upon a subject which has naturally much interest for old lovers of the oar.'[6]

While this research may cause a smile today it is worth reflecting that through all the benefits of modern science and the known effects of diet upon health, at the same time as using that knowledge to good effect, much of it comes back to a question of moderation. Thomas Harris, who died in August 1895, lived to the age of 84.

The Senior Common Room's interest in rowing was wider than Harris's activity on the river; the S.C.R. Betting Book is littered with Fellows challenging each other on the outcome of, typically, the Boat Race. The first recorded wager is between Harris and John Henderson in 1846 in which the Magdalen Blue bets Henderson that Brasenose will beat 1st Trinity B.C. (Cambridge) at Henley. Henderson's opinion paid off and Harris delivered up the wagered bottle of wine. Henderson, who was for many years Bursar of the College, developed a taste for the spoils of betting on rowing and frequently wagered Professor Marmaduke Lawson, the Sheradian Professor of Botany, on the outcome of the (by then) annual race between the two universities. Lawson had been an undergraduate in Cambridge and retained a loyalty to the light blue flag regardless of what the form book said in a particular year. The wager was invariably a bottle of Port. By 1874 the pair had agreed to 'make the bet every year so long as both able to pay for and drink same'.[7] For a while after the outcome is recorded but it seems the ink dried up before the money expired and ability to swallow failed.

Oxford aquatic dresses 1858. The first Magdalen rowing uniform and flag.

There are one or two insights that in the years immediately prior to the founding of the College boat club there was some activity on the river that must have had the makings of structure. A four-oared boat had been out in the Michaelmas Term of 1853, coxed by F.M. Millard (Demy 1853-67, Fellow 1867-70), and who had rescued a boy whose canoe overturned on a crowded river. Many of the other boats were preparing to race, it seems the Magdalen four were sim-

ply out for pleasure.[8] The start of the Frederick Bulley Presidency in 1855, succeeding Routh's 63 years as Head of House, may have given impetus to the foundation of the Boat Club. In the years to follow he was a great supporter and his son rowed in winning Magdalen crews. The publication *Oxford Aquatic Dresses* dated 1856, a pocket book with a college to a page, shows a cartoon of the oarsman's uniform and the flag for each club. Magdalen has an entry.

[1] G.C. Drinkwater and T.R.B. Sanders, The University Boat Race Official Centenary History, Cassell & Co. 1929

[2] J.E. Millard, Magdalen College School Journal 1839, Magdalen College School Archive

[3] W.E. Sherwood, Oxford Rowing, Henry Frowde 1900

[4] C.C.Knollys, Oxford University Challenge Races, OUP 1873

[5] H.T. Steward, Records of Henley Royal Regatta, Grant Richards 1903

[6] John Ed. Morgan, MD, MA Oxon, FRCP, University Oars, Macmillan 1873

[7] Senior Common Room Betting book, Magdalen College Archive, MC: O1/F1/2

[8] L.S. Tuckwell, Old Magdalen Days 1847-1877, Blackwell 1913

Below left: Foundationers' Four 1858. Below right: Commoners' four 1859. Opposite bottom: H.B. Middletons' medal, 1859

Left to right:

H.G. Alington    2
H.B. Middleton   Bow
G.W. Rawdon      Cox
H.R. Morris      3
L.S. Tuckwell    Stroke

Left to right:

A.H. Arnold      2
D.N. Mackenzie   Bow
M.F.B. Portman   Cox
G.H. Barne       3
G. Norsworthy    Stroke

# 2 1859-1879

## Foundation and the Fledgling Club

About the beginning of the year 1859 it was decided by those who were to found the Boat Club that the College should compete in the forthcoming Summer Races, and, in order to stimulate an interest in boating matters and in the hope of increasing the proficiency of the proposed eight, an undergraduate instituted an annual race between two four-oared boats which represented the two classes in the College of Foundationers and non-Foundationers (essentially Fellows, Scholars and Clerks; and the rest of the undergraduate population), and he generously covered the expense of silver medals to be awarded to the winning crew. This offer was accepted with the greatest enthusiasm, and crews were quickly chosen and training begun, and before the end of term the race was held.

So intense was the spirit of rivalry which drove both crews that their friendly relations were somewhat strained, and some of them felt this so keenly that they found it hard to keep on speaking terms with some of their opponents, and, as the date of the race drew near, the Foundationers agreed that it was advisable to take another route to the racing course to that which had been taken by their opponents. One crew took the road through Bagley Wood, while the other went through Nuneham Park to Abingdon.

The course was from Abingdon Lasher to Nuneham Island. The race was keenly contested, and at the close the Foundationers felt sure that it had ended in a dead heat, but the judges, two oarsmen of considerable experience, decided in favour of the non-Foundationers. The other crew accepted the verdict and after the result was announced good relations were re-established between the crews, they returned by the same route to College and that evening they dined together in Hall.[1] However, this newly structured activity took a little settling down within College. Bulley records in his President's Notebook that, on 5th April, he 'gave instructions to the Senior Dean not to allow the under-graduates to lounge about in College in their Boating Dress' or 'to wear within the College gates any head gear other than an academical cap'.[2]

# In Magdalen the foundation of the boat club was initiated principally by the influence of W.G.G. Austin, T.H.T. Hopkins and G. Norsworthy.

Whilst the change of President may have been a catalyst for the creation of the boat club, and the College undergraduate numbers were growing, other changes taking place on the river itself are probably part of the fuller picture that lead to the club's institution. The previous year, 1858, had seen the Eights racing changed to consecutive nights' competition thus adding to the importance of the event which had begun in 1852 with the Torpids moving to Hilary Term where they became feeders for Eights rather than mere second boats. In the same year O.U.B.C. began Trial Eights as a means of selecting men for the university boat for its race against Cambridge which had become an annual event from 1856; the year in which keel-less boats were first used on the Isis . A year later however, the O.U.B.C. President was to find himself short of men as the fears of an invasion of England by Napoleon III led to the formation of the Rifle Volunteer Corps across the country which was taken up enthusiastically at the University; Fridays on the river were relinquished to Corps activities and the Isis was almost deserted.[3] In Magdalen the foundation of the boat club was initiated principally by the influence of W.G.G. Austin, T.H.T. Hopkins and G. Norsworthy. These three men all came from rowing schools:

A pair of silver gilt claret jugs presented by G. Norsworthy in 1859 and R.C. Lehmann in 1895.
(see detail opposite)

William Austin, born in 1835, from Bath had been at Radley and arrived at Magdalen as a Demy in 1853. In addition to winning his Blue in 1858 he took a Third in Classics. He went on to become Chaplain to the Bishop of Guiana (which episcopate his father had previously held) and later Inspector of Schools there. Thomas Hopkins, born in 1831, was at Eton and was elected to a Demyship at Magdalen in the same year as Austin. He took a Third in Lit. Hum., and was ordained Deacon in 1858. A keen woodworker, he kept a lathe in his rooms. Having been elected a Fellow, he taught science in the Daubeny Laboratory and was Estates Bursar and Senior Tutor for various years and was Dean of Divinity. Hopkins was a keen supporter of the College School and its rowing and often coached the Four on the Cherwell. His health failed and he died at the age of 54; the first College Barge was commissioned from subscriptions raised in his memory. George Norsworthy, born in 1837, from Pinkneys Green near Maidenhead, began his education at Winchester, and was a Commoner at Magdalen from 1856. He became a barrister and was a noted rifle shot. In this first year of the Club, Norsworthy presented a silver-gilt claret jug bearing the Magdalen arms and inscribed as being a trophy for a pair-oared race. Having stroked the winning Trial Eight, he took the College's third Blue, and first after the foundation of the Boat Club, in 1860 rowing in the 2 seat of the losing Boat Race crew.

Four Oar Challenge Cup
presented by G. Norsworthy,
1859

**THE PROCCESSION OF THE BOATS, OXFORD.**

By G. Howse, Published 1st June 1859 by James Ryman, 25 High Street, Oxford.

Article in *The Times* 6th June, 1859.

These gentlemen, together with Messrs Mackenzie, Middleton, Morris, Stanhope (steerer), Tuckwell (a former chorister at the College School) and Westmacott formed the first Magdalen College Boat Club eight and prepared for the Summer Eights held in the first days of June 1859. Thus as the new boat of invited men including one Fellow, they started at sixteenth at the bottom of the order. They made a remarkable beginning achieving seven bumps at the expense of Queen's, Worcester, Corpus Christi, Wadham, Jesus, St John's and lastly Christ Church. Having bumped each of the seven nights, as was the custom of the time, Magdalen claimed an extra, eighth, night though they rowed over having failed to bump Trinity, on whom they had overlap, through the steering of an experienced Blue Boat coxswain. On that last night they finished eighth on the river (rather than ninth, Queen's having dropped out during the week). This achievement created sufficient attention that it was reported in

*The Times* as early as the morning after the fourth day's racing. The President allowed the crew to have a supper in Hall the night after the races, under the superintendence of the Vice-President.[4]

After the exam season, during Commemoration, the annual Procession of Boats was staged, at 7.30pm on 22*nd* June. This spectacle was therefore a week or two after Eights Week. The crews lined themselves up at Iffley in the finishing order and rowed up the river to salute the Head Boat stationed at the O.U.B.C. barge where a band was playing. The recognition of the Head Boat was performed in a style used at Eton for the '4th of June' festivities to mark the birthday of King George III. As they passed the Head Boat each crew in turn raised ('tossed') its oars vertically, sometimes standing up at the same time. This salute was returned by the Head Boat. Each crew then rowed on, before losing way, under Folly Bridge to turn and come back downstream through the other arch to the Gut and then to their barges. The barges were decked with the college boat club flags, while the coxswain also had a large flag fixed behind their seat; the crews all wore hats and boating jackets.

# As they passed the Head Boat each crew in turn raised ('tossed') its oars vertically, sometimes standing up at the same time.

The period from foundation in 1859 to 1887 is poorly documented in that the early Captains' and Secretaries' log books no longer exist. Information on this period comes from a number of other sources though with little detail. It was typical of college clubs in this period to elect the stroke as Captain. The Appendices to this book make that assumption in the absence of any other evidence. Norsworthy competed in the University Pairs in M.C.B.C.'s founding year, partnering L.P. Evans of Corpus Christi. They lost the final to a St John's pair by 6 seconds. In 1860 he again competed in this event, this time with A.H. Arnould, also of Magdalen, losing to Wadham in the third heat. Norsworthy's brother Henry raced with W.B. Monck in the 1862 challenge losing 'easily' to Brasenose in the final.

In the Hilary Term of 1860 Magdalen entered its first Torpids and started at fourteenth, the bottom position. Rowing over on the first

MAGDALEN COLLEGE EIGHT, 1892.
HEAD OF THE RIVER
Bow W. M. Poole... 10.5.
2. R.S. Medlicott. 11.0.
3. T. Royden.... 11.5.
4. G.H. Foster... 11.0.
5. A.H.P. Clarke. 12.8.
6. V. Nickalls... 12.12.
7. R.P.P. Rowe... 11.12.
Str. H.B. Cotton... 9.12.
Cox. G.B.H. Fell... 8.6.
Coach. F.P. Bulley

R. A. Talboys.

day they bumped Exeter II on the second, rowed over again on the third day and bumped Lincoln next. Queen's and Oriel fell to them on the remaining afternoons, thus they finished tenth. A week or so later athletic sports for the first time took place on the water meadow by the Cherwell. This activity emulated similar events at Christ Church, Exeter and Oriel.[5] For their second season in Summer Eights Magdalen, buoyed up by the success of their first year, backed themselves very heavily to make four bumps.[6.] In fact they achieved only two. Over the next two years both the Torpid and the Summer Eight crews rose up the table without conceding a bump. By the end of 1862 they were lying fifth in the Torpids and fourth in Eights. In 1863 there

was a shortage of oarsmen and the Revd Thomas Hopkins substituted as an emergency measure to prevent the first bump against Magdalen in Eights. This action did not save them and they fell one place to University College. The Torpid had already slid three places in March. This panic action of substitution, using old members, was repeated in Magdalen and three other colleges in 1865. Magdalen dropped in Middleton who along with the other substitutes was training at the recently-founded Kingston Rowing Club. O.U.B.C. then brought in a rule to prevent old members substituting unless they had been in residence for at least the preceding ten days.

Away from these principal inter-collegiate events, E.B. Michell won the O.U.B.C. Sculls in 1864 and the Diamond Challenge Sculls in 1865. The following year he repeated his win at Henley and also took the Wingfield Sculls along with the Championships of the Clyde, Ouse, Severn, and Wye. Edward Michell was also a champion boxer at heavy, middle and lightweights. He later purchased the site at Wimbledon for the All England Croquet Club.

In the spring of 1866 the Club was only just able to boat a Torpid but it was bumped on each of the first three days, lastly by New College, their first year on the river. Clearly disappointed by their arrival at the bottom of the table Magdalen took their boat off the river for the remaining three afternoons. They failed to appear for

Top left: Open Pairs 1863 won by E. B. Mitchell and H. B. Middleton.

Above: Thames National Regatta, Putney 1866, Gentleman Amateur Sculls won by E. B. Michell.

Opposite: Magdalens' first Boatman who served from 1872 to 1911

Summer Eights but returned the following year. It was not until 1870, after a rule (changing an earlier, more draconian, edict) had been brought in preventing anyone who had rowed as many as four nights for his college's Eight from rowing in the Torpid, that the Club put out another Spring boat. This was a struggle and the average weight of the crew was under 10 stone, the heaviest being 10 stone

4lbs. The Torpid hovered around the middle of the order for the next six years while the Eight also went through fluctuating fortunes.

1872 saw the second great individual achievement when C.C. Knollys won the O.U.B.C. Sculls, the Wingfields and the Diamonds. Both he and A.W. Nicholson rowed in the Oxford boats of that year and 1873. Later Sir Courtenay Knollys, he published *Oxford University Challenge Races* which was the first work on the subject of rowing in Oxford.

The same year the Boat Club moved from its small quarters in the back of Saltor's Green Barge to one rented from the same firm for their sole use; at the same time taking on the Club's first boatman, R.A. Talboys. Dick Talboys came from a family of Oxford watermen; his son was boatman to O.U.B.C.

It was also the first year that slides were used in Oxford initially only in Fours - indeed they were specifically banned from Torpids on the grounds that 'if a man cannot row on a fixed seat he cannot slide'. A year later they were allowed in Eights and Magdalen made good use of them, rising three places. They might have risen four had they not experimented with having the hull French polished. The boat became covered in oil and went very heavily; the polisher seemed to think that gentlemen liked their boats to look shiny,[5] some words were doubtless had between crew and artisan. The following year, 1874, even without this hindrance the boat dropped from sixth to thirteenth. Nicholson was elected Magdalen's first President of the O.U.B.C. for the academic year 1873/74 and won his third Blue.

# OSCAR WILDE

The start of the new academic year in the autumn of 1874 saw the arrival of Oscar Wilde at the College as an undergraduate, aged 20. He was very muscular and doubtless this had something to do with his being invited down to the barge in his fresher term to be tubbed with G.T. Atkinson. Wilde at stroke, Atkinson at bow, they were coached by someone whom Atkinson described as 'very unaesthetic, a Philistine of Philistines'.[6] Wilde's back was not an inspiring one to watch and he was criticised for not rowing with a straight spine. Nonetheless he stroked the putative Torpid until one afternoon when the Varsity Eight was coming downstream and heading for the Magdalen crew, their coach told them to 'put their backs into it and pull to the side'. Wilde took no notice and after uncomplimentary remarks from the two coxes he observed to Atkinson that he saw no *a priori* reason for rowing with a straight back and did not believe that the Greeks had done so at Salamis. After that day the Isis was not graced with Oscar's presence again. The boat club survived without him.

Having rowed for no more than a term and a bit, Oscar Wilde nonetheless still made his mark in dealings with members of the Boat Club; he famously announced: 'I don't see the use of going down backwards to Iffley every evening'. He had no regrets and heeded the advice given in John Ruskin's art lectures against 'fruitless slashing of the river'. After his departure from the river in Hilary 1875 and his alienation from the athletes of the College a cartoon appeared in 1881 summing up his feelings for all things sporting. His relationship with the oarsmen of Magdalen is perhaps best portrayed by the story of his tussle with J.H.T. Wharton.

AESTHETICS V.

AESTHETE. THIS IS INDEED A FORM OF DEATH, AND ENT
BELIEF IN THE IMMORTALITY OF THE SOUL.

The river is not for Oscar Wilde
and he is not for the river.

John Wharton was a Blue in 1878, 1879 and 1880 and had been at 7 in the first Magdalen crew to go Head in 1880. Along with some other undergraduates he decided to pay a visit to Wilde in his rooms to rag him and break up some of the furniture he was so proud of. They underestimated the extraordinary muscular strength of the lazy, lumbering, long-haired Oscar, this son of Irish farming stock, not at all a flabby aesthete as they reckoned. In an inebriated state they went to their victim's rooms followed by some spectators. To the astonishment of all the first was returned to their midst propelled by a hefty boot-thrust down the stairs; the next received a punch in the wind that doubled him up onto the top of his companions below; a third was lifted up bodily from the floor and hurled on to the heads of the spectators. Then came Wilde triumphant, carrying Wharton, the biggest of the gang like a baby in his arms. He was about Wilde's size and weight. His struggles were fruitless and he was borne by the poet to his own room and solemnly buried by him under a pile of his splendid and very expensive furniture. When the debris of tables, sofas, chairs and pictures had reached the height of a respectable mausoleum Wilde invited the now admiring crowd to sample the victim's cellar. The corpse pinned down beneath the ruin of his rooms was soothed in his dying agonies by the gurgle of expensive liqueurs and choice vintages being poured down the throats of his uninvited guests. [9]

In November 1878, following Wilde's departure from the river, Magdalen won for the first time the O.U.B.C. Fours, stroked by F.P. Bulley, son of the President. The Fours had been coxwainless since 1873 and was raced from Abingdon Lasher to Nuneham Island; they beat Univ. in the final. The following year Frederic Bulley and Charles Fletcher won the O.U.B.C. Pairs for Magdalen for the first time, beating Hertford; the prize being silver oars and a cup. In 1877 Herbert Pelham, who had been schooled at Haileybury and therefore had not rowed before Oxford, won his Blue in the only Boat Race to be declared a dead heat. The following year he became Magdalen's first Blue to win a Boat Race. In 1879 the Eight rose from sixth to second and was only denied the Headship through a broken rowlock: they had overlapped Balliol on the first night of the races before Balliol made their bump on Keble and subsequently rose to head over the week. Magdalen had rowed straight past Brasenose on the fourth night and were clearly the fastest crew.

[1] L.S. Tuckwell, Old Magdalen Days 1847-1877, Blackwell 1913

[2] President's Notebook, Magdalen College Archive PR/2/1

[3] W.E. Sherwood, Oxford Rowing, Henry Frowde 1900

[4] as [2] and [5] as [2]

[6] H.C. Wace, Nineteenth Century Brasenose Rowing, Oxford University Press 1909

[7] W.E. Sherwood, Oxford Rowing, Henry Frowde 1900

[8] G.T. Atkinson, 'Oscar Wilde at Oxford', Cornhill Magazine LXVI May 1929

[9] Sir Frank Benson, My Memoirs, 1930

1886 Head Crew, note the coxswain's silver rudder in a case

# 3 1880-1895

## Making a Mark: Warren, the Nickalls brothers and Cotton

Over the first twenty one years of its life, Magdalen College Boat Club had achieved a considerable degree of success, sometimes in the face of significant difficulties brought about largely through the numbers of undergraduates available to row. It had won all the O.U.B.C. small boats events and had its share of success in Eights and Torpids mixed, as is inevitably the case with bumps racing, with a taste of the slippery half of this aquatic snakes and ladders.

1880 began with arctic temperatures and the river was frozen for some weeks as far as Sandford. The thaw brought flooding and boats confined themselves to the upper river. Nonetheless Torpids were held and Magdalen rose four places. J.H.T. Wharton, who had been at the College School, won his second Blue, this time in the 7 seat. The opening evening of Summer Eights provided the opportunity to avenge the missed bump of the year before and Balliol were bumped. For the first time the red flag of the M.C.B.C. was to fly at the top of the mast from the O.U.B.C. Barge where custom dictated the flags of the college boat clubs (as with Magdalen, they often vary from that of their college) are flown in the order on the river. That flag did fifty years' service and is now on display in the College Bar. The Magdalen boat retained the Headship for the remaining five evenings, stroked by A. H. Higgins who weighed only 9 stone 3? lbs. Two years later he won his Blue; and having gained only 3 lbs. was the lightest stroke ever for either university. Like Wharton he had learnt his rowing on the Cherwell at the College School, though only in Fours – the School had ceased to use Eights in 1870, principally because the Cherwell was not big enough to accommodate the whole club in the bigger boat. Wharton's presence in this crew was a testimony to working the then system of residence. He had failed his Finals, then been ill a year later and was allowed, in January 1880, having failed again, to stay on 'under special circumstances' at Magdalen rather than migrate to St. Alban Hall. President Bulley was doubtless thinking of the Summer Eight. Wharton became a solicitor and named his house near the River Itchen *Cherwell*. Alfred Higgins, who had also been President of the J.C.R., became a barrister and worked in the legal department of the Board of Trade.

The 1880 Head Crew was photographed on the Cloister lawn, a location unchanged in the history of the club. It will be noted that they are wearing high-collared boating jackets which were the fore-runner of the blazer.

To celebrate the Headship, the President's wife organised a Ball on 10th June in the College Hall; about 120 were present and dancing continued until 3.30am. The Fellows allowed the S.C.R. to be used for the dinner. The oars and flag of the crew were hung on the north and east walls, the names of the crew inscribed on the blades. Oddly the coxswain's name (A.E. Norman) was not included though that of the spare man, FP Bulley, son of the President, who had stroked the 1879 boat, was listed.[1] Alfred Norman took holy orders and was at one stage vicar of Selborne which has ties to Magdalen dating from William Waynflete's taking over the priory. Waynflete gave its lands to the College and Selborne became a Magdalen living.

left to right:
A.H. Higgins, J.H.T. Wharton

In a composite with L.R. West of Christ Church, A.E. Staniland won the O.U.B.C. pairs. In the Michaelmas Term 1880, Magdalen won the University Fours, again stroked by Higgins. In the first heat they gave away an average of 2 stone a man to the Hertford crew and subsequently beat Exeter and then Brasenose. The President's Notebook records that he did not allow a dinner in Hall by way of celebration but no explanation is given for this decision. That December Higgins, who had trialled for the University as a cox the year before, stroked one of the Trial Eights while his school friend and fellow Magdalen man Frederic Bulley stroked the other, Alfred Staniland was in Bulley's boat and Alfred Norman coxed Higgins' crew. The race was held at Moulsford over a course greater than two miles; Bulley's boat won by less than a foot. None of these four, however, was selected for the subsequent Boat Race. John Wharton, who had not been in a Trial Eight, won his third Blue and stroked his second winning Oxford crew.

The Summer Headship was not for long and Hertford, on a remarkable rise from fifth removed Magdalen before the 1881 week was over. The College however did not drop out of the first three places on the river between 1880 and 1906 and occupied Head for ten of those years.

Above: Magdalen College School 1st Four or 1st Eight Cap. The Lily was white for 2nd Boats.

Left: Magdalen College School Four, winners of the Henley Public Schools Challenge Cup 1882 pictured on a college barge.

This period of successful oarsmen from the School coming to the College, winning Blues and contributing to Boat Club, highlights co-operation between the two institutions with a number of undergraduates helping with coaching School crews. For Henley of 1881, the School's Henley Fund of £20, 4 shillings and sixpence, received its largest single sum from M.C.B.C. with a donation of £2 and 2 shillings; they lost to Radley in the first heat stroke having 'slipped his button'. In 1882 the College School Boat Club won its first (and only) Henley trophy. Having moved to Fours twelve years earlier, they were the dominant force of the Public Schools Challenge Cup that year beating Christ's Hospital School in the final.

In the period 1884 -1886 M.C.B.C. won the O.U.B.C. Fours each year whilst also taking the Sculls in 1883 -1885. W.S. Unwin, who had been at the College School, was the principal name in these

boats, also winning the Pairs in an 1884 composite, thus giving the College all the small boats titles that year. He also took the Wingfields and the Diamonds in 1884 and 1885. Amongst the amateurs he reigned as supreme sculler for this period. This was a time when the argument about the definition of an amateur was reaching its peak and wordings were being drafted, debated and amended. The Amateur Rowing Association, which had grown out of the Metropolitan Rowing Association in May 1882, was at the centre of this drafting, following closely the decisions being made by the Henley Stewards. However, the wording still excluded workmen and artisans, whether or not they made their living on the river, and this did not entirely meet with approval in the universities. Cambridge men in particular, working in the London missions, saw the inequity of the situation and it led eventually to the founding of the National Amateur Rowing Association as a rival organisation. Ten years later Oxford men fuelled the debate in the light of their experiences working in the Oxford House Mission in Bethnal Green where they had contact with the oarsmen rowing on the River Lea.[2] The uniting of these two Associations was not to occur until 1955 when another famous Magdalen oarsman, G.O. 'Gully' Nickalls, was to be a key part of that process.

William Unwin and Henry Girdlestone were Blues in 1885 and 1886, the former in the bow seat, the latter at stroke. Girdlestone's skill in the first of these races led to a memorable race, saving it for Oxford through a brilliant performance. He was to be the first of a line of three Girdlestones to row for Magdalen, coaching his son Peter to the Headship in 1923, and grandson Gathorne followed in 1966. Henry Girdlestone was later ordained and served in various schools, completing his career as headmaster of Melbourne Church of England Grammar School, Australia. He was also a canon of St Peter's Cathedral, Adelaide.

H.Girdlestone

The Presidency of the College changed in 1885 when Bulley died and Herbert Warren was elected to the post. The Boat Club had a friend in both men though Warren was to prove the more active supporter during his 43 years in the Lodgings. By the 1850s, inspired by the university and collegiate rowing, Oxford had more than a dozen city rowing clubs some attached to churches, pubs or social clubs. The first City Regatta was held in 1841. Bulley's son Frederic's interest in rowing did not diminish with his graduation. Living in north Oxford, long after his father's death, he became involved in the Rowing Club of St Philip and St James which was a club for boys of the parish and its school of the same name.[3]

# HERBERT WARREN

The influence of Magdalen's President Warren was central to the fortunes of the Boat Club. Sir Herbert Warren was the first President of Magdalen to recognise the importance of rowing in the life of the College, and was himself both scholar and sportsman. He had won a scholarship to Balliol and took a double first in Mods and Greats; but he also played rugby for the University and won the University Fives championship. He was also 'seen on the river' according to his biographer, Laurie Magnus, which presumably means that he rowed in a Balliol crew. When he became a Fellow and Classics Tutor at Magdalen in 1878 a contemporary wrote: 'Until Herbert Warren came to the College, no effort, so far as I know, had been made to know the men (i.e. the undergraduates) or to help them in any way. The knowledge that one of the Fellows was off to play Fives with three undergraduates must have been an eye-opener both to dons and men alike'. This is perhaps overstating the position a little as Bulley had clearly been supportive generally, not least through his son's involvement. Warren selected his undergraduates from a long waiting list, and was determined to rejuvenate the moribund college by excellence in athletics as well as academic pursuits. Etonian oarsmen were at the forefront of this endeavour.

Warren was President from 1885 to 1928. During those years, Magdalen's reputation grew from its nineteenth century obscurity to rival Balliol in academic achievement and Christ Church in social standing. Magdalen also became, in the last two decades of his Presidency, the top rowing college in Oxford. Warren's penchant for Etonians is well known and often criticised, but the success of the M.C.B.C. in those years was due largely to the number of experienced oarsmen from Eton who were attracted to the College. Eton consistently produced the best school crews. Warren welcomed them to Magdalen, and the successful link between rowing schools and the College became self-perpetuating.

In its obituary of Sir Herbert Warren *The Times* said: 'The life-history of Colleges is a curious one, and is often quite independent of their dons; nor is it easy to see why in those years Magdalen suddenly leapt to the front rank, both in the Schools (exam results) and in the more conspicuous field of athletics. The College went Head of the River in 1880. For the next quarter of a century our Eight was always in the first three boats'.

Warren's biographer added: 'The sudden and marked rise of Magdalen in the first 20 years of his reign to leadership on the river and in the fields ... meant something more than a list of athletic successes. ... Everyone knows what the presence in a College of men of this type means to its moral and social welfare - to its tone; how that is raised by the example of team-work, of keenness, of training'. Warren positively selected undergraduates with athletic prowess or promise as part of his unswerving aim to improve and modernise the College. The position was aptly summed up by a newspaper article written by the great oarsman Guy Nickalls, who had much to thank Warren for: 'who has wisely recognised the fact that it is not by honour in Schools alone that a college's good name and prestige are kept to the fore, and who has, therefore, always cleverly allowed his college full scope for that ebullition of high animal spirit which is inseparable from healthy young manhood, especially when it is gathered together in large quantities.' Warren pasted a copy of the article into his President's Notebook.

The Headship was recovered in 1886, moving up into pole position on the first evening bumping Corpus Christi off the top spot. The boat was stroked by Henry Girdlestone who had also stroked the Oxford boat that year and the year before. On both occasions the bow seat of the Blue Boat was occupied by William Unwin who sat at 7 behind Girdlestone for Magdalen providing an experienced stern pair for the College boat to follow. Unwin later became a cleric and his last parish was Beachamwell with Shingham, Norfolk. He and his wife retired to nearby North Walsham, where the local solicitors included M. C. Sanders who was at Magdalen in the early 1930s. Through him, Unwin's widow offered in 1962 his illuminated sculling blades for the College or the School, keen that they should have them in the centenary year of his birth. Despite endless letters backwards and forwards the College Bursary was not very efficient at arranging their collection. Eventually, after three years, a College tenant farmer in North Elmham was asked to collected them from the Reepham office of the solicitors and they finally arrived in Oxford after a Bursarial Progress to the Norfolk farms. Sadly, these important relics of one of the Boat Club's great men are not in evidence today.

January of that year saw the launch of a fund to provide the cost of a new barge with donors being invited to a meeting in Hall on a Sunday evening. After their success in winning O.U.B.C. races and the Headship, and gaining the facility of the Barge, the M.C.B.C.'s need for equipment and to appeal to a broader base of inexperienced freshmen was met by the College following Balliol's example and starting an 'Amalgamated Clubs' scheme in 1887. This had the effect of institutionalising the Boat Club as an integral part of College, and involving Fellows on a formal basis, some of whom were friendly towards the oarsmen, some joining them at the river.

Magdalen lost the Headship in 1887 to New College but recovered it on the first night in 1888. The cox of this head crew was John Frederick Randall Stainer, who had been schooled at Winchester, was son of the famous composer Sir John Stainer who was earlier Organist and *Informator Choristarum* at the College and had later gone to St Paul's Cathedral. In this year Sir John returned to Oxford, and composed a piece named '*Sicut Lilium*' (and sometimes known by its closing phrase '*Floreat Magdalena*') to be sung at a celebratory occasion in Hall. It seems probable it may have been written for the 1888 Headship Dinner, the Academical Clerks singing from the gallery. The piece was rediscovered in the College archives in 2002 and has been sung at Headship Dinners from 2004 onwards. Stainer's younger brother Edward who had been at St Paul's School also came to Magdalen and followed J.F.R. into the cox's seat a year later when the boat went down three places. Neither of them followed their father's career in music, John became a barrister and was chief examiner at the Passport Office, and Edward a doctor. Sir John was appointed Professor of Music in 1889.

With the permission of the President, the 1888 Headship Dinner was followed by a party in the water meadow. Hard bargaining was needed with the tenant butcher but a bonfire and fireworks formed the celebration while the President arranged for coloured fire to be burnt on the top of the Great Tower. The only untoward circumstances of these festivities was an invasion, via the railings on the High Street, of the Brasenose crew who had finished second on the river. The President wrote to the Principal about it the following day.[4]

The 1888 crew contained Guy Nickalls who was to become one of the great oarsmen of all time. This was his second year in Oxford and he already had to his credit the second of his five Blues. He was elected Captain of Boats for the ensuing year (the Secretary's Book records that he took the title of 'President' rather than 'Captain', a habit that lasted a year or two and was repeated for a period in the 1930s). A.P. Parker, who was with Nickalls in the 1888 Blue Boat, sat behind him at 6 in the College eight and succeeded him at President the following autumn. They formed half of the College crew to win the O.U.B.C. Fours in 1889, beating New College in a heat before they dismissed Brasenose in the final. Nickalls, along with his brother Vivian who shortly followed him from Eton to the College; and son Gully, left an unrivalled family mark on the sport. Arthur Parker changed his surname to Dodds-Parker following a bequest from an uncle who had had been Lord Mayor of Newcastle-upon-Tyne. He became a surgeon and worked at the Radcliffe Infirmary, teaching anatomy for over forty years. During the First World War he oversaw the provision of 7,000 beds in the Examination Schools. He coached for O.U.B.C. and Magdalen for many years. Arthur Dodds-Parker's son Douglas, born in Holywell Street

J.F.R. Stainer

E. G. Tew. (8).          W. M. Poole (6)          H. W. Cotton (Str) M. C. Pilkington (7)

H. C. Middleton (Cox)

The 1885 Eight

in 1909, was also to become a Magdalen oarsman. R.P.P. Rowe was also in the 1889 four. Reginald Rowe took four Blues 1889-92 and was President of O.U.B.C. for the last of those races, having been captain in College the year before. He rowed in the Summer Eights that were Head in 1888 and 1892. Knighted in 1934, he was chairman of the Improved Tenements Association, a Governor of the Old Vic and of Sadler's Wells. He served in Flanders during the Great War and was afterwards Under-Treasurer and Steward of Lincoln's Inn.

# GUY AND VIVIAN NICKALLS

Guy Nickalls, by Spy,
for Vanity Fair July 1899

Guy Nickalls born in 1866 was the older of the famous Nickalls brothers, Vivian being five years younger. Their father Tom, who had not been an oarsman, sent them both to Eton where their love of the river began. Tom, who spent his childhood years living in Chicago, worked in the city of London and was one of the two leading jobbers in the American market. He acquired the nick-name 'Erie King' in 1872 and retained it for the rest of his working life [5] (see also Chapter 5, the 1912 Olympic Games). The contribution of these brothers to the life and success of the Boat Club is so extensive that it is woven into much of this chapter.

Guy arrived at Magdalen in 1886 aged 20. He took his B.A. in 1890. During his final undergraduate year he was President of the J.C.R., having been 'President' of the Boat Club the year before. In 1890 he was President of O.U.B.C. and President of Vincent's Club. Guy got into a few scrapes during his time in Oxford. On 26 May 1891 the Vice-Chancellor wrote to President Warren informing him that Guy had been involved in (and not helped to quell) a disturbance at Pembroke where he had been a guest. The incident must have been serious as it was referred to the Vice-Chancellor by the Proctors. He was fined £20 and sent down until he could obtain the leave of the Proctors to return. On 3 June Guy wrote to the President from Vincent's Club asking Warren to withdraw his name from the College lists and whilst apologising, also stated that he considered the Proctorial punishment to be over the top and unhelpful as he had left work unfinished. He thanked President Warren for his support, finishing the letter with the phrase 'Believe me'. [6]

He was Captain of Leander Club in 1892 and 1897. In 1898 Guy married Ellen Gilbey, making Harcourt Gold his brother-in-law. He died in 1935, aged 68, following a car accident at Bramham Crossroads where the Leeds-York road crosses the Great North Road; on the same day his school friend and rowing partner, Lord Ampthill, died. This coincidence led to the publication of the anonymous lines:

> Oarsmen they lived, and silver goblets mark
> The well-timed prowess of their trusty blades:
> In death their rhythm kept, they now embark
> To row their long last course among the Shades.

Guy's career was varied; he was a member of the Stock Exchange, a publicity and advertising agent, and a Captain 23rd Battalion the Lancashire Fusiliers. For some years he coached at Yale University. He won a blue in 1887, 88, 89, 90 and 91. At Henley he won: The Grand Challenge Cup in 1891, 1892, 1896 and 1905; the Ladies' Challenge Plate in 1885; The Stewards' Challenge Cup in 1893, 1895, 1896, 1897, 1905, 1906 and 1907. The Silver Goblets in 1890, 1891, ('90 and '91 with Lord Ampthill, New College), 1894, 1895, 1896 (these last three with Vivian) and 1897. The Diamond Challenge Sculls in 1888, 1889, 1890, 1893 and 1894 beating his brother Vivian, having scratched to him in the final in 1891. At the Olympic Regatta in 1908 he was in the VIII, aged 42, and won the gold medal. Of 79 races at Henley Guy won 67. Guy won the Wingfield Sculls in 1887, 88, 89 and 91.

Vivian

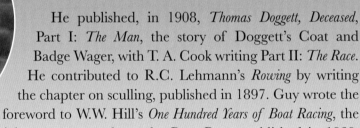

He published, in 1908, *Thomas Doggett, Deceased*, Part I: *The Man*, the story of Doggett's Coat and Badge Wager, with T. A. Cook writing Part II: *The Race*. He contributed to R.C. Lehmann's *Rowing* by writing the chapter on sculling, published in 1897. Guy wrote the foreword to W.W. Hill's *One Hundred Years of Boat Racing*, the

Guy

official centenary work on the Boat Race, published in 1929. In 1939 his son Gully posthumously published his autobiography *Life's a Pudding*.

Vivian matriculated in 1890, aged 19, and took his B.A. in 1893. He was Captain of Boats in 1892/93. In 1932 he published *Oars, Wars and Horses* in which he said:

'Rowing has never been so popular as it is now. …Undoubtedly it is the cleanest sport of any, it is the best exercise one can take, and it teaches a man discipline and unselfishness. After all a man in a crew is a cog in a machine, and if that cog goes wrong the whole machine suffers.'

He won a blue in 1891, 92 and 93. At Henley he won the Grand Challenge Cup in 1891, the Stewards' Challenge Cup in 1893, 1895 and 1896; the Silver Goblets in 1892, 1893, 1894, 1895 and 1896 (these last three with Guy), the Diamond Challenge Sculls in 1891. Vivian won the Wingfield Sculls in 1892, 1894 and 1895.

The brothers' list of successes on the Isis can be found in the Appendices.

His sons having won the Silver Goblets either together or with others for the previous five years, Tom Nickalls wrote to the Committee of Management of Henley Royal Regatta in 1895. The minute book records:

'The Chairman read a letter from Mr Tom Nickalls offering a Challenge Cup for Pair Oars.

On the proposition of the Hon. W.F.D. Smith M.P., seconded by Mr Russell Griffiths it was decided to accept Mr Nickalls offer with thanks, and to further inform him that the Committee were of opinion that a suitable inscription with the name of the donor and the date of gift should be engraved upon the Cup and that the names of past winners of the Silver Goblets should be recorded upon the stand or base.

It was further decided to inform Mr Nickalls that it was not within the power of the Regatta authorities to make the Cup carry with it the English Pair Oar Championship.'

In a subsequent meeting there is recorded the arrival of the cup and the letter from Mr Nickalls accompanying it is copied out in the minute book. He sets out a suggested arrangement for how the cup should be held by the winners during the year. The event was renamed 'The Silver Goblets and Nickalls' Challenge Cup'.

The Nickalls' Challenge Cup – a peg cup, note the interior protrusions, the origin of the expression ' to take you down a peg or two'.

There is little record from this period on the subject of coaching but until this time it had been conducted on horseback when not from within the boat by the captain/stroke. O.U.B.C. rules included a restriction that no boat could be followed by more than two horses; the towpath was often flooded in winter and in generally poor repair. It was even said that the regular horses could open the gates with their teeth! Running alongside the boat was not practical for some who might later have to row. Arnold Inman of Magdalen got round these rules and problems by introducing the use a bone-shaker bicycle. By 1896 O.U.B.C. was obliged to regulate this mode of

The 1893 Eight.

R.P.P. Rowe

transport too, limiting each boat to two persons on bicycles and that they were to observe the ordinary rules of the road. The same year saw the tightening of a rule, later lost only to be revived in the 21st century, of a swimming test for all who wished to row. It was suspected that men had sometimes taken the test and gained the certificate for their friends. Following an accident in which two who had certificates to show they could swim had to be rescued by others, a Captains' meeting swiftly introduced a rule making each Captain responsible for the validity of each certificate. Over one hundred years later these swim tests, taken by hundreds of students each year, are conducted in the University pool and the list is held centrally.

A record from 1889 gives some insight to competition within the

College, or at least its Boat Club. Perhaps engendered by that first Fours race in 1859, there were periodic small boats races on the Isis, typically for a prize of an M.C.B.C. silver medal. Thirty years on the Boat Club ran a 'College Regatta' on Saturday 15*th* June consisting of Dinghies, Cockles, Double Punting, Eights, Gig Pairs, Canoes, Sculling and Light Pairs, entries were limited to Magdalen members. That summer Guy Nickalls won the Diamond Challenge Sculls for the second time, beating C.J. Psotta, who was the American Amateur Champion, by a hundred yards. Nickalls was elected President of the O.U.B.C. for the forthcoming academic year; a post which Magdalen men would hold for six out of the next ten years.

The fortunes of M.C.B.C. on the Isis seemed to dip in 1891. R.P.P. Rowe (who reverted to the more conventional title; 'President' is crossed out in the Secretary's book and replaced with 'Captain' in the same hand) expressed his frustration at the state of the Torpid in robust terms:

'The only available Beef was so rough and unskilled … and the 1st [Torpid] settled to a truly Maudlin state of weakness and neatness. They would never do enough work, and didn't attend to their coach, whilst for the 2nd it was a great difficulty to get them over the course in under 10 minutes! Individuals plugged hard, but none had any form, except bow, who has never done a stroke of work in his life – like many other Radley eightsmen. They were a rather insubordinate crew. Most of them answered back when coached, if they happened to listen. Not men who could be trusted at all (NB. Three days before the races 5 in the 2nd went off to play footer!!)'. He went on to note that the 2nd Torpid simply turned round and grinned when bumped, something they suffered on four afternoons that week.

Of course the Torpid missed Vivian Nickalls who, in his first year would have been eligible, but he went straight into the Blue Boat. Rowe was also rowing in the Oxford crew while running the College Boat Club and this must have added to his difficulties. That year Magdalen provided the bow half of the winning Oxford boat, with Guy Nickalls taking his fifth Blue and W.M. Poole, at just 10 stone 7$^{1}/_{2}$ lbs., seated at bow. The Summer Eight rowed over every evening and so stayed in the third position. The Captain's Book shows that Rowe had not much joy this term either in dealing with his charges. He notes that he has had to admonish the Blues in the boat for muttering *sotto voce* and that they should leave the talking to the Captain.

W.M. Poole

# HUGH BENJAMIN COTTON

Michaelmas 1891 brought to Magdalen, fresh from Eton where he had not rowed, H.B. Cotton to read Law. 'Benjie' to his friends, he was to be one of the great oarsmen of his era but tragically died in the autumn following his B.A. Having taken up rowing in his first term, perhaps inspired by some of his wet-bob Etonian friends already at Magdalen, Vivian Nickalls in particular, he was in the bow seat of the winning Trial Eight less than three months later. He occupied the same seat in the Blue Boat of 1892, weighing a mere 9 stone 12 lbs. He kept the seat in the Oxford crew for the next three years, winning all four of his Boat Races. Cotton was elected President of O.U.B.C. for the academic year 1893-94, in which year his 'Spy' cartoon was published in the *Vanity Fair* 'Men of the Day' series. Its caption concluded: 'Tenacious, courageous, he keeps his blade covered, swings well, and never gets short. Socially retiring, though not a worshipper of the gentler sex in general, he is supposed to be not indifferent to the charms of some individually'.

His certificate of thanks from O.U.B.C. was signed by his successor, M.C. Pilkington, also of Magdalen.

In College, Cotton was chosen for his first Summer Eight which took the Headship by bumping New College and Brasenose. Considering the strength of the crew, which contained three other more experienced blues, it is a mark of Benjie's ability that he was

*Cotton certificate of thanks from O.U.B.C*

put in to stroke this boat. He went on to be a member of the 1893 and 1894 Head crews.

President Warren's Notebook records that on 20th May 1892 he approved the arrangements for a Bumps Supper, not to exceed 12 shillings per head. He ordained that the crews of Balliol and New Colleges be invited, being those Magdalen had bumped for the Headship. In addition he invited the Varsity eight, the Captain and Secretary of the Cricket Club and the President of the University Athletics Club. A bonfire was made in the meadow and there was no trouble. Warren asked the Senior Proctor to ensure there were no invaders. What is interesting is that this diary entry is for the evening Magdalen took the Headship; there were four more evenings' racing to be had but Warren was clearly confident there was no risk of his college being bumped off the top spot before the week was out. The dinner and festivities were not, however, held until racing was over.

Another striking example of the speed with which Benjie adopted rowing and achieved recognition and success came in his selection for Leander's winning Grand Challenge Cup crew of 1892, again in the bow seat. He repeated this two years later, Thames R.C. being the vanquished club on both occasions. Curiously, in the intervening year, 1893, he rowed for the College at Henley in M.C.B.C.'s first win in the Stewards' Challenge Cup (coxless fours) while the eight was beaten by Leander in the first round of the Grand. Elections to the College captaincy often take place by the division of the Trinity Term with the new Captain taking office immediately. It may be for this reason that

Cottons' room at
135 High Street, June 1890.

Cotton rowed for College at that year's Royal Regatta in a boat of Magdalen Blues that contained the Nickalls' brothers and W.M. Poole.

In 1894 Benjie Cotton was elected President of Vincent's Club, Magdalen's second holder of the esteemed post as the head of the University's exclusive club for distinguished sportsmen.

Cotton's love of rowing meant he was coaching for the College from his second year onwards. Ultimately this was to be his undoing, he was coaching in freezing weather in Hilary Term 1895 and though he was in the Blue Boat of that year, his health started to fail soon after. He added to this a bad chill caught cycling back to Oxford from Henley. Benjie coached the Summer Eight from the stroke seat but on one occasion could not cope and the boat was brought back to the barge where he was pronounced as having pneumonia. This was a particularly cruel fate as the College held the Headship for a fourth successive year. Not long afterwards, on medical advice, he went Davos Platz for the benefit of his health but died there of tuberculosis on 22nd October 1895. He had been accompanied to Switzerland by his close friend and fellow oarsman R.C. Lehmann. Rudie Lehmann's affection for Benjie was marked by his presentation to the College of a silver-gilt claret jug which matched Norsworthy's earlier gift. In the world of rowing he was a legend; the Magdalen Junior Common Room responded by publishing his memorial address, "The Strength of Life". To commemorate him the M.C.B.C. gave O.U.B.C. the silver base for the Summer Eights Trophy, inscribed to his memory.

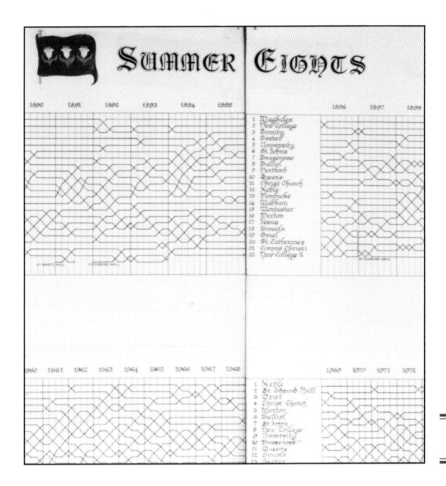

Summer Eights

1890 Bumps chart for Eights week.

1892 was to be the first of four successive years with Magdalen at the Head of Eights. H.B. Cotton's arrival and contribution was significant to this achievement though the College was also blessed with Blues such as Vivian Nickalls, R.P.P. Rowe and W.M. Poole.

Judging the finish of the O.U.B.C. Fours was conducted by the firing of a pistol. In the final that year the pistol was fired for Magdalen who believed they were anyway the winners. However their opponents Christ Church appealed that their pistol had misfired and that they were the rightful winners, producing many witnessed to testify to their case. The appeal was upheld but the incident brought about a change in judging with the pistols replaced by a semaphore to signal the first boat past the post.

Under Vivian Nickalls' captaincy there was careful deliberation over the Summer Eight seat order; Cotton was in the bow seat of

The trophies won by
H.B. Cotton, V. Nickalls and
W.A.L. Fletcher (Christchurch)
in 1893.

Bow section of the 1894 Eight, converted to a pipe rack by M.C. Pilkington.

Opposite: M.C. Pilkington.

the 1893 boat when it was stroked by another Magdalen blue, M.C. Pilkington. He was back at stroke in 1894; the Secretary's Book says of its captain Cotton:

'On the Saturday Magdalen were holding Head for the third year, strongly challenged by New College. Just opposite Weirs Bridge, one of the Eight caught a crab; the whole crew had to stop rowing. As they restarted, New College had come up on the Berkshire shore and were overlapping. Cotton, at stroke, immediately put in a magnificent spurt as New College came across the water and just missed the bump. The crew followed him to a man, and never gave New another chance. Foot by foot they drew away until, coming through the Gut, there was a quarter length clear. Along the Willows Magdalen obtained a further lead, but at the Barges New College came up rapidly and for a short time it looked as if Magdalen would lose their place after all; nevertheless, they managed to finish with a quarter length spare. *Floreat Magdalena*'. The cox of that boat was H.C. Middleton who died the following January of peritonitis. A short obituary was recorded in the Captain's Book. Before the year was out it would also contain a eulogy to Cotton.

1893 was the last year in which the Procession of Boats was held. The event had become unruly in that many oarsmen had left Oxford for the summer; some to row for Leander, and the boats were often manned by less able undergraduates. Magdalen entered the Grand and the Stewards at Henley, inviting Guy Nickalls, who had decided to have a go at the Diamond Sculls, to stroke both boats. Mackenzie of Fawley Court, who was an old Magdalen man, had just built a new house at the end of Wharf Lane and put it at the Club's disposal. They furnished it and christened it Magdalen Lodge. Fred Fenner came down to coach them; Guy Nickalls clearly felt he was more of a companion than a coach and they switched the seat order almost daily prior to the Regatta and between swivels and tholes with the same frequency. Nonetheless Nickalls won the Diamonds (for the fourth time) and the Four took the Stewards', beating Thames R.C. in the final, stroked by Muttlebury (a former President of C.U.B.C and the only person ever to have their Spy cartoon painted landscape rather than portrait). That crew was the only one which Guy Nickalls stroked over the Henley course not being also the steersman.

The Hilary Term of 1895 was especially hard: the Thames was

frozen and given over to skaters, four-in-hands and roasted oxen. Crews went daily to Sandford but in the end a truce was called, Torpids were cancelled and First Eight Colours awarded nonetheless. Trinity Term brought the fourth successive Headship but with Cotton's ill-health only G.H. Foster was in each of those boats. Foster, who had been at Haileybury, then a non-rowing school, later reverted to his father's style of Betton-Foster. This club of one became two in 2007 when L.J.A. Rooney also achieved four Headship titles. The 1895 Boat Race and that summer's Headship were the debut for another great Magdalen oarsman in his freshman year: C. D. Burnell. He arrived in Oxford having already won the Ladies' Challenge Plate with Eton and went on to be another of the growing collection of great Magdalen oarsmen.

M.C. Pilkington.

Other than the scullers, Magdalen had little success at Henley until the 1890s, although the College had a good many representatives in winning Leander crews. In 1889 Guy Nickalls and Lord Ampthill (New College) were beaten by two feet in the Silver Goblets. In 1890 they won; in 1891, they beat F. Wilkinson and W.A.L. Fletcher of O.U.B.C. by just one foot. In 1894 Guy and Vivian Nickalls won the Goblets, and contested the final of the Diamond Sculls against each other, Guy winning. In 1895 the brothers won the Goblets again, and thereby the new Nickalls' Challenge Cup presented by their father to celebrate one of his sons having been a winner of the Goblets for the last five years. Whilst it has been noted that during this period many oarsmen undergraduates came to Magdalen from Eton, it is interesting that most of those mentioned in this chapter went on to practice the law either as barristers or solicitors. Of the others, in the main they went into the diplomatic service or the armed forces.

[1] President's Notebook, Magdalen College Archive PR/2/6

[2] Eric Halladay, Rowing in England: a social history, Manchester University Press 1990

[3] The Record of the Rowing Club of St Philip and St James 1889-1909, Oxfordshire County Record Office, PAR21/17/N3/1

[4] President's Notebook, Magdalen College Archive PR/2/8

[5] David Kynaston, The City of London Volume I, Pimlico 1994

[6] President's Notebook, Magdalen College Archive PR/2/10

'Chasing the Boats' by R.Davidson. Note the Magdalen Blazer and cap fourth from the left.

# 4 1896-1906

## $\mathcal{L}$eander, Don Burnell, Harcourt Gold

Before moving on in the chronology of the Magdalen boat club's history it is worth pausing to explain the nature of the relationship with Leander Club. Originally set up in Lambeth in 1818, Leander's involvement in Henley Regatta was influenced by their inability in 1856 to produce an eight-oared crew to row there. The Oxbridge entrants had been affected by the success and participation of Royal Chester Rowing Club who that year carted off the Grand Challenge Cup and the Ladies' Challenge Plate. A new rule of 1857 limited the Ladies' to colleges from Oxford and Cambridge and to Eton and Westminster. Leander had been present, not as competitors but as spectators, and presumably returned to the Tideway to brood. A proposal to form a new London club had been mooted in April of 1856 and a meeting was called which culminated in the founding of London Rowing Club. Josias Nottidge, who had called the meeting, and his friends were irritated by the dominance of Oxford and Cambridge and clubs closed to non-university men, such as those formed for graduates as in the case of Leander which was limited to 25 members. This new club saw the end of over twenty small private clubs and moved Tideway rowing from Lambeth firmly to Putney, then still a country village.

Leander rose to this challenge which, unchecked, might have seen its demise. The 1857 Henley Regatta saw London beat Oxford to win the Grand. A year later, with both universities keen to meet this new challenge, and with Oxford unable to boat an eight and Cambridge with four not rowing in their University crew, these men approached Leander to enquire whether they might row under Leander colours. This would have caused complications to a club which restricted its number and had hitherto never elected anyone for the express purpose of racing for the club. It was agreed to. In the thirty years since the foundation of Henley Regatta this was to be only the third appearance of a Leander eight. This relationship flourished over the coming years which included a move to Putney 1866. These developments contributed to Leander's fortunes so that in 1891 an unprecedented run of success at Henley began.

1886 had seen a new committee to run the Royal Regatta, now run by rowing men rather than townsfolk, and a change to the Course. The Regatta was becoming established as a major

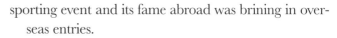

sporting event and its fame abroad was brining in overseas entries.

At a Special General Meeting of Leander Club, held in 1893, the rules were further changed: 'That a Resident Undergraduate of Oxford or Cambridge is not eligible for Election unless he has rowed in the University Eight, University Trial Eights, or in one of the first three boats on the river in Eights at Oxford or May Races at Cambridge, or has won the University Fours, Pairs or Sculls, or has rowed for the Grand Challenge Cup at Henley, or has won any other race at Henley except the Thames Cup.' One amendment (among several debated) was accepted, to add the words 'or may seem specially desirable to the Committee'.

E.C. Sherwood

The result came to be known as the University Qualification Rule and was to be the corner-stone of Leander election policy for almost a hundred years until it was swept away by a new Constitution in 1985. Whilst the new rule was intended to limit the intake of undergraduate candidates it had the reverse effect. By publishing a set of qualifications, to which only the most successful oarsmen of the day could aspire, Leander membership became something special in itself. Though the rule applied only to undergraduate candidates it inevitably set the standard for all other elections.

Leander's rise to its status as the world's premier rowing club was in train. In 1897 it opened its Henley clubhouse. Much is written elsewhere about Oxford's involvement in Leander and its successes of the last decade of the nineteenth century; many Magdalen men went to row for the club in that period and well in to the twentieth century.

The most notable of these were the Nickalls brothers, Harcourt Gold and Don Burnell, all of whom rowed for Leander while still in residence at Magdalen. Their huge list of achievements in one set of colours or the other can be found in their profiles or in the main text. In the same way, as will be shown later, men of the early twentieth century both before and after the Great War, rowed for College or Leander partly depending on the invitation and sometimes on who else best made up a particular boat. Where these boats were substantially made up of Magdalen men they have been included here.

Returning to the Isis of the Michaelmas Term 1895, three freshmen arrived from Eton where they had won the Ladies' Challenge Plate the previous term, an event which the school had dominated for the two previous years. R. Carr, D.O. Dunlop and H.G. Gold therefore added experience and ability to Magdalen. Carr went on to win three Blues while Harcourt Gold, nicknamed 'Tarka' won four. He followed Don Burnell into the Captaincy taking charge for the 1898-1899 season. In Trinity Term 1896 Rudie Lehmann came to coach the eight, following R.P. P. Rowe. He had been a close friend of Benjie Cotton at Leander Club and was clearly felt this was a way to support the College in its sudden loss. E.C. Sherwood, the captain of that year, was pleased to have such a respected oarsman to assist. Sherwood had won his Blue in that spring's Boat Race; his father was a Fellow of the College, Master of the College School and author of the definitive work on Oxford Rowing in the nineteenth century.

A Magdalen College School Four, W.E. Sherwood is on the landing stage.

# DON BURNELL

Charles Desborough Burnell, known as Don, was the first of a line of three Burnells to row for the College and to distinguish themselves in the sport. Don arrived at Magdalen in 1895, aged 19, having already rowed at Eton with whom he won the Ladies' Plate at Henley in 1894. Whilst at Oxford he rowed for the University in four Boat Races 1895-98, winning all of them. For College he rowed in the Summer Eights including the Headship crew of 1895. He won the O.U.B.C. Sculls in 1898 beating J. A. Tinné of University College by half a second. He only once won at Henley rowing for Magdalen when he was in the crew that beat Favorite Hammonia R.C. from Hamburg to win the Stewards' Challenge Cup in 1899.

C.D. Burnell also rowed for Leander Club and was their Captain in 1901-02. In the cerise colours he won the Grand Challenge Cup on four successive occasions from 1898 to 1901. In 1899 and 1900 he doubled up in a winning Stewards' four. He represented the Club in their eight which won the Cork International Regatta in 1902 and was selected, aged 32, for the Leander eight that represented the United Kingdom at the 1908 Olympic Regatta, held at Henley, taking the gold medal.

*C.D. Burnell in an early version of an M.C.B.C. 'Summer Blazer'.*

Don, who had for a time the curious nickname 'King of the Welters', was a member of the London Rifle Brigade from 1894. He left the Brigade in 1912 but rejoined in 1914 on the outbreak of the Great War with the rank of Major. Major Burnell was in charge of the enlisting process at the London Rifle Brigade's Bunhill Row headquarters and found he did not have time to select the men individually owing to the numbers if the mobilisation programme was to keep to schedule. So in order to speed up the process, and of course to ensure the usual sort of L.R.B. man was selected, he resorted to an expedient: being a former Rowing and Rugby Blue himself, he ordered all rowing men to leave the queue and fall in on the other side of the street; these men were then marched into the Drill Hall. Next he ordered all rugby men to do the same. According to one source,

HENLEY ROYAL REGATTA, 1901.
LEANDER EIGHT, WINNERS OF GRAND CHALLENGE CUP.
                                              St. lbs
C.A. WILLIS, ----- 11.1          5. C.D. BURNELL, ----- 13.4    NEW COLL. OXFORD.
                                   6. J.E. PAYNE, ----- 12.12   CLUB NAUTIQE OF
W. DUDLEY WARD, 12.7               7. C.J.D. GOLDIE, ----- 12.1 GHENT. BELGIUM.
G.M. MAITLAND, ----- 12.1      Str. R.B. ETHERINGTON-SMITH, 12.6 UNIV. OF PENNSYLVANIA
            Cox. G.S. MACLAGAN, ----- 8.9                       PHILADELPHIA. U.S.A.

HENLEY ROYAL REGATTA, 1903.
MAGDALEN COLL. EIGHT, WINNERS OF LADIES' CHALLENGE PLATE.
Bow. J.D. STOBART, 10.11                                      TRINITY COLL.
2. E.L. COLES, 11.11          6. G.C. JAMES, ----- 12.4       ETON COLL. B. CLUB
3. J.H. MORRELL, 11.4         7. C.A. WILLIS, ----- 11.1
4. C.P. ACKERS, 11.10        Str. H.C. ROSE, ----- 10.5
          Cox. L.E. DETMOULD, 9.3

HENLEY ROYAL REGATTA, 1899.
MAGD. COLL. FOUR, WINNERS OF STEWARD'S CHALLENGE CUP.
Bow. M.C. THORNHILL, 11.4        3. C.D. BURNELL, 13.11
2. R. CARR, 12.10            Str. H.G. GOLD (Stroke), 11.11

C.D. Burnell's collection of oars.

HENLEY ROYAL REGATTA, 1900.
LEANDER EIGHT, WINNERS OF GRAND CHALLENGE CUP.
Bow. R.O. PITMAN, ----- 10.6        5. C.D. BURNELL, ----- 13.9
                                    6. PAYNE, ----- 12.9
LORD GRIMSTON,                      7. M.C.M. THORNHILL, 11.0
4. F.W. WARRE, 12.4                Str. F.O.J. HUNTLEY, 11.2
              Cox. G.S. MACLAGAN, 8.12

these two categories appear to have provided the L.R.B. with all the men it needed.[1] Among them were a number of Magdalen oarsmen. Burnell was awarded the D.S.O. in 1918.

In 1903 Don Burnell married Jessie Backhouse and had two sons and two daughters. One of these sons was Richard Burnell who came to Magdalen in 1936, in turn, both of his sons also came to Magdalen and rowed. He was Churchwarden of St. Nicholas, Remenham; served as a J.P.; was President of Leander Club from 1954 to 1957 and also President of Henley Rowing Club, which holds his collection of illuminated oars. His rowing medals are on display in Leander Club. From 1927 to 1930 he was Umpire of the Boat Race. Burnell was elected a Steward of Henley Royal Regatta in 1919. He was made O.B.E. in 1954, and died in 1969, aged 93.

The S.C.R. Betting Book has a rather curious entry for 28*th* May 1897, between Mr G.E. Underhill and Mr C.R. Carter. Carter was a stalwart supporter of the Boat Club and though one may only guess what prompted the wage of some wine, his knowledge of the river was clearly the wiser of the two, though proving this issue at stake was doubtless an entertaining summer afternoon's work.

Mr Underhill bets Mr Carter that nowhere between the College Barge and the Berkshire bank is there now more than 8 ft of water. Lost by Mr Underhill.
28 May 1897.

Entry in the S.C.R. betting book

Cyril Carter was in fact a cleric who held the posts of Home Bursar and Dean of Divinity. When, in 1902, he left the College, the boat club was without one of its most loyal coaches. For six years he regularly tubbed freshmen as well as coaching the eight and the fours. He insisted on hard work and did not allow 'sugarers' to stay in a boat. He returned to Magdalen in 1910 as Estates Bursar; after the Great War he took up coaching again and retired from the towpath in 1921 but remained Senior Treasurer of the Boat Club. He was presented with a silver stopwatch that had originally belonged to Harcourt Gold, this was perhaps a slightly curious thing to give someone who had just ceased to have use of such an instrument but it was a mark of gratitude and esteem: Harcourt Gold's watch was not just any stopwatch.

In the summer of 1899 Magdalen won the Stewards' Challenge Cup at Henley for the second time. Harcourt Gold stroked the boat with Don Burnell at 3, Carr at 2 and Thornhill at bow. They beat New College in the first heat, Trinity College, Cambridge in the second, and Favorite Hammonia R.C., Hamburg in the final.

The 1900 Summer Eight recovered the Headship from New College after a six day battle. Stroked by Harcourt Gold, in the crew with him were two blues oarsmen H.H. Dutton and C.P. Rowley, the latter being the College Captain that year. The cox was G.S. Maclagan who had also steered Oxford that year and the year before; he was to do so for the next two Boat Races as well. The result of the 1901 Boat Race proved to be not unlike that of 1896. Harcourt Gold was now coaching rather than stroking and Maclagan bided his time behind Cambridge while both crews hugged the Surrey bank after Hammersmith through appalling conditions. Maclagan, whose crew had the Middlesex station, dropped the rating and waited until the bend was in their favour at Barnes Bridge; taking them out into the stream he steered them to a half length victory. The number of crews who win from behind at Barnes Bridge can be counted on a pair of hands. Tarka Gold married Maclagan's sister Helen the following year. Maclagan was killed at Ypres in 1915, one of many Magdalen oarsmen to lay down their lives in the Great War.

The Torpid of 1901 contained no less than seven Etonian freshmen and despite their experience of fine boats and sliding seats, were put in the clinker fixed seat boat. This crew was preceded in the Michaelmas Term by five Fours which was about the typical number that Magdalen would put out at the start of each academic year.

# SIR HARCOURT GOLD

Harcourt Gilbey Gold is one of three Magdalen oarsmen to have an entry in the Oxford Dictionary of National Biography for their prowess on the river. He was born in 1876 at Wooburn Green, Buckinghamshire, the ninth and youngest child of Henry Gold. His father was a director of W. and A. Gilbey, wine merchants, and his mother was Charlotte Gilbey. Harcourt went to Eton from where he sent a telegram home asking his parents whether he should become a dry-bob or a wet-bob. His elder brother opened the telegram and replied saying wet-bob. Eton was therefore the first beneficiary of this advice and he stroked the College to victory in the Ladies' Plate of 1893. He repeated this feat in 1894 and 1895 and went to Oxford in the autumn of that year.

Invariably known to his friends as 'Tarka', Gold was immediately picked to stroke the Blue Boat of 1896; the race proved to be one of the classic contests. Cambridge who were the strong favourites took a length and a half lead. With the station conditions against him, Gold nursed his crew to the calmer water around Barnes Bridge then produced a spectacular spurt gaining a hard-fought victory of just two-fifths of a length. Harcourt stroked the next two Oxford Boat Race crews, both of which won. He was President of the O.U.B.C. for his fourth clash with Cambridge in 1899, he was still at stroke but Cambridge won convincingly, ending a run of nine successive defeats.

In College, Gold was a constant member of the Eight and though Magdalen was knocked off Head in 1896 by New College, and then bumped by Trinity, they rose back from third to second below their old rivals a year later. In 1900, though he had not rowed in the Blue Boat that spring, Harcourt Gold stroked the Magdalen eight to take the Headship from New College.

During his time at Oxford Tarka stroked the Leander eight to victory in the Grand Challenge Cup at Henley in 1896, 1898 and 1899, in the latter years he also notched up wins in the Stewards' Challenge Cup, once with Leander and the second for Magdalen. He was Captain of Leander Club from 1898 to 1900.

On the turn of the century, Gold completed his brilliant if relatively brief career as an active oarsman. However, his contribution to the sport was far from over. He proved himself as a coach for the College and as finishing coach at Putney for eighteen Oxford crews, as well as the victorious Olympic eights of 1908 and 1912.

In 1909 Harcourt Gold was elected a Steward of Henley Royal Regatta - Magdalen's first man to hold that honour. Ten years later he became a member of the Committee of Management, the Regatta was struggling with the Edwardian financial crisis and it was he who conceived the foundation of the Stewards' Enclosure. The subscriptions for this convivial viewing area for the Regatta soon put Henley on a sound financial footing. He saw to it that fears about the cost to competitors were met with reduced rates for membership. His initiative proved crucial to the survival of Henley as a regatta of international quality. Gold became Chairman of the Committee of Management in 1945 and its first President in 1952. He died in London later that summer.

During the First World War he served with the Royal Flying Corps, reaching the rank of Lieutenant-Colonel; in 1918 he was appointed O.B.E. For many years Harcourt Gold represented Oxford University Boat Club on the Committee of the Amateur Rowing Association, of which he was Chairman from 1947. Under his leadership the A.R.A. affiliated to Fédération Internationale des Sociétés d'Avrion, the international rowing federation, in the same year.

In 1920 he wrote a small book entitled: *The Common Sense of Coaching*, published by *The Field*. He was knighted for services to rowing in 1949, the first man to be so honoured; a distinction not to be repeated until Steve Redgrave was dubbed in 2000.

At this change of the century it is perhaps the moment to reflect on the development of equipment that had taken place over the past few decades for though boats and oars continued to evolve thereafter, this point is perhaps a milestone. For a while afterwards the debate that raged was more about rowing style than design.

In Oxford the increasing popularity of boating in the 1830s had led to the development of local boat building. Isaac King's business at Folly Bridge was taken over by Salter in 1858, building both pleasure and racing craft. By the 1880s Fred Rough had added to his Tideway business with a yard at Long Bridges on the Isis in what was later to become Tims' yard. Rough's boats had a high reputation and his business built the eight that won the gold medal at the 1908 London Olympic Games. He died in 1913 a few months after his business was burnt down by suffragettes who left 'Votes for Women' cards in the gutted building. Rough's apprentice Tom Tims rebuilt the boathouse and that business continued until after the latter part of the twentieth century.

Competitiveness led to changes in boat design and technology, and that in turn raised the argument on style. The 1829 Oxford boat was 45 feet 4 inches long, 44 inches wide, weighed 972 pounds, had fixed seats, and fixed pin rowlocks. The 1929 Sim's boat was 62 feet 6 inches long by $23\frac{1}{2}$ inches, weighed 350 pounds, had sliding seats and had swivel rowlocks on the outriggers.

In 1841 Oxford had had the first carvel (smooth-skinned) boat, still with a keel, but as they were unsuccessful they blamed the boat and reverted to a clinker boat. By 1846 carvel hulls had become the match boats of choice.

The development of the outrigger was a crucial stage. Boats of very wide beam had been the only way to get leverage on the oar. A metal frame rigger with conventional fixed pin rowlocks secured over the top with a button down strap, out from the side of the boat was the start of the outrigger. Moving the pivot outboard immediately enabled boats to be slimmer, lighter and offer less water resistance. Initially they were made to fold into the boat for convenience in packing. Henry Clasper proved the outrigger design on a four, and by 1846 the design was adopted by both universities. He then introduced a keel-less boat in 1847. He built a keel-less eight which won the Grand and Ladies' in 1858. Friction was substantially reduced and the craft was more streamlined. Exeter College bought

Magdalen rowing over
Head of The River in 1899,
New College chasing.

the boat and went Head. The next innovation for the keel-less boat came in 1883 when Oxford added the fin – a very small midships keel that assisted straight running.

Sliding seats were first used in England and America in 1871, and in 1872 London Rowing Club proved them at Henley. In 1873 they were used in 58 foot boats for the Boat Race. At first they were offset, only slid 9 inches, and did not have wheels, but with the opportunity for enhanced leg power and longer stroke 23 seconds were immediately clipped off the Boat Race record, though average times in the Boat Race and at Henley were actually slower after the introduction of slides.[2] In 1883 the slides had developed to 16 inches length, and were becoming common by 1885 when wheels and vulcanite runners replaced the earlier bone runners in brass, and later even glass, running grooves; in 1892 they were used by Magdalen, exploiting the school training of a largely Etonian crew to go Head. As a result of this development in technique, in 1898 the slide with wheels was invented by an Oxford don, and this increased the length to 20 inches. As slides lengthened, so did boats, from 57 feet to one of 62 feet in length and 23 inches beam by 1896.

The last major invention was swivel rowlocks patented by Ayling in 1887; an 'improved' design by W.A.L. Fletcher of Christ Church in 1902 has disappeared. A small but important addition was the rubber ball on the bow of every boat, introduced in 1888 after a fatal accident at Cambridge.

The frozen Isis, 1896

The invention of outriggers and slides radically changed the mechanics of rowing. It did not standardise the dimensions of oars, their leverage, and outboard-inboard ratios, which remained open for experiment. The 'usual' oar in the 1890s was 12 foot 6 inches, with blades 3 foot 3 inches long and 5 inches wide. But these proved heavy to pivot for the work produced, and were soon adapted to blades 2 foot 8 inches or 9 inches long and 6 inches wide, more curved at the tip, and by 1882 the inboard length was usually 3 foot

# The invention of outriggers and slides radically changed the mechanics of rowing.

$8^{1}/_{2}$ inches. After inventing swivels in 1887, Ayling improved the design of oars to the tubular type of the same shape but with improved weight and balance. This sufficed until 1906 when the Belgians used short oars to capture the Grand, becoming the first overseas crew to win at Henley. A debate in which Magdalen played its part then ensued and continued for some time. More recent developments in oars, starting with the arrival of the asymmetric blade, have led to just as many arguments over the best refinements and their benefits.

Through all this progress in boat design it should be noted that, on the Isis at least, these advances were used only by first boats. Novices were taught in heavy clinker boats with fixed seats and raced in these for Torpids. Emphasis in novice coaching was on style, body movement being all-important as always but the fixed seat demanded attention to swing and the catch. Bank Tubs and Tub Pairs were used extensively and oarsmen of all levels of experience used them to improve their blade work and harmonise their style. Today they have fallen out of fashion (relatively recently) and oarsmen finding them, and the blades with holes in needed for the bank tub, at the back of the boathouse wonder what they were for.

Back in College, where these various changes in design had been watched closely and experimented with to good effect; the boat club spent the first years of the twentieth century just off the top of the first division of Summer Eights. In 1902 Magdalen had slipped to third and in July sent a crew to the Cork International Regatta, the first such regatta to be held in Europe. Their first week they were billeted at the Metropole Temperance Hotel; they lost to Newry R.C. then to Berlin R.C., one wonders if the domestic arrangements had been less than congenial. However in 1903, after being in the top three boats for the past 25 years, M.C.B.C. again entered the Ladies' Plate at Henley, still open to academic entries only (though now widened outside of the 1857 ruling), and coached by Harcourt Gold they beat Jesus College Oxford, Trinity College Dublin and then Eton in the final. This was to be the only time in the history of the M.C.B.C. that the College would win the premier academic eights event at the Royal Regatta, and it did so with just one Blue on board. New College, who were Head of Summer Eights, entered the Grand. A four that was a subset of the Magdalen eight entered the Visitors' Challenge Cup but lost to University College.

So far little has been said about Magdalen's achievements in Torpids. In the winter of 1904 the river was flooded and the towpath was too deep for the coaches to navigate. The coaches would stand in the stern of these broad boats and coxes would only be put in a few days before racing began. This was the period before the sluices and when the river flooded, as it often did, racing would be held even when the Green Bank was under water. Torpids were rarely cancelled. Magdalen reached fourth position and held it in the following year.

Summer 1905 saw Magdalen take the upper hand once again in the almost continual tussle with New College, bumping them off Head on the first night. The crew was stroked by E.H.L. Southwell of whom the Captain's Book said: 'Magdalen are lucky enough to have at last found another good stroke. Nothing could destroy his habitual *sang froid*. To him is the credit for having kept away from University College; if he had lost his head in the slightest degree, and hurried us ever so little when they were within a quarter canvas, there was every possibility of our going to pieces. Instead he kept the stroke long and enabled us to settle down. It is exceedingly satisfactory to have gone Head after having chased New College so hard for two years. The future looks hopeful as the crew was by no means composed of veterans'. Evelyn Southwell won Blues in 1907 and 1908.

One of the stalwart coaches of this period was A.P. Parker, later Dodds-Parker having changed his surname to reflect a bequest from his godfather who had been Lord Mayor of Newcastle-upon-Tyne.

He had won his Blue in 1888, been in the Head crew of that summer, and Captain of Magdalen the following autumn (giving it up to Inman of bicycle fame for the remainder of the academic year). He was to be a guiding light from the towpath for many years. In the autumn of 1905 he coached the all-Eton boat which won the O.U.B.C. Fours, steered from bow by the first of the Garton family to come to Magdalen. A year later the same crew and coach prepared for the event once again but the captain, Gatehouse, in the 2 seat, took ill the day before racing began and Johnson was substituted. They lost to New College on the second day. More remarkable is that this was the first year Magdalen entered a second boat for this event and they went on to win; Harcourt Gold had joined Parker in coaching both crews. This second boat, which had begun on its own initiative, contained three men who were to achieve the highest sporting honours for Somers-Smith, Gillan and Cudmore were to be part of the international success which Magdalen would enjoy in the coming years. Torpids 1906 was full of mixed emotions. There was considerable difficulty in putting together a second boat but, like the first boat having switched to lighter craft two weeks before the races, they took no less than 7 bumps and out of the third division where they had started third. The first boat however, having bumped Brasenose on the second afternoon, failed to bump New College despite having overlap down the Green Bank. It was two days later before they succeeded. On the last afternoon they failed by inches to knock Univ. off Head; the cox whose poor steering had been blamed earlier in the week was now chastised for his weak voice which could not be heard over the huge crowd. It was to be another six years before Magdalen would take the Headship of Torpids for the first time. 1906 was the first of A.G. Kirby's four Blues, the last of which, in 1909, he was to be joined by no less than five other Magdalen men. Despite being described by their coach Harcourt Gold as 'bad' and 'featureless' the eight held off New College to retain the Headship in Trinity Term.

It had become a tradition that the Head of the River crews at Oxford and Cambridge entered for the Grand at Henley. Magdalen had not previously done so, but in 1906 they decided to take up the challenge and made their first bid for the Grand, with only one crew change at seven. Their boat was considered not stiff enough, so they tried one built for Leander and decided to use it; they also tried new oars. The crew acknowledged a great debt to their coaches. Dr A.P. Dodds-Parker again coached and sought 'strong finishes throughout early practice, and after this we travelled as fast between strokes as any other crew. Then Mr Harcourt Gold insisted on more beginning, so that by the time we got to Henley we had more pace than at Oxford'. Leander had not entered the Grand to face the Belgians whom they had beaten in the final the year before when, on the fifth stroke of the race, the Sport Nautique de Gand stroke had caught a crab. Magdalen faced another Belgian club Club Nautique de Gand who had first appeared at Henley in 1900. There they were unlucky to meet the Belgians in the first round, losing by one and a quarter lengths. The foreigners were to beat Trinity Hall in the final and become the first overseas winners of this most prestigious event. The Belgians had rowed with 12 foot oars, and maintained a higher rate of striking than most English crews, who used oars of 12 foot 6 inches. They also seemed to row a shorter stroke, and were thought to be shorter in the water, but there was no doubt that they had found a winning formula. This shocked the orthodox rowing world, and provoked intense argument about oars and rig for several years. The debate concerned not only the length of oars, but also inboard ratios, leverage, and width of blades.

Magdalen had given a good account of themselves and the following Michaelmas Term the whole eight plus the spare man were still in residence. They were joined by J.R. Somers-Smith fresh from being Captain of Boats at Eton and A.W.F. Donkin who had coxed him. The story of the autumn Fours has already been recounted but it was the dawn of a great period for Magdalen rowing.

[1] K. W. Mitchinson, Gentlemen and Officers, The Impact and Experience of War on a Territorial Regiment 1914-1918, Imperial War Museum 1995

[2] R.D. Burnell, Swing Together, Oxford University Press 1952

# Henley Regatta 1902

Underneath a light straw boater
  In his pink Leander tie
Ev'ry ripple in the water caught the Captain in the eye.
  O'er the plenitude of houseboats
Plop of punt-poles, creak of rowlocks,
  Many a man of some distinction scanned the reach to Temple Island

As a south wind fluttered by,
  Till it shifted, westward drifting, strings of pennants house-boat high,
Where unevenly the outline of the brick-warm town of Henley
  Dominated by her church tower and the sheds of Brakspear's Brewery

Lay beneath a summer sky.
  Plash of sculls! And pink of ices!
And the inn-yards full of ostlers, and the barrels running dry,
  And the baskets of geraniums
Swinging over river-gardens
  Led us to the flowering heart of England's willow-cooled July.

Sir John Betjeman
(Matriculated 1925; Knighted 1969, Poet Laureate 1972)

The 1908 Olympic Games 'Diploma' awarded to victors. Magdalen's Coxless Four's copy.
Drawn by Bernard Partridge (1861–1945)

TO Magdalen College, Oxford
WINNER of FIRST PRIZE
FOR Four-oared Race
AT·THE·OLYMPIC·GAMES·LONDON·1908·

PRESIDENT OF THE
BRITISH OLYMPIC COUNCIL·

| Bow | C. R. CUDMORE. | 11. | 10. |
|-----|----------------|-----|-----|
| 2 | J. A. GILLAN. | 12. | 9. |
| 3 | D. MACKINNON. | 12. | 12. |
| STR | J. R. SOMERS–SMITH. (Steerer). | 10. | 10. |

# 5 1907-1918

## *H*enley Victories, Olympic Glories, War

1907 began with another near-miss at the Torpids Headship. Magdalen had on board J.R. Somers-Smith and Duncan Mackinnon. Whilst Somers-Smith had been captain at Eton, Mackinnon only took up rowing as a freshman the previous term. He had been at Rugby as a schoolboy and this was his first taste of the river. They took the Headship on the first day but were knocked off it again by Christ Church to go down to second by the end of the week. Kirby, Southwell, Gillan and Donkin were all in the Blue Boat. Kirby was the O.U.B.C. President, a position he held, most unusually, for two years. This was the first year that the College put out a *2nd* Torpid boat.

This year was set to be the start of what became known as 'The First Golden Era' in Magdalen rowing, a period that lasted until 1913. It is true; it was to be a period of huge success on the Isis, at Henley and the Olympic stage but it was really Magdalen's second Golden Era. The measurement of success is driven by the opportunities available and the period 1892 to 1895 warrants equal veneration. Then the College had its four years Head of Summer Eights and enjoyed success in small boats on the Isis and at Henley; this was the period before the founding of the modern Olympic Games and though the eight-oared events at Henley were being won by other Oxbridge Colleges they tended to be the larger and more established ones. It was well represented in the Boat Race and at Leander. By the same token it can be argued that the period 1953-1954 was a third era, a time when the development of the sport generally was beginning to reduce the status of collegiate rowing and yet Magdalen took the top academic positions. By 2004 when the College was next Head the world of rowing had changed much further. The successful defence of that headship over the three succeeding years and the recovery in 2008 after seventy four years, of the Torpids headship, surely merits similar adulation. By this time the opportunity for a College Boat Club with a turnover of members and size of field that Magdalen has to win an event at Henley or nurture international talent has long passed to bigger institutions, club rowing and squad structures. However, this period from 1907 contains the most remarkable set of achievements of which the College and its Boat Club can be justly proud, covering the greatest variety of success of any of the five periods argued for.

# Magdalen College BOAT CLUB.

## HENLEY · 1907.

| Winners of Stewards' Cup. | | | Winners of Visitors and Wyfold Cups. | | |
|---|---|---|---|---|---|
| BOW. | Hon. R. S. Stanhope | 9 st. 10 lb. | BOW. | C. R. Cudmore | 11 st. 12 lb. |
| 2. | E. H. L. Southwell | 12. 0 | 2. | J. A. Gillan | 12. 9 |
| 3. | A. G. Kirby | 13. 6 | 3. | D. McKinnon | 12. 13 |
| STROKE. | Guy Nickalls (Steers) | 12. 11 | STROKE. | J. R. Somers-Smith (Steers) | 10. 10 |

COACH: H. G. Gold.

STEWARDS' CUP.

We the undersigned, Past Members of the Magdalen Eight, desire to express our sincere gratification at the distinguished position at present held by Magdalen Rowing, and our appreciation of the successes it has recently gained at Henley, the achievements of the Crews representing the College this year in Winning the Stewards', Visitors' and Wyfold Cups — being without parallel in the whole history of the Regatta.

VISITORS' CUP.

We are especially gratified at the triumph of the old Magdalen traditions of good Coaching, good Watermanship, Style and Pluck and it is our earnest hope and expectation that future generations of Oarsmen will be impelled to uphold these traditions — and, if possible, to achieve similarly brilliant results.

WYFOLD CUP.

As a testimony of the very high esteem in which we hold those who have so worthily upheld the honour of the College, We beg their acceptance of this Address — and herewith subscribe ourselves.

| | | | | |
|---|---|---|---|---|
| W. D. Mackenzie 1858, 60, 61 | S. T. H. Burne 1872, 73, 74, 75 | G. S. Bazley 1884, 85, 86. | T. Royden 1891, 92, 93. | H. E. S. Lambert 1898, 99, 1901. |
| L. S. Tuckwell 1858, 60. | P. W. G. Filleul 1874, 75, 76. | W. S. Unwin 1884, 85, 86. | W. M. Poole 1893, 93, 94. | H. G. Frank 1899, 1900, 01, 02. |
| E. Norsworthy 1858, 60, 61, 62, 63. | G. B. Hulme 1875, 76, 77, 78, 79. | G. T. Prior 1884. | R. S. Medlicott 1892. | R. C. Boyle 1899. |
| H. B. Middleton 1859, 60, 61. | J. H. T. Wharton 1876, 77, 78. | A. C. Maclachlan 1885. | E. Tew 1893, 94, 95. | G. S. Maclagan 1899, 1900, 01, 02. |
| A. H. Arnould 1860. | F. J. Bulley 1877, 78, 79, 80, 82. | H. E. V. Bull 1885, 86, 87. | Wm. C. Pilkington 1893, 94. | H. H. Dutton 1900, 01, 02. |
| H. Daman 1864. | A. S. Commeline 1878. | H. G. O. Kendall 1886, 88. | P. Bowman 1894, 95. | E. D. P. Kelly 1900. |
| W. Caldwall Masters 1864. | C. W. Cave 1878. | R. du P. Bryans 1887, 88. | J. M. Steward 1895, 96. | Stanhope 1900. |
| R. H. Anstice 1864, 65. | C. R. L. Fletcher 1878, 79, 81. | A. P. Parker 1888, 88, 89, 90. | C. D. Burnell 1895, 96, 97, 98, 99. | T. Fleming 1901, 03, 04. |
| E. Worsley 1864, 65, 66, 68. | A. H. Higgins 1879, 80, 81, 82. | W. E. Young 1887, 88. | | J. H. Morrell 1902, 03, 04, 05. |
| A. J. Richardson 1864, 65. | J. H. Philpot 1879. | J. H. W. Riches 1889. | H. Graham 1895, 96. | C. P. Ackers 1902, 03, 04, 05. |
| S. L. Scott 1867, 68, 69. | H. W. Boustead 1880, 89, 90, 91, 92. | R. P. P. Rowe 1888, 89, 90, 91, 92. | P. R. A. Baker 1896. | P. R. James 1902, 03, 04, 05. |
| W. O. Massingberd 1867, 68, 69, 70, 71, 72, 73. | A. E. Stamland 1880, 81, 82. | C. R. Gilliat 1889. | E. H. Chapman 1897. | F. D. Stobart 1903, 04, 05. |
| W. A. Clarke 1868, 69, 70. | A. W. Bainton 1882, 85. | W. F. James 1889, 90. | M. C. Thornhill 1897, 98, 99, 1900, 01. | E. L. Coles 1903, 04. |
| A. du B. Hill 1870, 71, 72, 73. | A. G. Daubeney 1882. | E. L. Pilkington 1889. | C. P. Rowley 1897, 98, 99. | C. L. Garton 1905, 06, 07. |
| H. M. Faber 1871, 72. | F. J. Watkin Davies 1883. | H. C. Stewart 1889. | A. J. Jex-Blake 1897. | L. R. Gatehouse 1905, 06, 07. |
| A. W. Nicholson 1871, 72, 73. | H. C. W. Radcliffe 1880, 84, 85. | E. Stainer 1889, 90, 91. | J. Koppel 1897, 98. | H. F. Macgeagh 1905. |
| F. G. Bampfylde 1871, 73. | W. D. Lindley 1884, 85, 86. | H. G. G. Mackenzie 1890. | R. Duckworth 1898. | A. C. Clarke 1905, 06. |
| | | A. Mahaffy 1890. | | J. L. Johnston 1906. |

1907 was a crucial period for rowing, the beginning of 'scientific analysis'. At Oxford the debate was complicated by the fact that Torpids were rowed in slower clinker boats with fixed seats. Some argued that slower boats needed shorter oars and less inboard ratios, and so were not comparable to shells. In the 1907 Torpids, Christ Church (who bumped Magdalen to go Head) and Trinity (who made five bumps) used the short oars and seemed to have proved this point, as Magdalen had stuck to the old measurements.

At University level the question had been tackled by putting all the Christ Church men (who favoured short oars) into one Trial crew, "and then they were utterly defeated by their opponents with the old measurements". Oxford continued to use 12 foot 6 inch oars but lost the 1907 Boat Race. When training for Eights Week, the argument was still unresolved within the M.C.B.C. The Captain's Book for 5*th* May records: 'At this point we began to try experiments with measurements. This crew experimented with Belgian oars of 12 foot length, 7 inch blade, and 3 foot 7 inches inboard (the same as the Belgians had used in their win over Magdalen). As long as things went well, these were found to be a powerful combination. We were a very heavy and generally powerful crew, and very nearly man enough to wield these oars'. After two fast courses and much

Magdalen crews at Henley, 1907.

dissecting of fears, the Captain and coaches decided on Belgian oars. The log continues: 'The next feature of the preparation was the feeling throughout the crew that the thing was becoming impossible. These were not very short oars, and with such large blades they required a terrible amount of effort to get them through. It was held that times had proved them fast, and they were kept. On May 14*th* the riggers were put out one inch to 32, making the leverage a little easier. The labour was greatly reduced, but the boat got away from us badly, and a slow time was done with this arrangement. We therefore returned to the 31 inches leverage.'

On the third evening Christ Church bumped Magdalen for Head and though no one was willing to blame the experiments that had been made, the House was very fast and they were untroubled in the top spot for the remainder of the week. After this the confidence of the club was not high and C.L. Garton decided not to enter the Grand at Henley. Instead two Fours were arranged, one for the Stewards' and the other for the Wyfolds' and the Visitors'. The outcome was an astonishing success and Magdalen took all three trophies – an achievement never equalled by any other club. Guy

Magdalen II winners of the O.U.B.C. Fours, 1908.

Blazers, at this stage still usually called Boating Jackets, were common enough to warrant a separate entry on the College laundry tariff, at a price of 4d., a penny more expensive than any other kind of jacket.

*Magdalen IV. 1908.*
*Winners of O.U.B.C. Fours.*

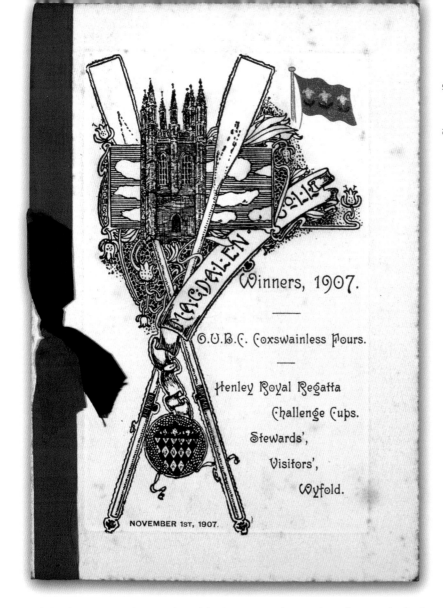

Winners, 1907.

O.U.B.C. Coxswainless Fours.

Henley Royal Regatta

Challenge Cups.

Stewards',

Visitors',

Wyfold.

MAGDALEN · COLL.

NOVEMBER 1ST, 1907.

Menu from the dinner to celebrate the 1907 success.

Nickalls, who had not taken his degree and was therefore technically still in residence, at the age of 41 stroked and steered the Stewards' Four with three other Blues onboard; he had won the event in the two preceding years for Leander. They beat London R.C. and met Leander in the final. The men in pink shot off the start at 42 strokes per minute and were out of sight by the top of the island. Magdalen, who had gone off at 40, got even around Fawley and went on to win by 3 lengths. Harcourt Gold had been coaching them and at dinner that evening proposed a toast to Nickalls: 'The greatest oarsman of all time'. He had yet to win an Olympic gold medal the following year.

The other Four, stroked by J.R. Somers-Smith still a freshman,

# the Olympic Committee, on the advice of the A.R.A. Selection Committee, invited the Magdalen crew to represent their country.

beat Trinity Hall II, Kingston R.C., Jesus College Cambridge 'B' and London R.C. to win the Wyfold Challenge Cup. Their doubling-up in the Visitors' brought them wins against Trinity Hall I, Merton College and First Trinity Cambridge. They were coached by Guy Nickalls who noted that Somers-Smith had steered all seven races without once looking round. This feat of the three four-oared events caused a stir in Magdalen and a congratulatory banner was produced by subscription, copies of which hang in the Leander Club bar and the Captain's Room in College. These successes fuelled the debate about oars and dimensions and further experimentation took place the following autumn but proved inconclusive during Torpids.

Trinity Term 1908 was to be an un-noteworthy beginning to a summer of glory. The Summer Eight failed to bump Christ Church off Head. It was not possible to enter this crew for the Grand as Kirby and Cudmore were in the trial eight for the Olympic Regatta, but when Cudmore was dropped by the selectors it was decided to enter the Stewards' and the Visitors' with the same crew as had won the latter event the year before. In both events they set new course records. In the Stewards' they achieved 7mins 28secs in a heat against Thames R.C., 2 seconds better than the previous record. They went on to beat London R.C. in the final. In the final of the Visitors' against Jesus College Cambridge, despite having the race well in hand at Fawley, they rowed themselves to exhaustion and clipped a remarkable seven seconds off to establish a new record of 7mins. 30secs. As a result of these records the Olympic Committee, on the advice of the A.R.A. Selection Committee, invited the Magdalen crew to represent their country. The United Kingdom was allowed two entries for each event, the other four being a picked Leander crew. The Magdalen Four of Cudmore, Gillan, Mackinnon and Somers-Smith's record-breaking time in the Stewards' stood until 1925.

# The 1908 Olympic Regatta

The Henley course was lengthened by 330 yards to a mile and a half for the Olympic Regatta, this was a time before there was any standardisation of course length and presumably it was felt a greater test was needed than the conventional Royal Regatta distance. The Belgians entered the Eights with a combined crew of the two Ghent clubs. Given their recent success on this stretch of water, the United Kingdom Selection Committee had, earlier in the year, invited a crew of 'old heavies' to form a second Leander eight. Coached by 'Tarka' Gold from April onwards, the crew included three Magdalen men: Guy Nickalls, by then aged 42, at 4, Charles 'Don' Burnell, aged 32, at 5 and G.S. Maclagan, 29, coxing. Cambridge were the other home eight but this older crew averaged six pounds a man heavier and rowed a very different style. Leander easily beat Hungary and then defeated the Canadians by a length. The Belgians did for the Cambridge crew. In the final the Belgians had the early lead but the Leander heavies had taken a length by Fawley and went on to win by two, giving three old Magdalen men Olympic gold. It was noted by G.C. Drinkwater that: 'a triumph for the traditional style of University rowing'. By this he meant the Orthodox Style of a long swing, a firm grip of the water behind the rigger, and a true combination of body and slide finish, not the lure of high-rate 'rowing-in''[1].

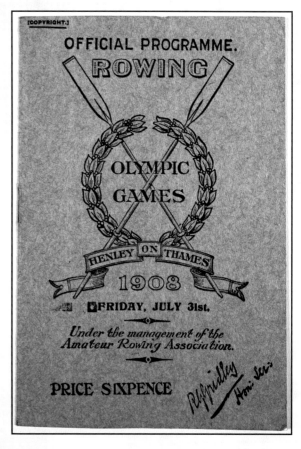

[COPYRIGHT.]

OFFICIAL PROGRAMME.
ROWING

OLYMPIC GAMES

HENLEY ON THAMES
1908
FRIDAY, JULY 31st.

*Under the management of the Amateur Rowing Association.*

PRICE SIXPENCE

The Magdalen Four had taken a ten day rest after Henley, a considerable length of time generally and given the proximity of the two events. They set 'the work 2 inches aft in order to cause the boat to run more level and steer more easily'. In the first heat they beat Canada after a hard race by 2? lengths in 8mins. 34secs. In the

5

TIME.
3.45.                                                        Final.

# FOUR-OAR RACE.

**No. 1 Berks.**

### UNITED KINGDOM.
(Magdalen College B.C., Oxford.)

|  | st lbs |  | st lbs |
|---|---|---|---|
| C. R. Cudmore, bow | 11 10 | 3 D. Mackinnon | 12 13 |
| 2 J. A. Gillan | 12 8 | J. R. Somers-Smith, str. strs. | 10 13 |

Substitutes : Hon. R. P. Stanhope, E. H. L. Southwell.
Colours : Red, Black and White.

**No. 2 Bucks.**

### UNITED KINGDOM.
Leander Club, Henley-on-Thames.

|  | st lbs |  | st lbs |
|---|---|---|---|
| P. R. Filleul, bow | 10 13 | 3 J. R. K. Fenning | 12 2 |
| 2 H. R. Barker | 11 12 | G. L. Thomson, stroke and steers | 11 12 |

Substitutes : E. Majolier, G. Nickalls.
Colour : Cerise.

## NOTE TO COMPETITORS.

Immediately after the last race this afternoon the winners of the Sculls, Pairs, Fours, and Eights, together with all competitors who have started in any race at this Regatta will assemble near the Grand Stand, and at a Quarter to Five o'clock, exactly, the Gold Medals will be presented by Lady Desborough, the Commemoration Medals by Baron Pierre de Coubertin, and the Silver Oars by the Mayor of Henley.

Above: Angus Gillan's medal collection

Left: The Magdalen Olympic Champions in Coxless Fours

Top left clockwise:
D. Mackinnon (3)
C.R. Cudmore (Bow)
Guy Nickalls (coach)
J.A. Gillan (2)
J.R. Somers-Smith (stroke)

other heat Leander beat Holland easily. Magdalen then beat the Leander crew by $1\frac{1}{2}$ lengths in the same time as their heat, to add Olympic victory to their record. A great achievement for a crew who, only a year earlier, had been the College second four.

Magdalen was sufficiently engaged and enthused by the prospect of some of its number competing for their country that it sent a donation to the British Olympic Association appeal (a funding method that remains today, for the association has never been in receipt of public money). The Honorary Secretary of the B.O.A. and International Olympic Committee member, the Revd. R.S. de Courcy-Laffan, wrote to the President after the event asking him to acknowledge safe receipt of a Commemorative Medal struck to mark the London Games and presented to those who had responded to the appeal.

Champions at the 1908 Olympic Games were presented with gold medals (solid gold, not gilt as now) about the size of the modern two pence piece, in the form of a coin (no eyelet and ribbon as was adopted later). They also received a model silver oar and a diploma. The commemoration medal was given to all participants including medal winners. The Olympic Regatta medal ceremony was conducted to the sound of the drums and bugles of the Irish Guards; the medals being presented by Lady Desborough, wife of the Chairman of the Organising Committee.

A 'diploma' was presented to each gold medal winner and one for their Club. The M.C.B.C. one now hangs in the Captain of Boats' room; above the names of the crew and the title of the event they won is a scene of Greek gods and goddesses at the Temple of Hera, Olympia, site of the ancient games and at which temple the prizes were presented.[2]

At the concluding banquet The Rev. Robert de Courcy-Laffan, IOC member, said in a speech: '…I must warn those who organise future Olympiads that they must be prepared for times of trial.'[3] *Plus ça change, plus c'est la même chose.*

1908 Olympic Gold Medal.

In the autumn of 1908 Olympic champions Angus Gillan and J.R. Somers-Smith were joined by Blues Kirby and Southwell for the O.U.B.C. Fours and without a regular coach they beat Christ Church. The run-up to this event had been another experiment, this time with swivel rowlocks. Duncan Mackinnon and W.G. Forest disliked them and dropped out but the final crew noted that: 'Swivels gave us more length, and enabled us to be smarter with our wrists at the finish'.

A letter to the editor published in the *Morning Post* on 13*th* November 1908 provides a glimpse of the sporting rivalry between Oxbridge colleges (perhaps an era before they became quite so concerned about academic league tables). The writer was the author of the Trinity Hall volume of the *College History Series* then published. He complains that the newspaper has a bias in favour of Magdalen's rowing results compared to the Hall's. 'Magdalen has won eights, fours, pairs and sculls at Oxford 10, 12, 10 and 6 times respectively; Trinity Hall 13, 9, 9 and 5 times respectively. Magdalen has had 59 places in the University Boat Race, Trinity Hall 66. Magdalen has won all four-oared events at Henley Royal Regatta in one year, Trinity Hall all eight oared and 2 four-oared in same year. *Par nobile fratrum*.' [brothers of equal achievement].[4] In fact at that point Magdalen had 68 Blues (see Appendices). It is not known if the editor was a Magdalen man but the aquatic record of the two colleges was certainly well matched.

Top: A.S. Garton

Above: A.G. Kirby.

Left: Winners of The Grand Challenge Cup, Henley Royal Regatta, 1907.

The 1909 Boat Race crew had six Magdalen men onboard: A.G. Kirby was President (whilst also President of Vincent's), Gillan, Cudmore, Mackinnon and Garton were also rowing and A.W.F. Donkin was coxing his third Oxford crew. The new stroke of the Oxford crew was R.C. Bourne of New College who was an outstanding oarsman and brought the O.U.B.C. a fresh run of success. A.S. Garton had arrived at Magdalen the previous October straight from Eton; he was a powerful man and was plucked out of the Torpid and put straight into the Blue Boat.

The Summer Eight, despite having five Blues, seemed to have seating problems. Duncan Mackinnon was put in at 5 where he was valued for his power though the Secretary's log book notes: 'a very painstaking oarsman who always rowed hard and with any amount of pluck. His worst fault was bad watermanship'. Not, perhaps, the remark one might ordinarily make of an Olympic gold medallist. Somers-Smith stroked the boat but had to drop out after the first night; it is not clear why this was, though the log book does, with its now familiar candour, say that he: 'is never big enough to control the man behind, so he got stiffer, and the boat lost its 'go''. Failing to catch the House, Magdalen remained second on the river. Henley beckoned and the College entered the Grand, Stewards' and Visitors'. Kirby had been elected Captain at Leander, whilst the College Captain was the Olympian Angus Gillan. The Magdalen fours, by the Secretary's admission, neglected to practice spending all their efforts on the eight. The Visitors' crew was beaten by Thames R.C. in the final, while the Stewards' four 'took things too much for granted'. This was a year of strong wind on the course and in the final of the Grand Magdalen lost out to the Belgians (who had seven previous winners onboard), despite considerable efforts by Stanhope at stroke. Donkin was obliged to use a lot of rudder and it was thought this cost them at least half a length. Richard Burnell, in his book on Henley, notes that had the stations been reversed so might have the result; that year there were forty-five races won on the Bucks station to only eighteen on Berks. It was to be another year before Magdalen would win the Grand Challenge Cup for the first time.

Michaelmas 1909 was Magdalen's fifth successive win in the O.U.B.C. Fours. They beat New College by a huge margin despite having a bad row; the second boat beat University College by five lengths and the final was an all-Magdalen affair. Mackinnon, who

D. Mackinnon by 'Spy' for supplement to 'The World', March 1910

had been President of the Magdalen J.C.R. they year before, had been elected to succeed Kirby as President of O.U.B.C.; trials were rowed for the first time in light boats. Mackinnon, Garton and Philip Fleming rowed at 5, 6 and stroke with Donkin as cox for the fourth time in the winning 1910 Oxford boat.

Summer Eights opened with Magdalen starting second and despite a bad start including some crabs, they bumped Christ Church off Head the first evening. Owing to the death of King Edward VII, racing was curtailed to four days; Magdalen remained Head despite a strong challenge from a reputedly fast New College. Stanley Garton and Philip Fleming won the O.U.B.C. Pairs.

While Kirby went off to prepare the Leander eight for Henley, the College, captained by R.E. Burgess, entered its Head crew for the Grand and the two crews met in the semi-final. The same south-westerly 'Bushes' wind was blowing as the previous year, which favours the Bucks Station. Magdalen were on Berks and their coach, once again Harcourt Gold, advised them to get in front early in the race and by the end of the island they had a clear length, having gone off at 13 to Leander's 38. Leander, who bar one were all Blues, clawed this back to half a length by the quarter mile signal but Donkin began to steer Magdalen across Leander's bows over towards the shelter of the Bucks station. Two minutes into the race Magdalen were directly

*Above: miniature replica Grand Challenge Cup, presented to each of the 1910 crew.*

| | | |
|---|---|---|
| C. P. ACKERS | C. L. GARTON | J. H. MORRELL |
| A. W. BAINTON | STANLEY GARTON | W. L. NEWTON |
| P. R. A. BAKER | L. R. A. GATEHOUSE | W. D. NICHOLSON |
| G. E. BELCHER | J. A. GILLAN | GUY NICKALLS |
| H. W. BOUSTEAD | C. R. GILLIAT | J. H. W. PILCHER |
| R. ov F. BRYANS | H. G. GOLD | E. S. PILKINGTON |
| H. E. U. BULL | HARTLEY GRAHAM | M. C. PILKINGTON |
| F. P. BULLEY | I. B. M. HAMILTON | W. M. POOLE |
| S. T. H. BURNE | A. H. HIGGINS | G. T. PRIOR |
| C. D. BURNELL | ARNOLD DOMAN | N. C. W. RADCLIFFE |
| RUSSELL CARR | C. B. JAMES | R. P. P. ROWE |
| C. R. CARTER | WALTER J. JAMES | C. P. ROWLEY |
| A. W. CAVE | J. L. JOHNSTON | TOM ROYDEN |
| B. H. CHAPMAN | H. G. O. KENDALL | W. F. SHERWOOD |
| L. C. CHOLMELEY | A. G. KIRBY | GEORGE SLADE |
| A. C. CLARKE | J. M. KNAPP | EDWARD STAINER |
| E. L. COLES | P. A. KOPPEL | J. F. R. STAINER |
| A. S. COMMELINE | H. E. S. LAMBART | RICHARD STANHOPE |
| CHRISTOPHER COOKSON | S. G. LEE | A. F. STANILAND |
| A. E. COWLEY | W. D. LINDLEY | H. C. STEWART |
| KENNETH CROSSLEY | S. C. LONG | F. G. TEW |
| G. D. DAKYNS | DUNCAN MACKINNON | P. F. TINNE |
| A. P. DODDS-PARKER | A. C. MACLACHLAN | W. S. UNWIN |
| A. W. F. DONKIN | G. S. MACLAGAN | THOMAS HERBERT WARREN |
| R. DUCKWORTH | A. W. MAHAFFY | F. F. WATKIN-DAVIES |
| A. H. FASS | F. N. G. MASTERS | H. B. WELLS |
| P. W. G. FILLEUL | FRANCIS H. MEADE | C. J. H. WHEATLEY |
| VALENTINE FLEMING | R. S. MEDLICOTT | L. G. WORMALD |
| C. R. L. FLETCHER | E. MILLINGTON-DRAKE | W. G. YOUNG |

*I*N making a presentation to R. *A.* TALBOYS to commemorate his long and faithful service as Boatman to *M*agdalen College we wish to place on record our high appreciation of the loyalty and zeal with which he has performed the duties of his office for a period of thirty-nine years (1872 to 1911) and to express to him our warm personal regard.

| | | |
|---|---|---|
| C. P. ACKERS | C. L. GARTON | J. H. MORRELL |
| A. W. BAINTON | STANLEY GARTON | W. L. NEWTON |

Waiting to start Eights Week,
1909.

in front of Leander and with only half a length ahead of them. Fleming at stroke judged the race with precision knowing that, in that position, one touch from Leander would have led the College's disqualification. After Fawley, Donkin, who until now had not turned round, moved his crew back to Berks. Leander crept up steadily through spurts led by stroke man Bourne. Magdalen had thrown everything at the early stages of the race but held on to win by three-quarters of a length. Stanley Garton's own programme reveals that he was sick at the end of the race.

In the final the following day, Magdalen raced Jesus College Cambridge, both had three Blues onboard. The previous day Jesus had beaten Thames R.C. by two feet. For the final the weather was calm and Magdalen took its first Grand title in 7mins 19secs beating the Jesus crew by two lengths. The Captain's book concludes the report with 'FLOREAT MAGDALENA', indeed it was flourishing.

Much of the crew was back for Michaelmas Term and the 1st Four won the O.U.B.C. Fours for a sixth successive year, setting a new record for continuous holding of that title.

The 1911 Blue boat contained six Magdalen men including the College Captain A.S. Garton, who with D. Mackinnon, was wining his third Blue with Wormald, Burgess and Millington-Drake winning their first Blues as did Wells in the cox's seat. Despite this talent the Summer Eight was bumped off Head by New College on the first evening only to remain there for the next four years. Bourne

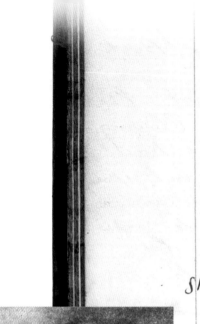

*Jeander just ½ a length clear It was a most extraordinary race Fawley was reached in 3.26 and from here Bourne began a marvellous series of spurts. Donkin however as cool as ever only gradually veered*

Start     M    M     M      M     M      Finish

Angle Pile

O

H.B. Wells

Captain's Book entry for Henley
1910 (see page 98)

stroked the New College boat with the longer yet narrower blades while Magdalen used the shorter, wider ones. The debate continued. The *2nd* boat however made five bumps.

For Henley the College entered the Grand, the Stewards' and the Goblets, the small boats both went out in the first round. In the Grand however, Magdalen exacted swift revenge on New College beating them in the first round and then taking Ottawa in the next. In the final they once again faced Jesus Cambridge, after a slight early lead for the men from the Isis the crews were level at Fawley. Magdalen lengthened out and took charge of the race to win by $2^{1/2}$ lengths. This was the first time an Oxford college had won the Grand in successive years. Once again the Captain's book gratefully acknowledged that: 'This was undoubtedly due to Harcourt Gold'.

Dick Talboys, who had been boatman to M.C.B.C. since 1872 decided to retire at the end of the Michaelmas term 1911 as his health was failing. Reginald Rowe, who had been captain in 1890-91 contacted former oarsmen seeking subscriptions for a Presentation Fund. This raised £20 and 19 shillings and the subscribers received a letter from him stating that Talboys was to be given a stop-watch with split-hand, suitably engraved; a pair of fieldglasses, and a testimonial address. This all came to £17 and he was given a cheque for the balance. The presentation was made at 3.30pm on Wednesday 6 December by the President, Rowe and C.R.L. Fletcher. According to the President's Notebook, the venue, the College Barge, was chosen

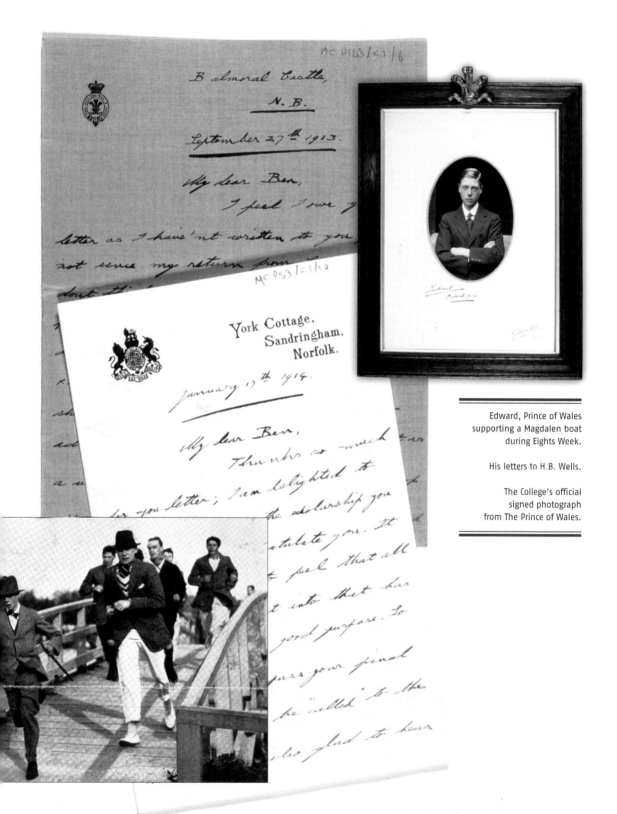

MC·P163/c1/6

Balmoral Castle,
N.B.

September 27th 1913.

My dear Ben,

I feel I owe y

letter as I have'nt written to you

not since my return from

MC·P163/c1/10

York Cottage,
Sandringham,
Norfolk.

January 17th 1914.

My dear Ben,

Thanks so much

you letter; I am delighted to

the scholarship you

tulate you. It

peel that all

into that has

good purpose. To

pass your final

be "called" to the

also glad to hear

Edward, Prince of Wales
supporting a Magdalen boat
during Eights Week.

His letters to H.B. Wells.

The College's official
signed photograph
from The Prince of Wales.

# HÔTEL BELLEVUE DRESDEN

R. Ronnefeld. Vorstand u. Leiter.

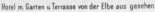

Hotel m. Garten u. Terrasse von der Elbe aus gesehen.

Front nach dem Königl. Opernhaus und Schloss.

Telefon-Anruf:
5254. 5255. 5256.
—
Direktion 5257.
—
Auto-Garage
(abgeschlossene Boxen)
—
Lieber's Code
Internationaler Hotel Code.

Dresden, d. July 13th 1913.

My dear Ben,

Very many thanks for your letter telling me all about Henley; you must have had a ripping time & I was very sorry to miss it. I am so glad the Leander crew won the Grand; I am sorry Joy was not rowing. I hear he was rather seedy. Eddie must also be very pleased with the Oriel crew for winning the Thames Cup. Life is not exciting out here but the time is going fast which is the great thing. I am now nearly at the end of a very pleasant motor trip from Munich to Neu Strelitz. I left Munich last Sunday & spent the next nights at Ratisbon, Nuremberg, Marienbad, Prague &

...esden where I have been since Thursday. I leave
...morrow for Leipzig, & then spend 3 nights
...Berlin before reaching Stretty on
...iday. Up to now I have done nearly 500 miles
...the car, & have driven the whole way myself. I
...ope to get back to England early in Sept. We
...ad a capital time in camp but that march
...as an awful sweat. You must have been
...ather sick at missing that Gray's Inn
...cholarship; very bad luck that it should
...ave come the same day as the race. I will
...rite again later when I have more news, so you
...ust excuse this dull letter.
...ood luck for a very good vac & "so long".
                    Yrs ever
                    Eddie.

## THE "BLUES" AND THEIR COLLEGES.

The table given below shows how many men in the different Colleges have taken part in all races, to-day's included, and the numbers of men from the different Colleges in the winning crews, counting the race of 1877 as a win for each University. The coxswains as well as oarsmen are included:

| OXFORD. | In all Races. | In Winning Crews. | CAMBRIDGE. | In all Races. | In Winning Crews. |
|---|---|---|---|---|---|
| Magdalen | 95 | 57 | Trinity | 276 | 126 |
| Christ Church | 76 | 38 | Trinity Hall | 97 | 37 |
| Brasenose | 66 | 36 | Jesus | 73 | 37 |
| New College | 76 | 46 | St. John's | 47 | 18 |
| Balliol | 62 | 33 | Caius | 35 | 20 |
| University | 49 | 29 | Magdalene | 21 | 11 |
| Exeter | 35 | 19 | Corpus | 18 | 4 |
| St. John's | 22 | 9 | Christ's | 11 | 3 |
| Pembroke | 24 | 12 | Emmanuel | 14 | 5 |
| Merton | 22 | 9 | Clare Hall | 8 | 5 |
| Corpus | 19 | 9 | Queens' | 6 | 3 |
| Trinity | 21 | 15 | L'dy M'rg'r't BC | 7 | 3 |
| Wadham | 15 | 7 | Peterhouse | 4 | 2 |
| Oriel | 10 | 6 | Pembroke | 9 | 3 |
| Worcester | 10 | 6 | Sidney | 4 | 2 |
| Lincoln | 10 | 3 | King's | 3 | 2 |
| Hertford | 13 | 11 | Downing | 2 | 0 |
| Queen's | 6 | 1 | St. Catharine's | 1 | 0 |
| Jesus | 2 | 0 | Cavendish | 2 | 0 |
| Keble | 3 | 2 | | | |
| New Inn Hall | 2 | 2 | | | |
| Magdalen Hall | 1 | 1 | | | |

The Oxford coxswains have belonged to Christ Church (14), Magdalen (11), New (9), Brasenose (6), Exeter (5), Corpus (4), St. John's (4), Hertford (3), Merton (3), Balliol (2), University (2), Trinity (2), Wadham (2), Worcester (1), Keble (1), and Jesus (1) ; the Cambridge to Trinity Hall (14), Caius (10), First Trinity (9), Third Trinity (6), Jesus (7), Clare (5), Corpus (4), Queens' (4), St. John's (4), Trinity (3), Magdalene (?), Cavendish (2), and Lady Margaret (1).

*The Times 1911*

because it was thought Talboys' health would not stand the excitement of a trip to College. It probably says at least as much about his devotion to duty, love of the river and the proximity of his home to the barge. One may wonder why a retiring boatman would wish for a stop-watch but Dick's son, who bore the same name, was then boatman to O.U.B.C. After these 39 years' service, he was succeeded as boatman to Magdalen by Jack May.

A large number of the crew left Oxford that summer and the blues autumn returnees included just Wormald and Wells. They were joined by E.D. Horsfall fresh from stroking Eton to win the Ladies' Plate and he stroked the Magdalen 1st Four that Michaelmas. He had acquired the nickname 'Dink' at school and was to become another of Magdalen's great oarsmen. He went straight in to the 1912 Blue boat to join Wormald and Wells.

That winter Magdalen took the Headship of Torpids for the first time in its history. They made four bumps against Trinity, Christ Church, New College and Balliol and held the top spot the following year.

Henry Bensley Wells had not tried rowing, or coxing, before coming to Oxford. It is interesting that this was the year both crews sank in the Boat Race, Cambridge opposite Harrods and Oxford at Chiswick, but perhaps the more so because Edward, Prince of Wales, followed the race in the Umpire's launch. He had arrived as an undergraduate at Magdalen that year and expressed a desire to cox. The Palace forbade it but it is not clear whether this edict was issued before or after the race. He became a close friend of 'Ben' Wells and maintained a flow of correspondence with him, typically about rowing and Wells' involvement. Of the O.U.B.C. Fours in 1913 H.R.H. wrote to Wells saying that College had allowed Eddie Burgess to stay up for the purposes of winning the event, but he felt that New College were sure to win, which they did.

# The 1912 Olympic Regatta, Stockholm

The summer was thin with no success in trying to retrieve the Headship of Eights from New College and the Olympic selectors taking Wormald, Horsfall and Wells to join, at Leander, Gillan, Garton, Kirby and Fleming to make them part of the crew for the eight preparing for the Stockholm Olympic Games that was also to race in the Grand at Henley. Unlike 1908 the Stewards did not ban overseas entries and when Leander, coached by Harcourt Gold, lost to the Australians from Sydney R.C. in the final he brought 'Long' Burgess in to the boat to replace C.E. Tinné of University College, thus making the Olympic Eight a crew of eight Magdalen men. S.E. Swann of Trinity Hall filled the 2 seat. New College's recent form meant that they were invited to be the other representative boat at the Games.

At the Olympics Games in Stockholm the other eights competing were Australia, Canada, Sweden, Norway, Germany and Hungary. A wide variety of oars were in use from 11 foot 10 inches to 12 foot 6 inches. Leander who had taken 12 foot 3 inch blades cut the three inches off in Sweden. Leander beat Canada in the first round then had the chance to avenge their defeat by the Australians a few weeks earlier. They too had made one crew change and had a lead of three-quarters of a length at the 1,000 metre mark. Fleming stroking the Leander crew put in a determined spurt and they passed the Australians to win in a fast time. Leander went on to beat the Germans to meet New College in the final who had disposed of Norway and Sweden on the way. The final was in the evening of the race against the Germans, New College had had a bye in the morning.

The Leander Eight at Stockholm

DEN FEMTE OLYMPIADEN DEL 17

RODD

OLYMPISKA SPELEN I STOCKHOLM 1912 I BILD och ORD

For many years there had been an intense rivalry between Magdalen and New College. Both clubs had been in the first three on the River for 25 years in Eights, and both had won the Grand. Their fortunes swayed to and fro in Torpids and O.U.B.C. Fours, but they worked together every year in University crews. The M.C.B.C. record books regularly record tributes to New College crews or named individuals, in a way that it does not do for other colleges, suggesting a rivalry based on personal and mutual respect. It seems that it was an incident at the final of the Stockholm Olympic Regatta which brought the long-standing rivalry between Magdalen and New College to a head. The Magdalen and Leander Club records are silent on the matter, the New College Captain's book suggests that something – deliberate or otherwise – went on with the allocation for stations. Having won the toss N.C.B.C. did the usual gentlemanly thing of offering the choice to their rivals who would have been expected to decline. In fact, it is suggested, Magdalen chose the station that had been nicknamed 'Bucks' which was thought, by New College at least, to be worth $1\frac{1}{2}$ to 2 lengths, as it avoided the hazard on the 'Berks' station of having to steer round a bathing shed to get a straight line for the bridge which was at a bias to the river, thus needing more rudder.

Fleming took no chances against a crew stroked by R.C. Bourne who that year had stroked Oxford to a lead of a length after 500 metres and to victory for a fourth successive time. At the Olympic final Leander had a lead of a canvas after 500 metres and three-quarters of a length at 1,000 metres. When the bend turned in New College's favour, Bourne put in a spurt and reduced the lead to a third of a length, but the bend then switched in Leander's favour and they drew away to win by a length.

It seems unlikely that even a regatta course of that period could have had a bias of the degree suggested. Further, though New College had been on 'Bucks' for the first two days, the toss for stations was renewed for each round and thus the notion that it was theirs by right is debatable. As the N.C.B.C. log suggests, it may have been an error on the part of an official at the start, though if that is so there is no record of anyone challenging it; they leave un-stated the possibility that it was dirty work by someone. New College reinforce their version by saying that King Gustav V was so impressed with the manners of New College that he conferred his royal colours on their Boat Club, so that their blades have had gold stripes ever since. No written account is known to confirm this claim. What makes this more curious is that the Nickalls family was known to the Swedish Royal Family in whose country Tom, Guy's and Vivian's father, had bought an 100,000 acre estate complete with a lake 8 miles long and where he built a large house for parties each August. Guy was coach of the Leander crew; Harold Barker that of the New College boat who were more typically coached by Bourne's father, Dr G.C. Bourne (New College 1882-85). Much more has been written elsewhere to try and explore the real cause of the tension felt by New College. In the final analysis the most likely explanation put forward is one of a mixture of resentment felt against Leander who may have treated them very much as the second boat, a decision to take an older craft to Stockholm and use the younger one for Henley, and the long-felt rivalry with Magdalen.

In any event, the Leander crew brought home Olympic gold and Magdalen, providing eight of the nine men therein, and who were still in residence, can rightly claim credit for this success. Angus Gillan, at 5 in the Olympic boat, had also rowed in the Magdalen winning four at the 1908 Games and so at Stockholm became the first Briton to win two Olympic rowing titles.

1912 Olympic Gold Medal

Back on the Isis in Michaelmas 1912, the traditional rivalry continued for the O.U.B.C. Fours. Magdalen's 1st four was stroked by Horsfall, with Wormald as steersman and Burgess both of whom had rowed at Stockholm, and freshman C.L. Baillieu. They beat New College in the first round thus avenging the previous autumn's defeat; they went to beat Balliol in the final.

In the Torpids of 1913 Magdalen stayed Head. The 2nd Torpid made six bumps and finished fifth on the River - a record place for a second boat. 'The effort was remarkable, and their triumph over New College I very welcome' says the Captain's Book. For New College I to be bumped by Magdalen II must have been the ultimate humiliation, and perhaps the remark hints at the feeling after Stockholm.

Wormald was President of O.U.B.C. and one of five Magdalen men with a seat in the Oxford crew for the 1913 Boat Race. Wells was cox once again and Horsfall was at stroke. Cambridge underrated Oxford for much of the race and led until Corney Reach where the conditions went against them. Oxford edged back before Barnes Bridge but Cambridge still had a lead of a length and a quarter and in Oxford's water. A hard push by Horsfall had the boats overlapping at The Queen's Head and both coxes gave way, avoiding a foul. Oxford inched up and the boats were level at the Mortlake Brewery. Despite a strong push from Cambridge they then wavered and Horsfall drove his crew on and took the race by a verdict of three-quarters of a length.

# After some good training, Magdalen bet 7-1 on themselves taking the headship before the Gut.

Magdalen badly wanted the Headship of Summer Eights back from New College who were now without Bourne at stroke. After some good training, Magdalen bet 7-1 on themselves taking the headship before the Gut. They didn't and for the rest of the week they didn't either. The 2*nd* eight went down two places to Trinity and Oriel. Magdalen did not enter the Grand at Henley that year. Their four blues Wormald, Garton and Horsfall rowed for Leander, coxed by Wells, and coached by Guy Nickalls. They equalled the course record of 6 minutes 51 seconds in a heat against the Toronto Argonauts, and went on to win the final against Jesus College, Cambridge.

Most of the College's best oarsmen left that summer and Magdalen lost the Torpids Headship in 1914 to Christ Church. The 2nd Torpid bumped St. John's I to rise from fifth to fourth on the river, a record that has never been approached by any college until Oriel were head and third in 1989. Torpids racing was still in clinker boats with fixed seats, the mantra being that Oxford oarsmen should learn to swing before using slides.

In the fateful summer of 1914 Eights week was not kind to Magdalen. They fell to fourth on the river, though the 2nd boat rose three places to 11*th* and the highest position yet seen by a second boat.

On 4*th* August the Great War erupted and for the next four years sport was forgotten and Oxford all but deserted of undergraduates. Many Magdalen men enlisted with the London Rifle Brigade. Don Burnell had joined the L.R.B. in 1894 and left in 1912; he rejoined in 1914 and recruited Magdalen oarsmen to this volunteer brigade. Among his recruits were J.R. Somers-Smith, G.H. Foster and A.G. Kirby.

1st Torpid cap

Bottom: 1913 Torpid on the start.

Capt. J.R. Somers-Smith M.C.
killed 1.7.1916

Capt. J. R. Somers Smith. M.C. (Killed 1.7.16)

The horrors of this war were to claim the lives of 192 Magdalen men amongst whom were many oarsmen, including six Blues. Three of them, K.J. Campbell, A.C. Hobson and W.L. Vince were in the Torpid head crew of 1912-14 and were not part of the greater successes enjoyed by the more senior summer crews. They went straight to war and the cycle of the College register is such that it does not list them until they are in the obituaries section. Vince was Captain of Boats in 1912-13.

Maclagan had been elected a Steward of Henley in 1914 but his death at Ypres, serving with the Warwickshire Regiment, a year later meant he was to be one of the shortest lived of their number, serving at only one Regatta. He had also been the Honorary Secretary of the Amateur Rowing Association.

President Warren's Notebook records an obituary for Duncan Mackinnon who died on 17th October 1917; he had joined the Scots Guards as a Lieutenant, having returned from the family business in India to fight. He was the third and last surviving brother of three, his elder brother William who had also been at Magdalen having been killed the summer before Duncan. He was also predeceased by A.G. Kirby, G.S. Maclagan, J.R. Somers-Smith, E.H.L. Southwell (Rifle Brigade) and the Hon. R.P. Stanhope (Grenadier Guards). Warren says: '*Unde pares invenias?*' [From where will we find their equals?] and reflects on Mackinnon's close friendship with Angus Kirby recalling that they were the life and soul of the Sunday evening Smoking Concerts in Hall (known as 'Afters'). He calls Kirby Mackinnon's '*fidus Achates*'[5] [a true friend; Achates was the friend of Aeneas]. Mackinnon had gone to war anticipating the risks; his love of Magdalen was such that he had prepared for the worst and had provided for a scholarship to be set up in his name. It remains the largest scholarship awarded by the College. C.P. Rowley (Royal Garrison Artillery) was the other Magdalen blue who fell after Mackinnon. Captain John Robert Somers-Smith, London Rifle Brigade, was awarded the Military Cross. He had been recruited to the L.R.B. by Don Burnell; they were both involved in the 1914 Christmas Day Truce which saw them playing football with the Germans. He died aged 29 and his body was never found; his name is inscribed on the Thiepval memorial.

[1] G.C. Drinkwater and T.R.B. Sanders, The University Boat Race Official Centenary History, Cassell & Co. 1929

[2] J. Swaddling, The Ancient Olympic Games, The British Museum Press 1980

[3] D. Miller, Athens to Athens, The Official History of the Olympic Games and IOC; Mainstream Publishing 2003

[4] President's Notebook PR/2/16, Magdalen College Archive

[5] President's Notebook PR/2/19, Magdalen College Archive

1920 Four training on the Isis, passing the College barge, watched by the Boatman, Jack May.

# 6  1919-1930

## Post-War Triumphs, Antwerp 1920, Gully Nickalls, Second Boat Success

When the Great War ended with the Armistice on 11*th* November 1918, Magdalen had just forty undergraduates in the Hilary term that followed. The College had lost 192 of her sons, many of whom had not finished at Oxford when the War broke out. The position was much the same in the other colleges and at a captains' meeting it was decided that Torpids could not be held in the usual way but that some 'special Lent races' be held on the American tournament system. Magdalen won rowing in the 'English Style' and, as the Captain's log notes, 'not influenced by the Australian coaching at Oxford now'. M.C.B.C. had just eleven members.

The outbreak of the War had brought the 'first golden era' to an abrupt end. One might wonder how it would have continued had hostilities not intervened. Magdalen was fortunate to have a mixture of returning oarsmen and freshmen of ability, mostly from Eton. Ewart Douglas Horsfall, always known from his school days onwards as 'Dink', had matriculated in 1911, at school he had stroked the Eton crew to win the Ladies' Plate of 1911 in a record time. Once at Oxford his pre-war rowing had been essentially confined to Leander and O.U.B.C. with whom he had won three blues and been their President in 1913-14, though he did also do some rowing with the College. He volunteered for military service and was commissioned as a Second Lieutenant with the Rifle Brigade. He was later transferred to the Royal Flying Corps and was awarded the Military Cross for operations behind enemy lines during which he was severely injured in the back while swinging a propeller. He rose to the rank of Major. In 1919 Horsfall became President of Vincent's Club and set about helping Magdalen rowing, and though no record exists of any elections or positions held, effectively he fulfilled the role of captain for Hilary and Trinity Terms. His experience with O.U.B.C. and as a member of the winning Eight at the Stockholm Olympic Games made him well suited to the task. Also returning to College were R.S.C. Lucas and W.H. Porritt. Richard 'Luke' Lucas had come from Eton to Magdalen for just the Michaelmas term of 1914 before serving with the King's Royal Rifle Corps. William Porritt had been at Wyggeston School until spending Hilary and Trinity 1917 in Oxford. After the War, together with Horsfall, they were to be instrumental in the restart of the Boat Club. They were joined by three freshmen who were experienced oarsmen from Eton. A.T.M. Durand, S. Earl and W.E.C. James (later 4th baron, Lord Northbourne), 'Jimmy' James had served with the 2nd/4th Northumberland Fusiliers.

Eights Week 1919 was confined to four days' racing. The starting order was drawn by lot and Magdalen obtained third place, one position higher than they had ended in 1914. The strength of the crew was quickly demonstrated and they bumped Christ Church and then New College to take the Headship. There had been no University Boat Race and five of the Magdalen men took the opportunity to row for the University at the Henley Peace Regatta. In view of the circumstances, the regatta put on a special selection of events rather than the usual pro-gramme. An Oxford University Service Crew entered the King's Cup, an international eights event for those who had served in the Allied Forces. The Magdalen contin-gent, entered with rank, were: 3: Pte. S. Earl, 4: Lt. R.S.C. Lucas, 5: Pte. A.T.M. Durand, 6: Major E.D. Horsfall M.C., 7: Lt. W.E.C. James. The crew beat the Canadians, then the Americans but in the final lost by a length to the Australians. This cup is still in use as a regatta trophy in Australia. Magdalen also entered the regatta in its own right, racing in the Elsenham Cup, offered for Colleges and Public Schools. Stroked by the Hon. Benjamin Bathurst (later 2nd Viscount Bledisloe) and made up mainly of Etonians and Harrovians most of whom went on to become barristers, this crew beat Radley in the first heat but lost to Shrewsbury on the second day.

The start of the new academic year in October 1919 brought G.O. 'Gully' Nickalls to Magdalen. The son of Guy Nickalls and nephew of Harcourt Gold, he was to make a mark on the rowing world equalled by very few but a match for his father and his uncle, Vivian. Canon H.D. Rawnsley, a Fellow of Balliol and contempo-rary of President Warren attended Magdalen Chapel on 11th November, the first anniversary of the Armistice. In his notebook Warren records this as being on St Martin's Day (Remembrance Day had not yet become the title for this anniversary) and that

E.D. Horsfall

Rawnsley was so moved by the remembrance service that he wrote a poem and later sent it to Warren. In the final verse he put emphasis on just how many of the College's lost sons were oarsmen.[1]

## At Oxford in May

*City of bells and sunny towers,*
*City of blossoming trees and flowers,*
*I who have been in Provence in May*
*Find her here in her haunts to-day,*
*Corcoris, lilac, cherry, laburnum,*
*All in their spring-tide gay.*

*No more now do the war-hawks hover;*
*Blackbirds call, and the lark hangs over,*
*Nightingales babble in Bagley lane –*
*They who listen forget their pain;*
*Captains and graduate brigadiers,*
*Students once, are students again.*

*Ah! but hark! how the brimming river*
*Mourns for her sons who return not ever!*
*- Men who with spirits bright as May*
*Poured the wine of their life away,*
*- Men whose names on the roll in Chapel*
*Bid us by service our debt repay.*

Cannon Rawnsley's reflection on The Great War.

The year started well with a comfortable win in the University Fours. Given the shortness of the previous year, it was essentially a freshmen's crew albeit an experienced one of Earl, who was steersman, Lucas, Durand and James. Earl had been elected Captain of Boats and held the position for the following year as well. Torpids 1920 were unremarkable but for Summer Eights the pre-war finish-

# The 1920 Grand Challenge Cup-winning crew was invited by the British Olympic Committee

ing order was restored for the first evening. Accordingly Magdalen started fourth and bumped Christ Church, University College and New College to take the Headship on the third day. The second boat first made two bumps to move into the first division and then rose to ninth place by the end of the week. By way of celebration, the President and Lady Warren (Herbert Warren had been made a K.C.V.O. in 1914) entertained the first and second boats to dinner in the Lodgings.[2] Lucas and Nickalls won the O.U.B.C. Pairs and Earl the University Sculls giving Magdalen a clean sweep of the small boats events; the Torpids headship alone eluded them. Dink Horsfall had gone down the previous summer and thus was not eligible to row for College on the Isis. He had coached the second boat, but he was able to row at Henley and came in to stroke the Eight which had entered the Grand. The eligibility rules for Henley Royal Regatta for this period took somewhat different approaches to circumstances. This was the year in which Jack Kelly, the famous American sculler, had his entry for the Diamond Challenge Sculls refused because, having been an apprentice bricklayer and now running his own building business, he was not classed as an amateur (this reason was never articulated and it probably was that his club, Vesper, was still banned for similar issues after the 1905 regatta)[3]. By contrast, the rules for the Ladies' Challenge Plate, an event for only certain academic institutions, nonetheless allowed a man to row who might have left his university or college but with a fairly generous restriction

on the time after graduating. It was this flexibility which allowed Magdalen to call upon Horsfall's services to strengthen the boat in 1920 and 1921. Jocelyn Proby, who was part of the 1919 intake from Eton, was the man to lose his seat though the order had been changed considerably from the Summer Eight. Earl, Durand, James and Horsfall doubled up to make a Stewards' Four while Nickalls and Lucas also entered the Silver Goblets. Magdalen, coached by Reginald Rowe, won all three of these open events, a remarkable achievement for any club. The second Eight entered the Thames Challenge Cup and beat Trinity Hall and then St Catharine's College, Cambridge before losing to Thames R.C. 'A' crew by three-quarters of a length. The following day Thames beat Caius College, Cambridge in the final. An indication of the general strength of the Boat Club is displayed by the fact that half this crew, plus their cox G.D. Clapperton, were still in the second boat (and the Thames Cup) a year later, the first Eight having had only one change.

The 1920 Grand Challenge Cup-winning crew was invited by the British Olympic Committee to represent the nation at the Games to be held in Antwerp. This was declined on grounds of cost though Sebastian Earl, writing sixty years later, observes somewhat enigmatically that the Magdalen crew refused 'because in the unlikely event of our being beaten the College would be unpopular for many years'. However

HENLEY
ROYAL REGATTA
(In accordance with the rules of the A.R.A.).

THE OFFICIAL
PROGRAMME
FOR
SATURDAY,
JULY 2nd, 1921.

they did agree to row under different colours and the Captain of Leander, R.S. Shove, had approached the Amateur Rowing Association, with the club's permission and despite objections from its President, George Rowe, to enter a Leander crew for the Olympic Regatta. Thus five members of the Magdalen crew became part of the Leander Eight along with two Cambridge Blues and Shove at stroke. They were coached by Cherry Pitman. Horsfall was in his second Olympic Eight whilst Earl, James, Lucas and Nickalls were making their debut for their country. The Olympic Regatta was held on the Brussels Maritime Canal, and the British crew found there an American crew that was essentially professional. They were all Navy men who had been together for two years and since January had no other

Rudder presented to R.P.P. Rowe who coached the two crews

duties to distract them. They came with a doctor, masseurs, a second crew to act as a pacemaker, and their own food and cooks. The cruiser which had brought them over acted at their hotel base near the course. Meanwhile the Leander crew had had barely five weeks together and were handicapped by poor British Olympic officials' administration – they had to stay some seven miles from the regatta site in a station tavern using rough roads and dirty trams to go between the two. Despite this they beat Switzerland, the reigning European champions, and then Norway to reach the final where they were narrowly defeated by the Americans.[4] Earl's 1981 letter went on to say 'during the race he [Shove] fainted on my shoulder when we were leading Annapolis [the Americans] by three feet, a

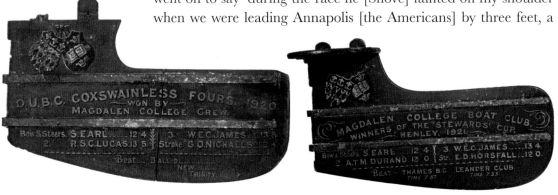

O.U.B.C. Pairs Cup 1921
A.T.M. Durand and S. Earl.

few strokes from the finish, and we were beaten by eight feet. The crew was nowhere near as fast as the Magdalen crew that won the Grand. They would certainly have won instead of being only second.'[5] Not only did the Magdalen Captain's book feel the silver medal had been won in the face of this adversity, there was comment by various rowing correspondents over the poor management of the British crew. Earl and the other Magdalen men may well have rued their original decision not to row the College crew.

The academic year 1920-21 had the benefit of the continuing presence of all the key figures of the Boat Club. Nickalls, Lucas, James and Earl won the O.U.B.C. Fours though the Captain's Book records that this was the first year since 1908 that they had used swivels and that 'it took them a while to adjust'. During Torpids 1921, when the fairly novice crew were still rowing on fixed seats in clinker eights, Magdalen dropped two places to fourth overall. The President and Lady Warren had entertained the crew to breakfast in the Lodgings on two mornings that week.[6] In the University Boat Race Jimmy James, who was President of O.U.B.C., was joined by his fellow Magdalen men of Earl, Nickalls and Lucas, with Porritt coxing. They lost a good race to Cambridge, a rare thing for these men of this era of such success. Earl won the University Sculls and with Tom Durand won the Pairs. Prior to Summer Eights, the President and Lady Warren entertained the three eights to dinner in the New Room. In his letter of thanks, Seb Earl says he is sorry the coal strike prevented them from hosting the occasion in the

1920. Magdalen A.C.:

Winners.

| Eights | Head of the River | Henley Royal Regatta | Grand Challenge Cup |
|---|---|---|---|
| O.U.B.C. | Fours | " " " | Stewards " |
| " | Pairs | | Silver Goblets |
| " | Sculls | Olympic Eight (Brussels) | |

Boat Club. 1921.

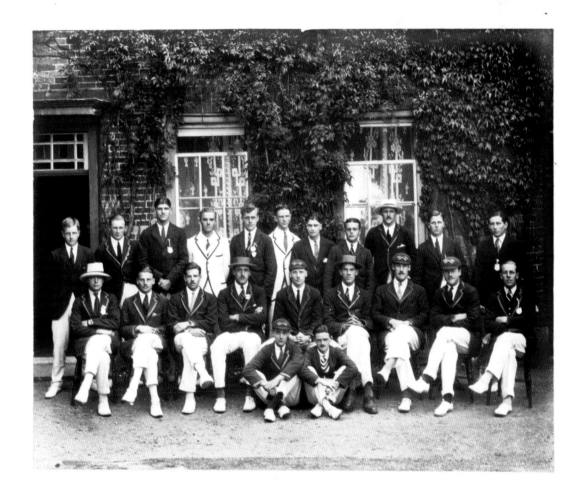

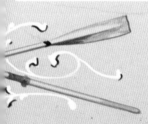

Winners

| O. U. B. C. Fours | Henley Royal Regatta |
|---|---|
| ,, Pairs | Grand Challenge Cup |
| ,, ½ Sculls | Stewards Challenge Cup |

President's Lodgings but hopes the Club will uphold the traditions of the College.[7] It was not to be – they were bumped by New College on the second night and thus lost the Headship. Earl, in his second year as Captain, recorded that 'they never really learned to work hard, except Nickalls at seven who was a tower of strength as far as individual pulling was concerned, but scarcely ever followed stroke, to the detriment of the crew as a whole.' New College had no Blues onboard while Magdalen had four plus the cox, all from the previous year's Grand-winning crew. They turned this situation round when the beat New College in the second round of the Grand Challenge Cup at Henley where the 1920 crew was entered again with one change at the two seat and Horsfall again brought in at stroke. They had seen off London R.C. in the first round and then Jesus College, Cambridge in the final, crews they had beaten in the same event a year earlier. Earl, Durand, James and Horsfall doubled up in a four to win the Stewards' Challenge Cup beating Thames R.C. and then Leander. This was Dink Horsfall's last appearance in a College boat, but he continued to be an inspiration and a coach to M.C.B.C. for many years. The second boat entered the Thames Challenge Cup and beat Maidenhead R.C., Downing College, Cambridge and First Trinity B.C. before succumbing by one foot to Christiania Roklub, Norway, the eventual winners, in the semi-final. The bow pair of the Grand Eight, H.C. Irvine and R. Armstrong-Jones, doubled up in the Visitors' Challenge Cup with J.C.P. Proby, who was also in the Thames Eight, and Ben Bathurst who stroked this four. They beat Trinity Hall but then lost to Lincoln College in the final - probably the only time a Magdalen crew has been in the shadow of that college. Nickalls and Lucas doubled up from the Grand Eight to compete for the Silver Goblets and Nickalls' Challenge Cup but were knocked out by Campbell and Playford from Jesus College, Cambridge, the eventual winners; small retribution for the result in the Grand.

During the O.U.B.C. autumn Fours of 1921 the Magdalen first boat met the second. In the first boat, Tom Durand and Gully Nickalls were in the middle of the boat and the steersman at bow was Peter Girdlestone; they won the event. Girdlestone had stroked the second Eight the previous term and at Henley, he had arrived as a freshman in Michaelmas 1920 having learnt to row at Melbourne Grammar School and St Peter's College, Adelaide. His father, Henry, who later coached him in the 1923 Head crew, had been at

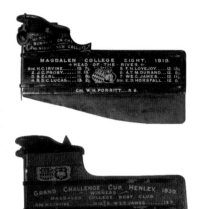

Magdalen and was a Blue in 1885. Peter's son Gathorne came to the College in 1968 and the Girdlestones became one of the few Magdalen families to have three generations at the College and rowing, the Burnell, Lewis and Dodds-Parker clans being the others. On 10th November the Boat Club held a 'Grand Night' in Hall to celebrate their success on the river at Henley and in the small boats events on the Isis. Ninety-six members were present of whom nine were Fellows.[8] It may well be that the 2007 Headship dinner was the next time so many members of the S.C.R. were to dine with the Boat Club. At the end of 1921 Cyril Carter retired from many years of coaching but remained at Treasurer of the Boat Club; he had first been involved in the club in the late 1800s.

W.H. Porritt's rudder collection.

Summer 1922 saw Magdalen row over behind New College; perhaps the problems of the previous Summer Eight remained. The crew split up for Henley. Nickalls and Lucas won the Silver Goblets and Nickalls' Challenge Cup for the second time and were both in

President Warren (seated)
in the O.U.B.C launch 'Etona'
in Iffley lock with the blue
boat, G.D. Clapperton coxing.

the Leander crew with Horsfall and Porritt that won the Grand. This took William Porritt's successes to three successive wins in this premier eights event alongside his three Blues for the same years and two Headships in Summer Eights. His decorated rudders now hang in the College's Old Kitchen Bar. A Ladies' Plate Eight was entered for Henley that was essentially the second boat. Again stroked by Girdlestone and coxed by Clapperton, they beat Beaumont College, Christ Church and Shrewsbury to reach the final against Brasenose. Despite an early lead Magdalen could not respond to the Brasenose push at Fawley and the cup was to rest further down the High Street; not a bad performance for a second crew against a first. On the strength of being beaten by Shrewsbury, Girdlestone was to send Gathorne and his brother to school there on the grounds that they must be good if they could beat Magdalen. Irvine, Philips, Proby and Bathurst entered both the Visitors' and the Wyfold but did not make the final in either. Earl won a heat of the Diamond Challenge Sculls but lost to the Australian A.A. Baynes in the second round.

The academic year 1922-23 was to be a first for M.C.B.C., now out of the era when only novices rowed in Torpids and containing six of the previous summer's Henley crew, for the first boat bumped New College for the Headship. In Trinity Term the Eight finally exacted its summer revenge on New College bumping them opposite the Worcester barge on the first evening. Despite some rocky rowing the following night when the bump was nearly reversed, they then held off Christ Church on the final three evenings to hold the Headship and thus a first Double Headship. The Captain, the Hon. W.B.C. Lewis (later Lord Merthyr), noted that they were probably the lightest Magdalen crew for 20 or 30 years with an average of 11 stone 3lbs. He also recorded the enormous contribution of Gully Nickalls for whom this was his last appearance for Magdalen.

# G.O. 'GULLY' NICKALLS

Guy Oliver Nickalls, always known as 'Gully', was to match his father Guy's rowing record, and to follow him though Eton and Magdalen. Born in 1899, eight years after his father had left the College, he was twice an Olympic Silver medallist both at Antwerp in 1920 and in Amsterdam in 1928, on both occasions in the Eight. Gully rowed for Oxford in three Boat Race crews, winning in 1923 when he was President of O.U.B.C. He won the Grand Challenge Cup at Henley on seven occasions – a record unlikely to ever be equalled or surpassed. He had an eventful time rowing for the trophy added to by his grandfather Tom to mark his father's and his uncle's success in the Silver Goblets. He competed for this cup on no less than eight occasions between 1920 and 1927, making the final on six occasions and winning twice in 1920 and 1921. There was considerable misfortune in some of the other years, often to do with woodwork of one sort or another. In 1923, rowing for Leander with H.B. Playford after a final in which they were practically level with their opponents from Trinity College, Oxford, they hit the pile just below the Judge's Box to lose by five feet. Rowing in 1924 with his College friend R.S.C. Lucas, again for Leander, they went out to the Magdalen pair of G.K. Hampshire and W. Phillips in the first heat. The entertaining, if unfortunate, story is best told by the race report: 'The result of this race was entirely unexpected for Nickalls and Lucas were considered the probable winners of the Goblets. It was not generally known, however, that as well as being famous oarsmen they were no mean amateur carpenters and always carried a set of tools. Whilst waiting at the Start, Stroke, thinking that the boat was unnecessarily heavy, cut away some of the bigger timbers and on the first stroke of the race Bow pushed his stretcher through the skin and she started to leak. However, they soon took the lead and before going far, Hampshire and Phillips hit the booms and Nickalls and Lucas waited for them.

On re-starting Nickalls and Lucas again took the lead and were a long way ahead at Fawley, reached in 5.30. Here it became obvious that something was wrong for the boat was floating lower and lower in the water. In spite of the handicap they kept well ahead and it became more of a race against the leak than against their opponents. At the Mile Post it was clear that the leak was gaining on

Nickalls' comic opera programme

them fast and at the bottom of the Enclosure the cut-water disappeared and then the boat sank amidst execrations that were visible but inaudible at the Winning Post.

All the time Hampshire and Phillips were entirely unconscious of what had happened to their opponents whom they had not seen since about half way up the Island. When they came up with them they were not a little surprised to find them swimming and so stopped rowing. Ultimately they paddled in to complete the Course in 12 mins. 0 sec. and immediately offered to row the race again. The Committee, however, could not allow this, pointing out that as they had passed the Winning Post the race was over and that a boat must abide by its accidents.'[9] The chivalry and respect for Nickalls and Lucas shown by their College contemporaries says as much about the awe in which they were held as for the sportsmanship of the period.

After Oxford, Gully continued his rowing at Thames R.C. and with them, at the age of 29, won the Stewards' Challenge Cup in

KENTON THEATRE

HENLEY on THAMES

KENTON THEATRE (PRODUCTIONS)
presents

REGATTA DAY

May 26ᵗʰ to June 1ˢᵗ 1991
at 7·30 pm

BY G. O. (GULLY) NICKALLS

REGATTA CHAMPAGNE SUPPER/SHOW, SUNDAY 26th at 7 p.m.

MATINEE: Saturday, June 1st at 2.30 p.m.

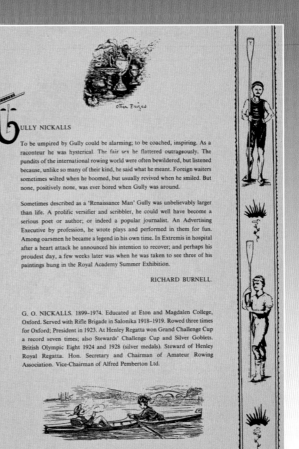

Other Pages

GULLY NICKALLS

To be umpired by Gully could be alarming; to be coached, inspiring. As a raconteur he was hysterical. The fair sex he flattered outrageously. The pundits of the international rowing world were often bewildered, but listened because, unlike so many of their kind, he said what he meant. Foreign waiters sometimes wilted when he boomed, but usually revived when he smiled. But none, positively none, was ever bored when Gully was around.

Sometimes described as a 'Renaissance Man' Gully was unbelievably larger than life. A prolific versifier and scribbler, he could well have become a serious poet or author; or indeed a popular journalist. An Advertising Executive by profession, he wrote plays and performed in them for fun. Among oarsmen he became a legend in his own time. In Extremis in hospital after a heart attack he announced his intention to recover; and perhaps his proudest day, a few weeks later was when he was taken to see three of his paintings hung in the Royal Academy Summer Exhibition.

RICHARD BURNELL.

G. O. NICKALLS. 1899–1974. Educated at Eton and Magdalen College, Oxford. Served with Rifle Brigade in Salonika 1918–1919. Rowed three times for Oxford; President in 1923. At Henley Regatta won Grand Challenge Cup a record seven times; also Stewards' Challenge Cup and Silver Goblets. British Olympic Eight 1924 and 1928 (silver medals). Steward of Henley Royal Regatta. Hon. Secretary and Chairman of Amateur Rowing Association. Vice-Chairman of Alfred Pemberton Ltd.

1928; his seventh win in the Grand was at the same regatta. For many years after this Gully coached University and Magdalen crews, and would often be seen with M.C.B.C. for Summer Eights and Henley through to the 1960s.

Prior to Oxford Nickalls, as a 2nd Lieutenant in the Rifle Brigade, saw active service in Salonika in 1918. He made a career in advertising, concluding as Vice-Chairman of Alfred Pemberton Ltd from 1945 up to his retirement in 1964. Gully was a great all-rounder exemplified by being a keen amateur artist and actor. Three of his paintings were hung at the Royal Academy Summer Exhibition. He wrote plays and a comic opera *Regatta Day* which was staged at the Kenton Theatre in Henley in 1951, and again 1991. Gully described it as a 'little Edwardian frolic'; it was commissioned by the artist John Piper who was one of the licensees of the theatre.

Gully, in succession to his uncle Sir Harcourt Gold, was Chairman of the Amateur Rowing Association from 1952-1968. While he was the Honorary Secretary of the Association for the five years prior to this elevation, he addressed the question of the inadequate funding of the cost of sending crews to represent Great Britain in Olympic and international regattas. This was resolved by Gully's proposal to levy a charge on domestic regatta entry fees of one shilling per person per entry. Until this crews covered their own expenses for international representation. He was Captain of Leander Club 1923-27, 1946 and 1948 and President of the club 1962-1966. He was elected a Steward of Henley Royal Regatta in 1935 and served on the Committee of Management for a period from 1945 to 1973, the year in which he died.

Nickalls wrote various books: *Rowing* (1939, with Dr P.C. Mallam); he edited and contributed to the chapter on rowing in *With the Skin of Their Teeth*, 1946; his own reminiscences *A Rainbow in the Sky*, 1974; and he edited and contributed to an autobiography of his late father *Life's a Pudding*, 1938. A keen cricketer, he was a member of the M.C.C. and a contributor to *The Twelfth Man*, produced by The Lord's Taverners.

Gully Nickalls as President of Leander Club

| Bow | A. F. Markham | 10 | 8 |
| 2 | G. L. Tysoy | 11 | 8 |
| 3 | G. R. R. Stevens | 12 | 1 |
| 4 | G. C. Carlisle | 11 | 2 |
| | | Cox | R. F. |

Gillman & Co Ld
Oxford.

5 &. D. Crisp 12 3
6 J. M. Buckley 12 1
7 F. R. Scott 11 13
Str. R. P. Slade 10 11
le. 8 13

At the Henley that followed the 1923 double Headship, Magdalen entered a four for the Visitors' and the same crew entered the Stewards' Challenge Cup. Though a very light crew they were fast and beat New College then Brasenose College to reach the final where they beat Trinity College, Oxford. Had the final of the Stewards' not been just one and a half hours later they might have had a better chance against Third Trinity B.C. who were the winners of the Visitors' the previous year. The era of success that culminated in 1923 was followed by a change in the fortunes of the Boat Club. Eton had been a major source of good oarsmen for many years and the successful Magdalen crews were often made up of a majority from the school. Over a period of twenty-six years R.S. de Havilland, who had been at Eton as a schoolboy and President of O.U.B.C. while at Corpus Christi College, had been coaching at the school where he was a Housemaster. He enjoyed great success producing eleven crews to win the Ladies' Challenge Plate at Henley. He retired from coaching in 1919 and died in 1921, aged 60.[10] His influence on the young men that came to Magdalen was a major contribution to the College's fortunes on the river. His passing led to a decline in rowing at Eton and meant that M.C.B.C. could no longer rely on a steady stream of experienced and successful oarsmen.[11]

# Eton had been a major source of good oarsmen for many years

The following year Magdalen lost both the Headship of Torpids, falling three places, and of Summer Eights dropping one place to Christ Church. Still a light crew, they entered the Ladies' at Henley and reached the semi-final where they lost to Jesus College, Cambridge. Jock Clapperton coxed his second Blue Boat; he had been educated at Magdalen College School and thus learnt his watermanship on the narrow winding Cherwell. His coxing career continued at Leander Club for a number of years. In 1953 he was elected a Steward of Henley Royal Regatta; for many years he lived in the Mill House at Sandford-on-Thames, at the head of the 'Radley' reach and at one time a College property. The story of the all-Magdalen (albeit Leander against the College) heat of the Silver Goblets is recounted in the profile of Gully Nickalls (pages 125-127). The unlikely winners who were rowing in College colours did not survive the next round but were more successful in later life. Hampshire became a director of I.C.I. and the father of the actress, Susan Hampshire. Wogan Phillips eventually became Lord Milford, the Communist peer.

A year later, 1925, Magdalen dropped another place in Summer Eights. Charles Horsfall was Captain; his photograph albums survived the ravages of the white ants of Northern Rhodesia and they

1923 crew at Henley. Note the finish angle.

later came to the College providing a record of crews of this period. The year 1925-26 was to be an unusual one on two counts. In November Magdalen won the 'College' freshmen's Fours with a crew that contained His Imperial Highness Prince Chichibu of Japan, The Marchese Paolo Misciatelli, Alexander Davidson and Derek Richter, coxed by Christopher Fuller. Herbert Warren was clearly proud of this modest achievement in the rowing firmament as he mentioned it in his President's Notebook. All of them had arrived at Oxford that term and had been taught to row by other members of the Boat Club. Prince Chichibu was the younger brother of Emperor Hirohito and he had to return to Japan after just one term at Magdalen owing to his father's death.

Warren was clearly pleased by his arrival as it worthy of comparison with the matriculation of the Prince of Wales in 1912, though it was later rumoured that the Imperial Palace was anxious about the Prince's exposure to Western values. Nonetheless he clearly enjoyed his short time in Oxford, even arranging his study in the Imperial Palace along the lines of his College room. He was a great anglophile and after his death in 1953, aged 50, his widow did much to restore Anglo-Japanese relations, and remained in close contact with the College. C.H.F. Fuller later became a director of the famous Griffin Brewery at Chiswick, Fuller, Smith and Turner Ltd. The firm has long been a supporter and sponsor of rowing events on the Tideway.

In Torpids M.C.B.C. bumped Brasenose on the second night and then rowed over, though Guy Jansen writing in the Captain's book speculates that Magdalen was probably the fastest crew on the river. Bumps' racing was ever to be thus: speedy but not necessarily rising up the division. Trinity Term brought the other unusual aspect to this year. The General Strike had an impact on Summer Eights and caused the event to be shortened to four days' racing (from the then usual six; they moved to four in 1954). At a Captains' Meeting on the second day of the strike the O.U.B.C. committee was empowered to cancel or postpone Eights Week, and practice if necessary. The following day all practice was cancelled. Large numbers of undergraduates volunteered to help maintain transport by driving trains, operating cranes and other essential services. The strike ended on 12th May after just nine days and on 19th May most students were back in Oxford. The Eight rowed over for the first three nights and then bumped Brasenose on the last evening. The stroke of the crew was Pat Johnson who was a physicist and in his third year. The following year he won a Blue and in 1928 was elected to a Fellowship; during the next twenty years held various College Officerships. He coached the Boat Club for many years and was instrumental in the regaining

of the double Headship in 1932. He was therefore the third Magdalen Blue (after Harris and Hopkins) to become a Fellow of the College. Also in this crew were Reginald Manningham-Buller who was Lord Chancellor from 1962 to 1964 and created Viscount Dilhorne of Greens Norton on his retirement from that great office; Kenneth Irvine was for many years a G.P. in Henley and, with his wife Phyllis, were generous hosts to Magdalen crews and old members of M.C.B.C. at their home in Henley. Many crews stayed with them for Regatta Week and enjoyed legendary hospitality including

Jack May, Boatman 1911–1936, punting the 1927 2nd Eight across the Isis

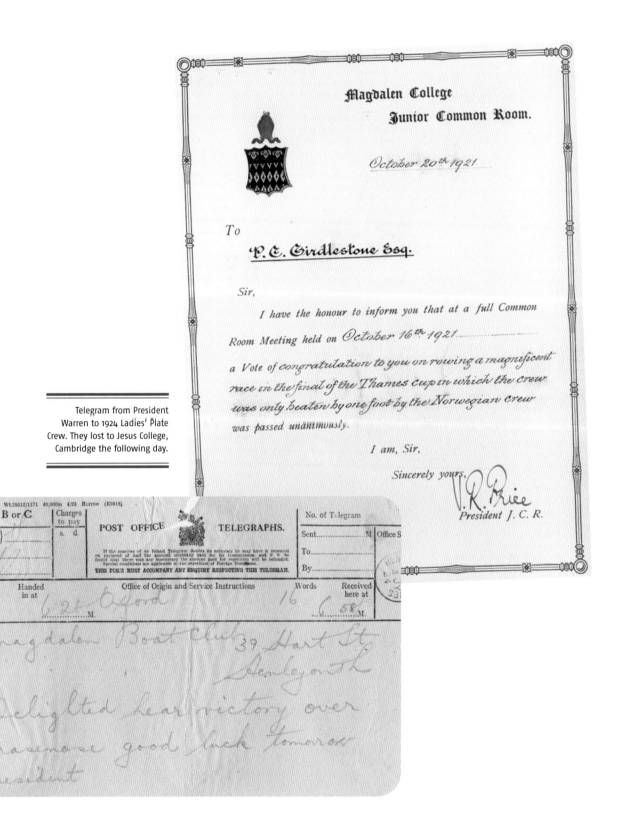

**Magdalen College**

**Junior Common Room.**

*October 20th 1921*

*To*

*P. E. Girdlestone Esq.*

*Sir,*

*I have the honour to inform you that at a full Common Room Meeting held on October 16th 1921 a Vote of congratulation to you on rowing a magnificent race in the final of the Thames cup in which the crew was only beaten by one foot by the Norwegian crew was passed unanimously.*

*I am, Sir,*

*Sincerely yours,*

*V. R. Price*
*President J.C.R.*

Telegram from President Warren to 1924 Ladies' Plate Crew. They lost to Jesus College, Cambridge the following day.

(9310) Wt.29512/1171 40,000m 4/23 Harrow (E9618)

**B or C**

**Charges to pay** s. d.

Recd from

By

**POST OFFICE** **TELEGRAPHS.**

If the receiver of an Inland Telegram doubts its accuracy he may have it repeated on payment of half the amount originally paid for its transmission, and if it be found that there was any inaccuracy the amount paid for repetition will be refunded. Special conditions are applicable to the repetition of Foreign Telegrams.

THIS FORM MUST ACCOMPANY ANY ENQUIRY RESPECTING THIS TELEGRAM.

No. of Telegram

Sent........M Office S

To........

By........

Prefix | Handed in at | Office of Origin and Service Instructions | Words | Received here at

6.25 Oxford — M. | 16 | 6.58 M.

Magdalen Boat Club 39 Hart St Henley on T

Delighted hear victory over Brasenose good luck tomorrow President

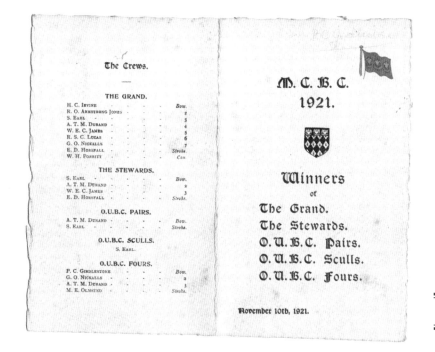

The Crews.

THE GRAND.
H. C. Irvine · · · · Bow.
R. O. Armstrong Jones · · · 2
S. Earl · · · · · 3
A. T. M. Durand · · · · 4
W. E. C. James · · · · 5
R. S. C. Lucas · · · · 6
G. O. Nickalls · · · · 7
E. D. Horsfall · · · · Stroke.
W. H. Porritt · · · · Cox.

THE STEWARDS.
S. Earl · · · · Bow.
A. T. M. Durand · · · 2
W. E. C. James · · · 3
E. D. Horsfall · · · Stroke.

O.U.B.C. PAIRS.
A. T. M. Durand · · · Bow.
S. Earl · · · · Stroke.

O.U.B.C. SCULLS.
S. Earl.

O.U.B.C. FOURS.
P. C. Girdlestone · · · Bow.
G. O. Nickalls · · · 2
A. T. M. Durand · · · 3
M. E. Olmsted · · · Stroke.

M. C. B. C.
1921.

Winners
of
The Grand.
The Stewards.
O. U. B. C. Pairs.
O. U. B. C. Sculls.
O. U. B. C. Fours.

November 10th, 1921.

Celebratory dinner menu.

the 'Irvine's Lunch' and generous Pimm's. Jansen, recalling his time as Captain, gave some insight to the training regimes of the day: 'we went round Adders [Addison's Walk] at 8am, ran the last 100 yards to breakfast in Hall at 8.15am. Rowing was usually two journeys to Iffley in the afternoon, then a training dinner in a lecture room at 7 and bed by 10 o'clock. No smoking, eating or drinking between meals, beer only, except an occasional fizz night, usually the Saturday before the races if we had done well.' The judgement of 'had done well' probably fell to Don Burnell and Dink Horsfall who were both coaching through this period. Like many Boatmen, Jack May did some coaching too. Jack had been Boatman to Magdalen since 1911; he was fond of sayings such as 'That there Mr So and So, he couldn't pull a sardine off a plate' and when the wind was blowing a gale upstream 'There's a nasty draft behind, sir'.

One of the best forms of needle within a boat club can be a second boat out-performing its senior crew. Bumps' racing, by its very nature, is unpredictable with any degree of certainty and can lead to glory for lower boats while the top boat does not shine in the same way. Summer Eights 1927 was to be a perfect example of this situation: the Eight dropped one place on the third night to Brasenose to finish the week in third position. Meanwhile, the Second Eight rose five places to finish eighth (and could have been seventh but for an accident on the last evening which caused them to be caught back by Worcester who had two Blues onboard). The Captain's Book is gracious enough to acknowledge their speed and even implies they were faster than the Eight as he suggests they were quicker than Christ Church, at Head, and Brasenose. Five of this Second Eight were overseas students, three of them graduates. Most of the crew had rowed at school and the graduates had all been at leading rowing universities prior to their arrival in Oxford. One of the crew was John Eccles, a Rhodes Scholar from Melbourne, who was to become a Fellow of the College in 1934, later to be knighted and awarded the Nobel Prize for Medicine for his work in neurophysiology. Derek Richter became a distinguished neuropsychiatrist. Charles Saltzman, another Rhodes Scholar, had a distinguished career as a general in the United States army during the Second World War and was later Under-Secretary of State. For many years he was Chairman on the American Friends of Magdalen and in 1991 he joined with the President, Tony Smith, to present the Boat Club with a women's eight named *The President*. Another was Humphrey Slade who spent his working life in Kenya, first as a schoolmaster, then an M.P., and was the first Speaker after the country's independence in 1963. The College's barge was replaced in this year.

Though the second eight of 1928 was not the same men as the year before, it continued the upward trend. Rowing over on the first three nights they then exacted revenge on Worcester and then bumped Wadham and Merton to finish sixth on the river, an all-time record for a second boat. The first night had not been without its drama: the four-man lost his oar and, amazingly, it was caught by the cox, John Bingham, who passed it back through the crew. During this St John's came up and overlapped Magdalen II but their bow-man caught a crab just before they would have bumped and they were themselves bumped by Pembroke. Lincoln then came within striking distance but Magdalen II had started again and drew away to finish only two and a half lengths off Worcester. Given the delay, this margin was quite small and one therefore wonders why they rowed over for the next two nights before catching Worcester on the fourth evening. The answer was that on the second and third evenings Magdalen overlapped Worcester entering the Gut but came out a length behind. The crew mutinied at this incompetent steering and Hervey Black, who had coxed the 1927 crew, was brought in on the fourth day. Black was later Chairman of General Accident Insurance. The crew was stroked by R.P. 'Harry' Hichens, his first summer at Magdalen. Douglas Dodds-Parker later recalled that Hichens 'led the singing while we waited for the start'[12] He stroked the Eight again in 1929. After Oxford Hichens joined the Royal Naval Volunteer Reserve and was killed in action, leading the Motor Gun Boat 8th Flotilla, off the Hook of Holland in April 1943. Lieutenant-Commander Hichens was the most decorated member of the R.N.V.R. with a D.S.O. and bar and a D.S.C. and two bars. His father and his two sons were all at Magdalen.

The Eight meanwhile, bumped Christ Church who slid three places from Head, but two days later were bumped by New College and thus remained third on the river. 1928 was M.C.B.C.'s fiftieth year in the top four on the river, a remarkable, and unrivalled, achievement. The Eight, starting from the Radley boathouse, rowed to Henley in one day, stopping for breakfast at The Queen's Arms in Abingdon and lunch at the Roebuck Hotel near Reading. They arrived in Henley by 6pm. Entered for the Ladies' Plate, they beat Monkton Combe School but lost to Jesus College, Cambridge in the second round. Four from this crew doubled up to make a Visitors' Four and beat Wadham before losing to First Trinity B.C. who went on to win the event and, later, the coxswainless fours at the Olympic Games in Amsterdam.

1929 and 1930 were to be disappointing. In Summer Eights Magdalen slipped to fifth and then to eighth, the lowest the Club had been since 1876. There were no Magdalen Blues in the Boat Race of 1930, only the fifth year since 1877 that the College had not been presented in the University crew. At its peak, Magdalen had provided six members of the University Boat, in both 1909 and 1911. Douglas Dodds-Parker was Captain in 1929-30 (though he changed the title to 'President', a form which had been briefly used in the 1880s) and decided despite the disastrous position in Summer Eights, to enter the Eight for Henley, not least because the majority of the crew would all be up the following year. They were beaten by Lady Margaret Boat Club, Cambridge in the first round of the Ladies' Plate.

The revival of M.C.B.C's fortunes was around the corner.

[1] President's Notebook PR/2/19, Magdalen College Archive

[2] President's Notebook PR/2/19, Magdalen College Archive

[3] Christopher Dodd, Henley Royal Regatta, Stanley Paul 1987

[4] R.D. Burnell and G.G.H. Page, The Brilliants, a History of the Leander Club, Leander Club 1997

[5] S. Earl letter, MC:O4/C1/5, Magdalen College Archive

[6] President's Notebook PR/2/19, Magdalen College Archive

[7] President's Notebook PR/2/19, Magdalen College Archive

[8] President's Notebook PR/2/19, Magdalen College Archive

[9] C.T. Steward, Henley Records 1919-1938; Hamish Hamilton 1939

[10] G.C. Drinkwater and T.R.B. Sanders, The University Boat Race Official Centenary History, Cassell & Co. 1929

[11] L.S.R. Byrne and E.L. Churchill, The Eton Book of the River, Spottiswoode Ballantyne & Co, 1935

[12] Roger Hutchins and Richard Sheppard, The Undone Years, Magdalen College Oxford 2004

The last night of Eights Week, photograph by Henry Taunt

THE EIGHTS, OXFORD, No. 12.
THE LAST NIGHT OF THE RACES.

TAUNT & CO. 135

# 7 1931-1945

## Double Headship, Money, John Garton, Richard Burnell, World War II

Until now there has been no mention of money or the financing of the Boat Club. From its inception, the Club raised subscriptions from its members and in the early years these dues were the only source of income. As was common in the nineteenth century, Magdalen did not own any boats but rented them from Salter's yard and other boat builders on the Isis, therefore the question of capital expenditure therefore did not arise and subscriptions covered the costs of hire as well as the other running expenses. Of course undergraduates of the period had to cover all their costs of being at the University and generally had the means to indulge in sports and other diversions if they so wished. Even so, the costs could be considerable, especially if a crew went to Henley or to other events away from Oxford. Once M.C.B.C. wanted to invest in boats the question of funding such purchases arose as the equipment would belong to the club. Some were bought through the generosity of individuals or a small group of members but the J.C.R., which was also funded by subscriptions, provided the means to buy boats. Periodically the College itself would pay for a new eight but in a hetærocracy this was usually at the instance of sympathetic Fellows and in the light of notable success. There has long been a debate as to the effect of sport on the quality of degree a student might collect and this perhaps became more polarised after the Great War. Authors of books on sport and sporting technique have often felt moved to comment on the relationship between study and physical activity. In his book *Boat Racing: or the Arts of Rowing and Training*, published in 1876, Edwin Brickwood wrote: 'The moral and physical man is connected closely and intimately, and if health, strength, and longevity are to be secured, it is of absolute importance that whilst the mind is cultured and refined, an equal attention should be paid to the training and education of the creature. With the body in health, the muscles in full and vigorous action, the mind is far better able to grapple with and overcome the more difficult problems of intellectual philosophy.' Whether or not Brickwood's dogma holds water, by 1930 the Boat Club was considering the future of its finances and seeking to ensure that equipment funding was not dependent on the mood of

College or Common Room. Thought was given to establishing an endowment fund and in February that year Dink Horsfall wrote to St John's College, Cambridge to seek the advice of the Secretary of Lady Margaret Boat Club which had already been fundraising from old members. Despite a helpful and encouraging reply, Magdalen did not act upon the advice and an endowment fund did not become established until the late 1990s. In the meantime M.C.B.C. finances operated on an eleemosynary basis, obtaining donations from old members towards a particular boat purchase, and sometimes receiving help from the O.U.B.C. Trust Fund; the J.C.R. too, continued to be a key provider of financial support. The Henley Fund received donations principally from Fellows.

Douglas Dodds-Parker, who had been President (sic) of the Boat

Club in 1929-1930, had privately funded the cost of casting new M.C.B.C. medals. First sunk in 1859, the original dies were found at Rowell's, the Oxford silversmith on the High, by Dodds-Parker who was keen to reinstate them and award them for the internal small boats racing, thereby encouraging members of the Club to learn to scull and to row in pairs and fours. In 1931, he contributed to the Henley expenses. The First Torpid had risen two places and only missed out on a third, for the Headship, through a classic bumps pile-up. Without any Blues or even Trial Caps, the Club was short on experience but had Pat Johnson as coach. Johnson was a Fellow of the College and Dean of Arts. For the first time in its history, Magdalen entered The Tideway Head of the River Race and finished 16th. An unchanged crew formed the Summer Eight and they made five bumps to finish third; a great restoration of fortune after the difficulties of the previous two years. Dodds-Parker had not been available for the Eight as he had been working for the Sudan Civil Service exams, but he was very keen that two eights should enter Henley to give the oarsmen, who would be the basis of the Eight the following year, a chance to experience the Regatta. His father, who had been Captain in 1889-1890, gave Douglas £50 'for surviving three years' and it was this sum that he placed anonymously in the Henley Fund. The Irvines helped with accommodation for the eighteen members of the club. Neither crew survived their heat but the benefits of the exposure to competition at this level, away from the Isis, was indeed to bring its reward the following year.

The six man of the Eight was J.H.E. Griffiths. James Griffiths was a graduate student; over the preceding three years he had not rowed but took the top First in Physics. He went on to win a Fellowship by Examination on the recommendation of the Nobel Laureate, Erwin Schrödinger. 1931 was to be his only year in a boat but when later

# Michaelmas Term 1931 saw a major development in equipment, and therefore rowing style, with the arrival of the swivel to replace the fixed pin.

he became President of Magdalen, in 1968, he remained a keen supporter of the Boat Club and kept open house for oarsmen with a barrel of beer always to hand.

Michaelmas Term 1931 saw a major development in equipment, and therefore rowing style, with the arrival of the swivel to replace the fixed pin. As with many innovations, this change caused concern for some, in particular with old members who were proponents of the 'Orthodox Style' and who saw it is an encroachment of the 'Fairbairn Style'. A summary of the differences in these two styles is perhaps best, and certainly most aptly, taken from Richard Burnell's book *Swing Together*, published in 1952. He does this by surveying the rowing stroke thus:

'*The Forward Position:* No difference.

Entry and Beginning: Orthodoxy saw the entry as a lightning drop, coupled with a spring off the stretcher which opened out the angle between shoulders and knees as quickly as possible. The leg-drive was not allowed to master this opening of the body angle. Faibairnism saw the entry and beginning as one movement, a running hit. There was no reservation about legs master-

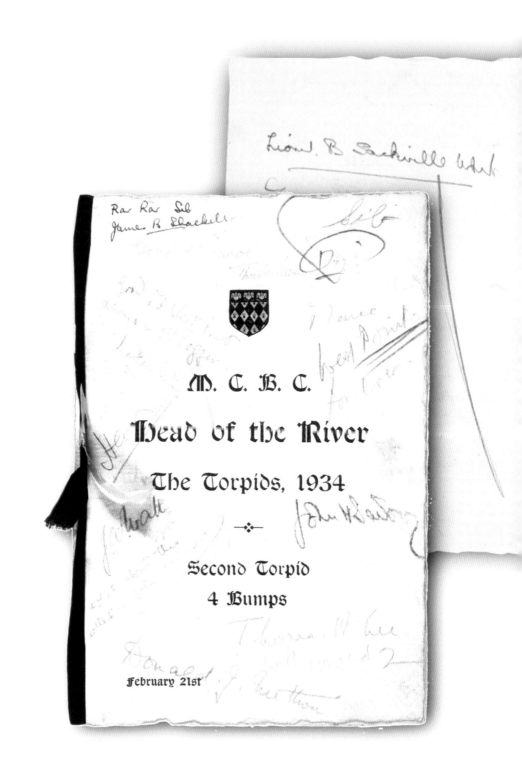

M. C. B. C.

Head of the River

The Torpids, 1934

Second Torpid

4 Bumps

February 21st

### First Torpid.

|  |  |  | st. | lbs. |
|---|---|---|---|---|
| Bow. | L. H. P. VAN DER GOES | . | 10 | 8 |
| 2. | A. K. SIBLEY | . . . | 11 | 0 |
| 3. | W. J. FLETCHER-CAMPBELL | . | 11 | 1 |
| 4. | J. H. TOWNSEND | . . | 11 | 5 |
| 5. | M. J. MORRIS | . . . | 14 | 13 |
| 6. | G. GREENE | . . . | 13 | 0 |
| 7. | B. ALEXANDER | . . . | 10 | 8 |
| Str. | J. STURROCK | . . . | 13 | 13 |
| Cox. | J. A. WATT | . . | 8 | 13 |

**HEAD OF THE RIVER.**

---

### Second Torpid.

|  |  |  | st. | lbs. |
|---|---|---|---|---|
| Bow. | P. B. SPILSBURY | . . . | 11 | 12 |
| 2. | D. J. METHUEN | . . | 11 | 7 |
| 3. | T. M. LEE | . . . | 12 | 0 |
| 4. | R. G. ETHERINGTON-SMITH | . | 13 | 0 |
| 5. | J. M. McC. FISHER | . | 13 | 2 |
| 6. | J. B. SHACKELL | . . | 13 | 9 |
| 7. | E. J. S. CLARKE | . . | 11 | 7 |
| Str. | J. C. BURGOYNE-JOHNSON | . | 11 | 8 |
| Cox. | J. N. SAVORY | . . | 8 | 12 |

**BUMPS:**
Keble II., Lincoln, Queen's,
St. Catherine's.

The M.C.B.C flag which flew on the O.U.B.C. barge until 1930

Pennants flown behind the bow seat of the First Eight

**Double Headship, Money, John Garton, Richard Burnell, World War II  143**

ing the opening of the body angle, but there was still the same ideal of the shoulders moving back faster than any other part of the body. Nor, of course, was the running hit specifically intended to dissipate any length forward.

*The Stroke:* Virtually no difference, except that Fairbairnism made no reservations about the leg-drive, or about bending of the arms.

*Finish and Extraction:* The position was the same, but Orthodoxy saw the extraction as a 'drop and away', whereas Fairbairnism taught to row the blade out 'round the turn'.

*Forward Swing:* No difference, except that Fairbairn allowed his crews to 'hook themselves forward with their toes'. Probably this was making a virtue out of a necessity, owing to the use of unlimited slides, with no backstops.

The essential difference between Fairbairnism and Orthodoxy was not in execution, but in the belief that Nature was the best judge of how to work a man's limbs.'[1]

Steve Fairbairn was one of the great Cambridge oarsmen from Jesus College. He coached for his college in the 1920s and for Thames and London Rowing Clubs, with extraordinary success. However, Reggie Rowe, Captain in 1890-1891 and a coach for years afterwards, in a letter to Peter Hewison (who was Captain in 1932-1933) wrote that it was 'hard to ignore such an authoritative a reproof'. Having tried out swivels in the O.U.B.C. Fours that term, M.C.B.C. ordered a new eight with these new gates; the resultant success in 1932 won over the sceptics. The new eight was built by 'Bossie' Phelps and funded by old members urged by Dink Horsfall and Pat Johnson. In fact the successes of this year on the Isis are unrivalled in the Club's history. The First Torpid, which still could not contain Trial Caps, righted the frustrations of the previous year's pile-up and bumped Wadham and Corpus Christi to take the Headship. On the final afternoon they rowed over in pole position and finished three lengths clear despite bow, four and five being unwell. The crew went on to win the 1*st* Clinker Pennant in The Tideway Head of the River Race. Though the College had no Blues in 1932, the Summer Eight was a different crew and it is clear that, in addition to the Trial Caps of Peter Hewison and Francis Barmby, there was some jockeying of persons and seats between the first and second boats from winter to summer. Notably, the Captain, Tom Warren-Swettenham, a Radleian, was in the second boat in both terms, though he is reputed to have said that if the Summer Eight did not go Head in three nights he would swap the crews over, such was the matching of the two crews. As it was they bumped University College on the first evening, half way up the Green Bank. Admirably steered by Chaloke Komarakul Na Nagara, who had been schooled at St. Paul's, they bumped Brasenose on the second evening at the crossing. Koma, as he was known, had also coxed the Torpid and thus was one of only five Magdalen men to have been Head of both Torpids and Eights in the same year. Koma was Siamese and for many years he was the Financial Attaché to the Royal Thai Embassy in London (the country changed its name in 1939). He would be a loyal supporter of M.C.B.C. for many years, often bringing a case of champagne up for Eights Week in his Rolls-Royce.

On the remaining three evenings Magdalen rowed over Head; the third and fourth days were comfortable but the final evening was not without surprise. Brasenose, aware that Magdalen had a relatively slow start, decided to change to shorter oars (11 feet 10 inches, 6½ inch blades) in the hope of making ground in the early stages. They went off at 44 to Magdalen's 39 and came up rapidly, closing to within eight feet in the Gut. Through the good steering of Koma and their length of stroke they drew away along the Green Bank and, with crucial support and instruction from Pat Johnson on the bank, finished Head better than the starting distance ahead of Brasenose. Percy Bristow, at 3, in a letter to his brother wrote: 'Half an hour later; a glass of beer in one hand, a strawberry ice in the other and a cigarette tasting like blotting paper in my mouth. But who cares?'. Arthur Smithies, at 4, a Tasmanian Rhodes Scholar, with caustic wit, remarked in ringing tones as they drew alongside Brasenose after they had bumped them: 'There's a brazen waste of money for you'.[2]

C. Komarakul Na Nagara with The Torpids trophy, 1932.

This was a reference to the fact that Brasenose had five Blues on board and the college was reputed to be generous with scholarships to 'men of outstanding character' – a euphemism for those with a gift for success in sports. The contrast was all the sharper as Magdalen had no Blues, and not even its Captain, on board. Bristow and Rod Sarell (the bow man) both recall how the Dean of Divinity, the Reverend Adam Fox, was present at the Bumps Supper with 'his dog collar at a distinct list and smiling benignly on all around' and yet hurled a strawberry Melba on its plate across the Hall. A surprising moment of decanal enthusiasm from Fox, who had already been the Warden of Radley College, supplier of so many undergraduates to Magdalen many of whom were good oarsmen, and was later Professor of Poetry and then a Canon of Westminster Abbey. It was the more unlikely for Fox was known to find the Boat Club irksome when it descended on Chapel *en masse* and proceeded to sing more loudly than the Clerks who threatened to strike.

## an excellent training regime had paid off and Magdalen had its first, and so far only, double Headship

The 1932 Second Eight, stroked by the Captain of Boats, also enjoyed success, climbing five places in the second division to become sandwich boat and then managing to bump into the first division. This crew was coached by S.G. Lee; Stephen 'Luggins' Lee was a Fellow of the College, a Tutor in Modern History, and a loyal supporter of the Boat Club: a patient coach he took a wide variety of crews, in particular the Second Eight, up and down the river for over thirty years. The Third Eight added to the share of success by making six bumps and finishing as the top third eight on the river. The First Eight decided to enter the Ladies' Challenge Plate at Henley, first beating Bedford School but losing by four feet in the second round to Shrewsbury School, who went on to win the event. Peter Hewison, who had been elected Captain of Boats for the ensuing year, could not row at Henley owing to Schools and Lionel Sackville-West replaced him in the two seat of an otherwise unchanged crew. They felt that they had just missed out on winning the Ladies' Plate as their time against Shrewsbury was the fastest of the event and quicker than Oriel College's, the losing finalist's, races. The Second Eight entered the Thames Challenge Cup and beat Walton Rowing Club but then lost to Trinity College, Dublin.

Douglas Dodds-Parker, who was now Assistant District Commissioner of Kordofan Province in the Darfur Region of Sudan, was riding his camel when a messenger arrived with a telegram. Written by Tom Whitley, Captain the year earlier, it said: 'We have gone Head. We have found out where the £50 came from ...'. A wisely-spent sum. Tom Warren-Swettenham had the satisfaction of a Captain's job well done. The continuity in the crews and an excellent training regime had paid off and Magdalen had its first, and so far only, double Headship.

In the two years that followed, Magdalen retained the Headship of Torpids but were bumped off the top spot in Summer Eights. Komarakul Na Nagara coxed the 1933 Blue Boat but Magdalen was otherwise bereft of University representation. Roger Black and William Whipple, two Rhodes Scholars from West Point, the United States of America's Military Academy, provided some horsepower, though the 1933 Eight were bumped by Oriel and New Colleges, and in 1934 another place was given up to Balliol. Only a successful appeal against a bump by Christ Church saved M.C.B.C. from falling further in 1935. Malcolm Morris, the 1934-35 Captain, wrote a ten page examination of the state of the Boat Club and reflected on their training, style and organisation. He reflected on the loss of the Torpids' Headship and was concerned that despite a wealth of willing old Blues, the Club had not made use of them and indeed had distanced itself. This was still a period when the trend of father-therefore-son was an unblinking expectation and Morris was worried that some old members, famous Magdalen oarsmen amongst them, might send their sons to other colleges. Despite the successes, the new equipment of 1931, the swivels, were blamed in part for the poor performance. Morris believed the riverbank was alive with talk of the 'Magdalen Dive' – holding back the body swing until after the legs were down. The cure prescribed was a return to the Orthodox Style and thus to fixed pins. Strictly speaking, there is no absolute relationship between the Orthodox Style and fixed pins though the Fairbairn Style could only be achieved with swivels.

The crew were fortunate to have Dink Horsfall and Gully

Nickalls return to coach them and in a very short time made something of a cohesive crew out of the manpower available, resulting in them rowing over each night of 1935. This was the first year in which the College put on a fourth eight and it began at 58*th*, the bottom of the last division.

A further insight to the Boat Club of the early 1930s is provided by Jock Fletcher-Campbell in an interview in his 96*th* year. Jock had been at Radley but had not rowed at school. On his first evening at Magdalen he was 'attacked by every society knocking on one's door', two Radleians who were members of the Boat Club were among them. They encouraged him to come and row but he explained he was a cricketer; nonetheless he was inveigled into going down to the boathouse where he expected to be made a coxswain. In fact almost at once an oar was put in his hand.

Though the barge was moored on Christ Church Meadow, oarsmen went down by bicycle to Folly Bridge and along the towpath to whistle for Jack May, the Boatman, who would come and pick them up in a punt. Fletcher-Campbell recalled that Jack was, more often than not, 'on the verge of being sober' but he always managed to get the punt across the river no matter what the current. If one was fortunate he might have put the fire on and had a small supply of warm water with which to wash – a small hand pump brought up the river water. Some went down to the barge by canoe from College along the Cherwell. The Magdalen boats and oars were kept in the University boathouse and Jack would either punt the crews across to collect them or he might fetch them himself and they would board at the barge. The fleet consisted of two shell eights and one clinker, plus a four; the oars were plain varnished – there was no lily to adorn the blade, for that change did not come until later part of the twentieth century. Boats of the 1930s did not have names but simply had the College coat of arms on the bows. Rowing clothing of the period was also relatively understated; crews trained in whatever they wished but those who had rowed at school would wear that kit. For the Torpids and Eights they would wear a white singlet with black trim and baggy towelling shorts, and there was a white sweater with a black line on the 'V'. Jock noted that the third boat did not have shoes fitted and so the crew strapped in their own footwear. Jackets varied from crew to crew: the first eight wore a red blazer with a dark blue trim and three lilies embroidered on the pocket, the second eight had a plain red blazer, and the Third Eight's was white with a black trim and lilies on the pocket, the same as the first Torpid. Bumps Suppers sometimes provided the greatest test of resilience of these blazers (which were typically owned by the Club, though some members would order their own). After one of these Torpids Headship dinners the first eight was rather lively and made their way to the room of a rather unpopular undergraduate in Chaplain's Quad. They succeeded in negotiating the awkward and steep stairs and removed his grand piano but not without some damage occurring. The Senior Dean of Arts, Pat Johnson, who was also their coach, was furious at their misbehaviour as he felt his good name has been besmirched. He therefore got the Boat Club together and made his views clear. He told them how much the piano would cost to repair and that the sum must be produced by the end of the day or they would all be sent down forthwith; somehow the money was found. On a slightly tamer note Fletcher-Campbell recalled that whilst there were few social occasions organ-

The Captains' Book

ised by the Boat Club, they did have crew dinners in Lecture Room A in St. Swithun's I. Though a special diet of food considered appropriate for those in training was served up, it is not clear who determined the menu. Adam Fox, the Dean of Divinity, had his rooms on the floor above and on one occasion when he was entertaining two elderly ladies to dinner had to send his scout downstairs with a note. The crew dinner, taken during a break in training, included champagne and thus some singing. The message was to ask the oarsmen to 'articulate the words less clearly'.

Jock Fletcher-Campbell was to be in the First Torpid for its three years Head of the River 1932-1934. Later he took Holy Orders and in retirement moved back to the Radley area. In 2008 he came down to the Isis to watch and meet the first Torpid just after it had taken the Headship for the first time since his era.

For the academic year 1935-1936, John Sturrock was Captain of Boats and he maintained the Orthodox Style. John Garton arrived from Eton as a freshman, he had already gained a Trial Cap but with the recent rule change he was eligible to stroke the 1936 First Torpid, coached by Gully Nickalls, which made three bumps to regain the Headship. Sturrock won the O.U.B.C. Sculls and was Magdalen's first oarsman to win a Blue in seven years. Augmenting the crew for Eights Week they rose one place, bumping Balliol. Sturrock was concerned that Henley Royal Regatta was becoming more difficult for Oxford colleges to enjoy success, indeed he felt it was partly at the hand of their Cambridge counterparts as much as to do with the increasing foreign entries. They entered the Ladies' Plate and lost to Trinity Hall in the second round. The Henley Fund this year received its smallest level of contribution on record, perhaps a reflection of the mood of the S.C.R. John Sturrock went on to win another Blue in 1937, and in 1938 he was in the six seat of the England Eight which won the gold medal at the British Empire Games held in Sydney.

Jack May, Boatman to M.C.B.C. since 1911, retired in the summer of 1936. He had been a professional sculler and Magdalen oarsmen remembered his ability to punt ten of them across the Isis in a fast stream with one hand, while gesticulating over some reminiscence with the other and yet managing to avoid other river traffic. He was succeeded by Edgar Dickens who thus became Magdalen's third boatman.

The autumn of that year brought to Magdalen someone who was to become one of the great men of the Boat Club's history. Richard Burnell arrived from Eton and won a Trial Cap that winter along with Robert Stewart, his contemporary at school, who went on to win his Blue that year. In College the Captain was William Baillieu, whose father, later Lord Baillieu, had also been at Magdalen and in the Oxford crew of 1913. Other branches of this Australian family were also at Magdalen. The 1937 Torpid retained the Headship and the two of its members came into the First Boat for Summer Eights. The Fourth Torpid was remarkable, making seven bumps before the Gut. It was coxed by John Stainer, a third generation Magdalen man, being grandson of the famous composer and son of the cox of 1888 Head crew. The following year Stainer says he 'was pressured into being the cox of the First Torpid' which was bumped off Head by St Edmund Hall. In Eights Week, starting third Magdalen bumped Oriel but then spent the rest of the week trying to catch New College, without success. The Second and Third Eights finished the week as the top second and third crews respectively; the thirds made five bumps but were eclipsed by the Fourth Boat which made seven. At Henley the Eight entered the Ladies' Plate and, stroked by John Garton and coached by Pat Johnson, beat Trinity College, Dublin, Corpus Christi College, Cambridge, and then Shrewsbury School to meet Clare College, Cambridge in the semi-final. It was a close race all the way with neither crew having a lead of more than a few feet though the ownership of the race changed three times only to end in a dead heat following a final push by Magdalen. In the evening re-row the race was as close as it had been earlier but Clare got ahead through the Enclosures to win by a quarter of a length. They won the final against First Trinity Boat Club, Cambridge.

J.L. Garton as President of Leander Club, by Paddy Page, 1985.

The next two years were to be unremarkable: the Torpids' Headship was lost and Magdalen fell to third place. Despite having three Blues (and Burnell who would have made the Oxford boat but for an injury) on board the Summer Eight fell three places to fifth. The stern four of the Eight entered both the Stewards' and Visitors' Challenge Cups at Henley but lost to Leander and to Oriel respectively. This crew, however, won the University Fours that autumn.

John Garton was Captain in 1937-1938; he was President of O.U.B.C. the following year. He coached Magdalen crews into the 1950s. Elected a Steward of Henley Royal Regatta in 1959, he chaired its Committee of Management though the period 1965-1978 and was subsequently the Regatta's President. The Regatta had not been immune from the financial difficulties in the country; it was Garton who recognised this and brought about change and a sure footing for the future. From 1969 to 1976 Garton was President of the Amateur Rowing Association. He also served on the British Olympic Association and the Board of the Thames Conservancy. He was President of Leander Club from 1980 to 1983.

The 1939 Blue Boat had Burnell, Garton, Forbes and Stewart representing Magdalen. Their loss may have affected the performance of the Summer Eight which slipped, despite being favourites, two places to seventh. The Second Eight also suffered, being bumped every night it dropped to eighteenth, a shock for a college that had spent 25 years as the highest second boat on the river. The Third Eight fell five places. Magdalen did not enter Henley that year though Burnell entered the Diamond Challenge Sculls and in the semi-final lost to R. Verey of Akademicki Zwiazek Sportowy, Poland, who was the reigning European Champion. Writing up the Captain's book after the war, and reflecting on the difficult times of recent years Burnell noted: '1. Generally speaking, it is best not to have Blues as Captains and Secretaries - certainly not both in the same year. They cannot give the time necessary to running the Club. 2. We relied far too much on a supply of ready made oarsmen from school. Consequently we had great difficulty in filling bow seats, and crews usually lacked cohesion. 3. We suffered desperately from shortage of numbers. I therefore suggest, humbly (as one who took part in the debacle!), that the first necessity is a big drive to increase the numbers of the Boat Club, and that infinite pains should be taken to teach any newcomers who show any signs of enthusiasm, even if unpromising'. His wisdom remains pertinent today.

# RICHARD BURNELL

**B**orn in 1917, Richard Desborough Burnell, like his father before him, was educated at Eton and then came to Magdalen, arriving in Michaelmas Term 1936. Already a veteran of three years rowing in the Ladies' Challenge Plate at Henley, once as a finalist and another as Eton's Captain of Boats, he rowed in the same event for Magdalen in his freshman year having been in the Summer Eight. A Trial Cap in 1937 and 1938, Richard was then Captain of Boats at Magdalen in his third year, 1938-1939, the year in which he won his Blue in the losing Oxford crew. The Second World War delayed his rowing career but afterwards he emulated his father by winning an Olympic gold medal. He and Bert Bushnell represented Great Britain in the Double Sculls at the 1948 Games in London. The Olympic Regatta was, as it had been at the 1908 Games, held at Henley. Writing in 1952, Burnell said 'A good rower needs the normal three years at university followed by a further three in which to develop a strong style. During the war there was no chance of this and the general standard fell considerably.' Burnell had ended the war, in which he served with the Rifle Brigade and the Royal Northumberland Fusiliers and at Tactical H.Q., in Hamburg and found it strange, as a member of the Occupying Forces, to be back in the city he had visited with an Oxford crew in 1937. Despite the heavy damage to the city, the Hamburg Club had survived and Burnell was able to row with them. On coming out of the Army in 1946 Richard Burnell won the Wingfield Sculls, the Amateur Championship of the Thames, held on the Tideway. A year later, he had intended to prepare to compete in the single scull at the Olympic Regatta but, aged 30, knew it was his only chance 'and the only decent coach, Eric Phelps, was in South America.' He decided to try and find a doubles partner and tried various scullers before he met Bert Bushnell, whom he had beaten in the Diamond Challenge Sculls in 1946. They started training together three weeks before the Olympic Regatta and as Richard put it 'Our respective weak points seemed to cancel themselves out, and our strong points were complementary.' They made it to the final against Uruguay and Denmark, though not without a

Three generations of Burnells: left to right: Don, Richard , Peter at Putney, 1962.

the social structure of rowing then still in place. Bushnell was a local man, brought up on the river in the family boat-building business at Wargrave. When he returned from home for the final he was not allowed to park at Leander Club; as he put it himself 'You see I was not a member – not posh enough.' Burnell and Bushnell were of quite different backgrounds and yet they ended up having great respect for each other. They beat the Danes 'safely' with the Uruguay coming third by five lengths.[3] At Henley in 1951, partnering Pat Bradley, Burnell won the Double Sculls for Leander, beating Davies and Kemp of Reading Rowing Club in the final.

Aside from his sculling, Richard Burnell continued to row on his return from Germany. With Leander Club he won the Grand Challenge Cup twice, in 1946 and 1949. He was their Captain in 1949-1950 and again in 1965. In 1950 Burnell captained the England rowing team at the Empire Games held in Auckland, New Zealand; he rowed in the 5 seat of the Eight which won the bronze medal. After being elected a Steward of Henley Royal Regatta in

1965, Burnell was Honorary Secretary of Leander in 1966-1967 and then President of the club from 1988 to 1993.

Richard Burnell married Rosalind Garton (daughter of A.S. Garton who had been at Magdalen and rowed for the College 1908–1911) in 1940. Their son Peter came to Magdalen and won a Blue in 1962. The Burnells lived in the Thames Valley, and Richard was a member of Berkshire County Council from 1957 to 1967.

At the time of the 1948 Games, Dick Burnell had already been Rowing Correspondent for *The Times* for two years and wrote a modest account of his own success. He held this post until 1969 and that of *The Sunday Times* until his retirement in 1990. He edited the British Rowing Almanack from 1948–1953. Burnell died in 1995. As David Miller put it in his obituary: 'To outsiders visiting the towpath at Putney once a year, Burnell was the Boat Race: a large man out of whom flowed a tide of information, the Bodleian of rowing.' In addition to his newspaper posts, Burnell was a prolific writer of books on rowing: *Swing Together*, 1952; *The Oxford and Cambridge Boat Race 1829-1952*, 1954; *Sculling, Training and Rigging*, 1955; *Henley Regatta, A History*, 1957; *Sculling, The Oxford Pocket Book of Training*, 1962; *A Short History of Leander Club* (with H.R.N. Rickett), 1968; *Sculling for Rowing*, 1968; *The Complete Sculler*, 1973; *Fitness Afloat*, 1978; *One Hundred and Fifty Years of the Boat Race*, 1979; *Henley Royal Regatta,*

*A Celebration of 150 Years*, 1989; *A Year to Remember, A Celebration of the 150th Henley Royal Regatta*, 1990; *The Brilliants: A History of Leander Club* (with G.G.H. Page), 1997. He also edited the Henley Royal Regatta Records 1969-1974, 1975-1979, 1980-1984, 1985-1989; and contributed to '*Well Rowed Magdalen*', published in 1993.

Mr Weldon bets Mr Lee 2 bottles of 1912 Port that "the Eights" will be held in Trinity Term 1940 in the usual way. 30.11.39

Paid by Mr Weldon 27.9.40

Mr Stevens bets Mr Bazell one bottle of (Sen. bone by armed forces) port that there will be a German Invasion of Great Britain by July 31st, 1940.

9.vii.40.

paid by Mr Stevens.

The declaration of war in September 1939 caused the suspension of the official racing order on the Isis. Many undergraduates volunteered for the Armed Services, conscription followed and with many going straight from school into the Forces, there were few in College. Degree courses continued to be offered in certain disciplines such as medicine. Against this background there continued to be some activity on the river, and the Club continued to operate in rather reduced circumstances. In the S.C.R. there was some debate about the way the war might develop and the impact it would have at home. Mr Weldon clearly felt Oxford life would not be affected while Mr Lee saw the troubles that lay ahead. One might have expected optimism to reverse their positions for Stephen Lee was a keen supporter and coach of the Boat Club while Weldon reputedly loathed it. It has been suggested he was responsible for disposing of much Boat Club's pre-Second World War archive material.

Robert Somervell was elected Captain at the start of Michaelmas 1939 but on being called up, was succeeded by Lancelot Thirkell. Both survived the war, Somervell became a director of K Shoes while Thirkell went into the Diplomatic Service and then the B.B.C. In a perhaps unlikely alliance, Magdalen joined with New College to make up an eight for both Torpids and Eights of 1940, there were three divisions for twenty eight boats and the 'N.C.M.B.C.', for Summer Eights, started third. They bumped the composite of St. Edmund Hall and Queen's College. An all-Magdalen four won the O.U.B.C. Fours. In 1941 the number of boats on the river was only thirteen, split into two divisions. N.C.M.B.C. bumped the Broad Street Alliance of Balliol and Trinity to take the Headship. The Magdalen men occupied the bow four of the boat. John Brocklebank was the bowman and Captain. He was killed in action in November 1943. The other three were Thirkell, Bob Southey from Australia, and Anthony Gell. For 1942 the number of boats was eighteen, N.C.M.B.C. was bumped off the Headship and ended up third.

# 'stressed the great benefit of rowing in combining good exercise with good fellowship - a camaraderie unparalleled in any other sport.'

1943 began with the second wartime Boat Race. The Oxford crew included D.G. Jamison at bow and A.G.C. Shurrock as coxswain. As with all the wartime University crews, these two Magdalen men did not win Blues; the race was held at Sandford over a 1¼ mile downstream course. Oxford won by two-thirds of a length. Summer Eights that year saw two all-Magdalen crews the first of which started sixth (the starting order not being the same as the previous year's finishing order) and bumped New College and then Hertford. For the 1944 Boat Race, held at Ely over a 1½ mile course, Magdalen again held the seat at each end with Jamison again at bow seat but this time Robert Ebsworth Snow coxing. They won by three-quarters of a length. David Jamison was now Captain, and at Summer Eights again Magdalen boated in its own right and made three bumps to regain the wartime order Headship. No record of the names of the crew has survived. That autumn Stephen Lee, who was Acting Home Bursar during the war years, spoke at a meeting of the Boat Club and the Captain's Book records he: 'stressed the great benefit of rowing in combining good exercise with good fellowship - a camaraderie unparalleled in any other sport.' Along with Pat Johnson, the physicist shortly to become Vice-President, and the newly-arrived Gilbert Ryle, as Waynflete

Professor of Metaphysical Philosophy, the Boat Club was well supported in the S.C.R.

The 1945 unofficial Boat Race had three Magdalen men onboard: D.G. Robertson Campbell at four, David Jamison at stroke, and Robert Ebsworth Snow again coxing. Racing over the Henley Royal Regatta course they lost to Cambridge by two lengths. In College two eights were entered for Torpids and three for Summer Eights. At a meeting of the Boat Club held on May Day, David Jamison aired the prospect that Henley Royal Regatta would be revived the following year and that he hoped those who would still be in residence then would be encouraged to row in eights. Though the war did not end for another week or so it would seem that both in College and outside, plans were being laid for a return to a more normal life. The war in Europe ended on 9th May, V.E. Day, and Eights Week was three weeks later though the wartime order was maintained and Magdalen rowed over Head each evening. The third eight was stroked by Colin Beaumont-Edmonds who had been blinded whilst serving as a Lieutenant in the infantry, and won a Military Cross; he had arrived at Magdalen the previous Michaelmas Term. Having explained his condition to the Boat Club scouts their response was to invite him to stroke and thus avoid the complications of following the man in front. A one-day regatta was held at Henley and Magdalen entered the Danesfield Cup, an eight-oared race for all comers. They beat Christ's College, Cambridge and the Royal Australian Air Force 'B' crew in the first heat but in the next round were beaten by the 'A' crew from the R.A.A.F. by only three feet, Middlesex Hospital coming third. Imperial College, who Magdalen had beaten in a private match, won the event. The cup for the event was provided by A.S. Garton who had rowed for Magdalen's Grand Challenge Cup winning crews of 1910 and 1911.

Throughout the war the Captain's Book records constant reminders to members of the Boat Club to look after the equipment as it would be nigh impossible to replace: the boatman, 'Dick' Dickens, was on active service and the local boat builders and oar makers were similarly absent. Etienne Gutt, the Hon. Secretary records: 'Coxes were told not to attempt to upset our American Allies into the Isis, if it were to be at the cost of 2 or more oars belonging to the club'.

Post-war M.C.B.C. would be a thriving hive of activity and something of a revival of its immediate pre-war doldrums.

[1] R.D. Burnell, Swing Together, Oxford University Press 1952

[2] Letter from R.F.G. Sarell, Magdalen College Archive

[3] J. Hampton, The Austerity Olympics, Aurum Press 2008

# Henley-on-Thames

I see the winding water make
  A short and then a shorter lake
As here stand I,
  And house-boat high
Survey the Upper Thames.
  By sun the mud is amber-dyed
In ripples slow and flat and wide,
  That flap against the house-boat side
And flow away in gems.

In mud and elder-scented shade
  A reach away the breach is made
By dive and shout
  That circles out
To Henley tower and town;
  And "Boats for Hire" the rafters ring,
And pink on white the roses cling,
  And red the bright geraniums swing
In baskets dangling down.

When shall I see the Thames again?
  The prow-promoted gems again,
As beefy ATS
  Without their hats
Come shooting through the bridge?
  And "cheerioh" and "cheeri-bye"
Across the waste of waters die,
  And low the mists of evening lie
And lightly skims the midge.

Sir John Betjeman

The Magdalen crew training at Henley, on the Leander raft.

# 8 1946-1955

## Post-War Headship, Fours at Henley, Dead Heats

In the October after the War was over, numbers of ex-servicemen returned to the College to complete their degrees and others arrived who came straight from the Forces. Magdalen had once again lost many of her sons, oarsmen among them, fighting for their Country's freedom. The new term, however, saw a revival of the Boat Club and its fortunes. Equipment was in short supply as nothing had been built during the war and the boatman, Edgar 'Dick' Dickens had been away fighting. He returned to Oxford and took up his post once again. The Club had four eights, two of them clinkers, and a handful of small boats; some had warped and were now difficult to row. Members of M.C.B.C. continued to be reminded of the need to look after the boats and oars; it was 1947 before a new eight was ordered from Sims for £180.

J.R.W. Gleave had arrived at Magdalen in 1943 and joined the Boat Club almost immediately. Though rowing became his passion, he won Blues for Eton Fives and Squash as well as going on to represent Oxford in three Boat Races. In Michaelmas Term 1945 he was one of seven Trial Caps from Magdalen and won his seat in the University crew for the 1946 Boat Race. Robert Ebsworth Snow translated his wartime Oxford coxing experience into this first official Boat Race to be held since 1939, back on its usual course from Putney to Mortlake. David Jamison, who had also been a pillar of the M.C.B.C. during the war, was selected for the number three seat but broke his arm on a training run in Addison's Walk. He was forced to wait another year for his first Blue to add to his three wartime appearances for Oxford. All of these three men were medical students who went on to successful careers in their various specialties. John Gleave became a consultant neurosurgeon at Addenbrooke's Hospital in Cambridge where, over a twenty year period, he gave his energies to the benefit of Lady Margaret Boat Club coaching principally their men's first boat. He also backed their women's crews and was and early supporter of lightweight rowing when it began in the mid 1970s. His record from his Magdalen days, for both College and University and his success with Leander in 1949, winning the Grand Challenge Cup, set him in good stead to swap one red cap for another. Of the 1946 Boat Race, G.L.F. Thompson, writing in *The Daily Telegraph*, commented: '[Gleave was] the most useful man

man in the boat, consistent, hard-working and strong'. Of Ebsworth Snow he wrote: 'outstanding, steering an excellent if risky course when he boldly put Cambridge's cox in difficulties by taking their water at Harrods when he only had a three quarter length lead.' Oxford was coached by Peter Haig Thomas, a Cambridge Blue (1902-05), who attributed the dark blue success in the race to 'we won because we adopted the old orthodox method followed since 1871. We had rhythm, and kept absolutely together.' This was to be the last Boat Race won on fixed pins.

# Post-war rationing had an effect on oarsmen's diets and to some extent their performance. In College oily whale steaks were served

Haig-Thomas was invited by David Jamison to attend a Magdalen Boat Club general meeting in January 1946 and gave a talk to the members. 'Haggers' was to become a key component of the Magdalen coaching team over the next several years. During that period he also coached one or other university (and in one year both); at Magdalen he became quite a part of the place for a while eventually taking up semi-permanent residence in College. Members of the Club took it in turns to keep him company; John Phipps recalls that 'he was treated by all with a respect mingled with amusement'. Despite painful arthritis, he still coached from the towpath, riding bolt upright on a large bicycle with a high saddle and even higher handle bars. His coaching technique was intensive: frequent tubbing to improve blade work and achieve the correct entry with coordination of body and legs; and short, very firm pieces of paddling.

The same month saw the opening of the new boathouse on Christ Church meadow, to be followed soon afterwards by the sale of the barge. The story of the barges and boathouse is in chapter 12.

The returning servicemen asked to be given a fair opportunity to show their worth among the other Magdalen oarsmen and it was agreed they would put on a scratch eight for Torpids. The first Torpid began and ended the week fourth on the river and went on to take second place in Reading Head of the River. Etienne Gutt,

Magdalen's Belgian law student, was one of the returning servicemen, used his R.A.F. savings to buy himself a Sims' sculling boat.

Summer Eights reverted to the finishing order of 1939, Magdalen therefore started seventh and had a real prospect of bumping each evening. However, having bumped Balliol on the first day, their bump on Christ Church on the second was not acknowledged and an appeal was lodged. Once the committee to hear the appeal was divested of the representatives of the House and Magdalen it was left with those from Oriel and New College, who were the next two colleges in the division. John Gleave recalled that: 'the appeal was therefore turned down'. Revenge was had the following evening the bump on Christ Church in the Gut with Magdalen going on to finish third, having failed to catch Oriel. Had the week gone as it should, Magdalen might have prevented Trinity's spell at Head being extended to 1949. The lower boats did well with the Second Eight rising six places, the Third four and the Fourth three. John Gleave partnered R.M.A. Bourne of New College to win the O.U.B.C. Pairs. Bourne had spent some time in a prisoner of war camp and had been in the Blue Boat with Gleave that spring. Having been knocked out of Henley on the second day of the first full post-war Regatta, Magdalen went on a tour of the continent first to Utrecht, Holland and then to Belgium to a regatta in Brussels.

Post-war rationing had an effect on oarsmen's diets and to some extent their performance. In College oily whale steaks were served, Kenneth 'Poppy' Everard, who had arrived in Magdalen in 1944, wrote that the Hall food was 'indescribably unappetising and insubstantial'. However, when he moved out of College to Mrs Richardson's digs at 159 Iffley Road, where generations of Magdalen oarsmen had stayed, the food was much better: "Mrs R' had a catering licence which must have been for a hotel, because we were never short of excellent food. Huge steaks appeared regularly. Man-sized joints filled the oven. Bacon and eggs were the staple at breakfast. Her Yorkshire puddings rose twice as high as anybody else's.' After 1951, and catering for himself, Everard found that two small chops were his weekly meat ration. Mrs Richardson continued housing Magdalen oarsmen for a further twenty years and lived to the age of 109. At a party given by her former lodgers in the New Room to mark her centenary she said she would 'remember it for years to come'. On the continental tour the crew arrived a week before the event and had to endure a carbohydrate diet which the Dutch had become accustomed to but which caused the Oxford students to lose a stone a man. They came fifth of five crews in the regatta on the Rhine Canal. Moving on to Brussels their fortunes were revived by their stay at the Gutt household. Etienne Gutt was a member of the crew; his mother was an excellent cook and, through his father who was Minister of Finance, had managed to pull strings to obtain supplies. The oarsmen regained the lost weight and went on to beat Liege, the Belgian Champions but lost to the Dutch.

After a year as J.C.R. President, David Jamison was elected President of O.U.B.C. for the year 1946-1947 and won his first Blue. He was also President of Vincent's for the same period. John Gleave became Captain of Boats in College and took his second Blue. Hilary Term training was severely hampered by a hard winter: the Isis was frozen over for two weeks and Torpids has to be cancelled. When the thaw came the ensuing flood was the worst the Thames had seen since 1896 and the Magdalen boathouse was under two feet of water. The general standard of rowing in Summer Eights had not returned to its pre-war form and though Magdalen managed to bump Oriel to take second position, they failed to worry Trinity. The O.U.B.C. News stated that 'Oxford, crowded and ill-fed, works hard; teaching hours extend; there is less time to row and coach. Yet many First Division crews showed fair form and good practice times over the course. Coaches perhaps conceded too much to food shortage in the matter of light outings with too few and too short pieces of rowing.' The lower boats made their mark in a variety of ways; the Second Eight dropped out of the First Division to finish 17th on the river, the third eight made seven bumps to finish 33rd. The Fourth Eight had the unique distinction of being double over-bumped twice. David Gallop, a member of the crew, recalls the circumstances of the boat which: 'was so weak that it was bumped by a boat that had started five places behind it, two ordinary bumps having occurred in its wake. This double over-bump was then without precedent in the annals of

Oxford rowing.' What made it even more noteworthy was that the tangle was disputed by the four crews in the middle and the whole episode was re-rowed the following day with the same outcome. Twenty yards from the finish line New College III caught them again. The matter created correspondence in *The Times*. At Henley Magdalen entered the Ladies' Plate, the Visitors' and the Goblets. The Eight rowed on fixed pins while the Four used swivels. Since the latter was a subset of the former these men had to row with both on the same day. McCulloch coached the four which was stroked by J.M.G. Andrews; Etienne Gutt steered the boat from three. Robert Southey was at two and the Captain, R.J.D.McC. Kinsman, was at bow. Knighted in 1976, Southey was Federal President of the Australian Liberal (Conservative) Party and held a variety of other posts including the Rhodes Scholarship Selection Committee. He had arrived at Magdalen before the war, saw service with the Second Battalion, Coldstream Guards and returned to take a First in P.P.E. Gutt had a distinguished career in the Belgian legal profession including the post of President of the Belgian Constitutional Cour d'Arbitrage from 1984 to 1989. Whilst at Oxford he had been President of the University Swimming Club and Captain of Water Polo.

The Four beat Jesus College, Cambridge but lost to Trinity Hall in the next round. The Eight lost to Trinity College, Dublin by six feet. Gleave and Jamison made the final of the Goblets, losing to J. H. Pinches and E.M. Sturges of London Rowing Club by 2½ lengths.

Reflecting on the support give to the Boat Club before and after the war, Gleave wrote: 'Jock Clapperton and Ken Irvine reminded the newcomers of the great traditions of the Club, and helped pass them on. The M.C.B.C. was relatively successful, and this engendered the Club spirit so essential to success. Other prominent support from Old Members came from Gully Nickalls, Seb Earl, Tom Durand, and 'Luke' Lucas, a giant of a man who had led with Gully in a pair. Vivian Nickalls was a great favourite; he used to appear before Eights with a small dog, to see how he could help. Above all, tribute should be paid to Don Burnell. He is reputed to have been somewhat irascible in his younger days, but by this time he was a mellow and most supportive father figure. In these years there were only four umpires at Henley, three of them from Magdalen.

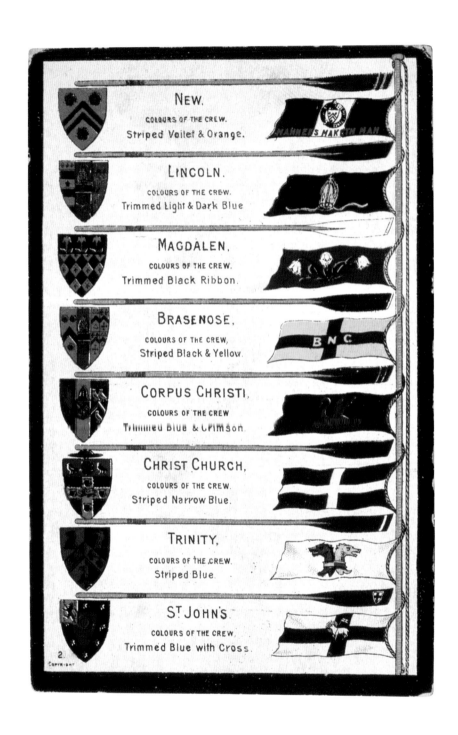

Accordingly the Magdalen coxless boat was always assured of a fair start.' In the period 1946 to 1966 Magdalen men dominated the Henley umpiring team. Over the period, Harcourt Gold, Don Burnell, Stanley Garton, Gully Nickalls, Jock Clapperton and John Garton all presided over the conduct of racing on the Royal Regatta course.

Michaelmas Term 1947 saw Oxford rowing examining its standards and the Long Distance Race was revived 'to encourage college crews to cover more mileage'. Following Oxford's defeat in the Boat Race, Dink Horsfall felt that a return to the Orthodox Style was needed. Another issue facing the rowing fraternity was the state of the towpath. The Thames Conservancy and the riparian owners could not agree on who was responsible for it and neither felt able to fund repairs. A year later the Oxford Preservation Trust had raised £7,000 by way of an appeal and O.U.B.C. noted that 'coaches have no longer to choose between a dive into the river or joining a baby in a pram'. Eights Week 1948 was uninspiring with Magdalen again rowing over second behind Trinity; but they seemed to make up for it off the water as the Captain's Book records that the members of the club 'were fined 5/- each to repair the damage to Mr Morgan's room after the Eights Party'. At Henley the Visitors' Challenge Cup was an exclusively Oxbridge college affair. Sandy Cavenagh, stroke of the Four, recalls steering the boat head on into the second four (which was entered for the Wyfold Cup) on the Saturday before the Regatta. Both boats were 'substantially wrecked' but Dick Dickens 'had them as good as new by Monday.' Magdalen beat Brasenose then Jesus College Cambridge then Pembroke College Cambridge to reach the final. New College fought off Oriel then First and Third Trinity, Cambridge and then Worcester to face Magdalen for the cup. Though they narrowed the lead in the middle of the race, New College could not overhaul Magdalen who won by 1½ lengths, making it M.C.B.C.'s first Henley trophy since 1923. They had again been coached by 'Mac' McCulloch who had been in the 1920 Leander crew which lost to Magdalen in the final of the Grand. McCulloch had also won the Diamond Sculls in 1908. Though not an M.C.B.C. man he was a highly successful coach for the College, generous with his time over many years.

In the 1949 Boat Race Sandy Cavenagh and John Clay won their first Blues in a crew that lost to Cambridge by a canvas, a lead that had been taken in only the final half minute of the race. Cavenagh was also the College Captain and had the first and second boats preparing for Torpids train from Godstow to gain some mileage. For four weeks before racing smoking was banned and drink reduced to no more than a pint of beer at dinner and an occasional port. As an experiment, racing was reduced to four days. Magdalen nonetheless fell two places to eighth. In Summer Eights the top order was unchanged. Having won the Visitors' the year before, Magdalen entered the Stewards' Challenge Cup at Henley but lost to Trinity College, Oxford stroked by C.G.V. Davidge. This Broad Street four went on to win the event beating Leander in the final. The Leander crew contained John Gleave and, like Trinity, it was a subset of their Grand Challenge Cup eight. Gleave noted once again he was rowing on fixed pins in one boat and swivels in another on the same afternoon.

As has already been noted, the College made periodic contributions to the purchase of boats. Colin Cooke, Senior Bursar from 1944 to 1970, was also Senior Treasurer of the Boat Club for the same period and therefore took a close interest in the affairs on the river. In a letter to Jock Clapperton dated June 1949, Magdalen's Blue Boat coxswain of 1923 and 24 and now Honorary Secretary of Leander Club, Cooke asked if they would like to purchase an Eight built in 1939 for a thirteen stone crew and no longer needed by the College. He suggests £150. Clapperton replied saying he would ask Leander. In the exchanges they noted that Neptune Rowing Club was very slow paying Magdalen for two boats they had bought, Clapperton agreed to chase them up. Income from the sale of old and unwanted craft have always been an important part of the Boat Club's economy.

There was an unusually large intake of 104 freshmen in Michaelmas Term 1949 which provided the M.C.B.C. with plenty of new recruits. Sandy Cavenagh, Captain for a second year, planned a comprehensive training programme. Quoting Steve Fairbairn, his favourite saying was 'Mileage makes Champions'; he entered three eights for the Long Distance race which was held on the Radley Reach, the first crew came in second overall. Torpids training was again conducted from the St. Edward's School boathouse at Godstow. On the first afternoon the First Torpid was bumped by

# The re-row was ordered for 7.30pm that evening. Magdalen again led by a length at the half mile but this time continued to gain and won by 1 ¼ lengths

Worcester but went up four places on the subsequent days. The Second Torpid had a collision with St. Edmund Hall which destroyed their boat so they used the third boat thus denying the Third Torpid any rowing that week. Cavenagh was convinced that Cambridge's large entry for The Head of the River Race each March was the key to their success against Oxford colleges at Henley, he therefore entered Magdalen. They first competed at Reading Head of the River and then made their way down the Thames to the Tideway, stopping for a day's training at Eton. This crew was the First Torpid augmented by John Moberly. Moberly's father, Sir Walter, was then the Principal of St. Catharine's, Cumberland Lodge, a Christian training institute in Windsor Great Park and he put the crew up overnight. Starting 112th, they finished 23rd in the First Division. Summer Eights 1950 was dogged by illness and Magdalen were bumped by New College who then knocked Trinity off the Headship. Magdalen did not catch Trinity over the remaining four evenings. The Second Eight made two bumps to finish 15th on the river, comfortably the highest second boat and thus gave testament to the efficacy of long distance work. The First and Second Eights combined to make a crew for the Ladies' Plate, but before competing at Henley they entered Reading Regatta where they nearly beat London Rowing Club's crew preparing for the Grand Challenge Cup. At Henley, the Eight beat St. Catharine's College, Cambridge by half a length on the first day. A four out of the eight entered the Visitors' and at 4.30pm on the first day they raced First and Third Trinity B.C., Cambridge to a dead heat. The re-row was ordered for 7.30pm that evening. Magdalen again led by a length at the half mile but this time continued to gain and won by 1 ¼ lengths, First and Third being unable to repeat their recovery over the last minute of the race. Magdalen then fell victim to a food poisoning incident attributed to some eggs and they were beaten by Emmanuel College, Cambridge in the next round. The Eight suffered from the same affliction and lost to Pembroke College, Cambridge. H.J.

Renton, who had won his first Blue that year, entered the Diamond Sculls and he won two rounds but then lost to the eventual winner, A.D. Rowe of Leander Club. Jeremy Renton was one of Magdalen's best scullers in the post-war period but he quit the sport after the 1951 Boat Race in which the Oxford crew sank.

The four which had competed at Henley entered the University Fours that autumn. Richard Burnell, writing for *The Times*, noted 'For the third year in succession, Magdalen rowed a dead heat, then went one better and repeated it in the re-row. Their opponents were Trinity, and it looks as though they are the two best Fours in the race'. The problem of dead heats arose frequently on the Isis because the judging depended on the reflex action of two separate signal operators. It had become customary to give a dead heat for any verdict of one second or less. Yet one second represented at least half a length in a fours' race, which would be a decisive margin in a side-by-side race. In the third re-row, the crews were still level at Long Bridges. Burnell continued: 'Trinity, hitting the beginning rather harder, looked to be travelling the faster, but Magdalen had the long drawn out finish that makes for run in a four, and at the University boathouse it was their signal that fell first by a bare half second. All the

Clockwise from left: current Boat Club tie

1960 Boat Club tie

Boat Club socks

boater band

Second Eight/First Torpid bow tie

First Eight bow tie

way up the barges, both crews gave all they had, and when the finishing signals dropped the most one could say was that this time Magdalen had definitely won. The verdict was 1 and $^4/_5$ seconds'. The crew went on to beat New College II, but four hard races in two days had taken their toll, and they lost to New College I in the final. In the University Pairs that same term, John Clay and Jeremy Renton won the event convincingly after a very hard race against Christopher Davidge and David Callender of Trinity College. All four were Blues and had rowed together at Eton. Davidge was probably the most successful oarsman of the 1950s. In 1955, rowing for Leander, he and Magdalen's James Gobbo reached the final of the Goblets. Davidge went on to win the Goblets in 1957 and 1958 with D.A.T. Leadley.

The 1950 Long Distance Race was marred by a result that 'was between farce and tragedy. Owing to laxity and incompetence on the part of O.U.B.C. officials concerned, the First Eight arrived at the finish before the umpire and timekeeper. Therefore, Magdalen had to be content with knowing that we were somewhere in the first three. This was a good performance, but the crew felt that they had been deprived of a clear win'. In Torpids, the same crew was bumped twice before finally finding their form and re-bumped University College on the last night. On the Tideway they did even better than in the previous year, coached by Jock Wise of London R.C. and Tony Rowe. In the Putney Head of the River race they came fifth out of 214 despite a collision with London University who would not give way when being overtaken. Reinforced by two Blues, Sandy Cavenagh and John Clay, the Summer Eight finally bumped Trinity on the first night, and New College on the third night, then rowed over at Head of the River on the fourth night. On the fifth night Merton were behind them, having also bumped Trinity and New College. They were obviously a fast crew, but were not regarded as a serious threat. At the University boathouse they had closed to half a length and then pushed hard all the way up the barges. Magdalen failed to push and

General Boat Club blazer, also First Torpid blazer before 1939.

the cox did not swerve. They were bumped right on the line, just before the signal fell. There was no chance of catching Merton on the last evening, and the misery was palpable. On the rebound of this frustration, Magdalen entered four events at Henley. The Eight entered the Ladies' Plate and the stern four also raced the Stewards' Challenge Cup while the bow four did so in the Visitors. A Wyfold four from the Second Summer Eight also competed. None of the crews made it past the first round though the Visitors' four had the partial satisfaction of knowing they were beaten by the eventual winners, Trinity Hall. P.G.P.D. Fullerton, now at the end of his second year at Magdalen, persuaded his father to house the crew at their house on the river near Henley for the Regatta period. They took over the house for three weeks and brought with them Reg Willis, a scout who competed in the College Servants' Rowing Club, and his wife as cook. A house full of fragile objects and full of oarsmen is a dangerous mix: the almost inevitable accident resulted and a large family portrait was damaged in an accident. Peter Fullerton recalls that the following year they were not invited back; they billeted with Henley doctor Kenneth Irvine and his wife Phil, longstanding hosts to M.C.B.C. and by then living in Peppard Lane.

Although six of the Eight of the previous year were still available, and three of them got Trial Caps, none of the 1951-52 crews per-

formed well. Tom Moon had to give up the Captaincy half way through the year because of work, and D.G. Penington inherited a morale problem. The First Torpid went down five places. After a succession of others during Trinity Term, Peter Haig-Thomas coached the Eight during the final stages of preparation but they succumbed to Balliol and then New College. Rowing over in front of Trinity for the last three nights was perhaps remarkable as David Penington, at stroke, had chronic asthma though his rhythmic wheezing set the rating with audible precision. His condition did not prevent him becoming Professor of Medicine at Melbourne University and later its Vice-Chancellor. At Henley 1952, reinforced by two freshmen from the Second Eight, D.P. Wells and L.P. Shurman, the crew came on well and won their first race in the Ladies' Plate against Queens' College, Cambridge. In the autumn, after more coaching at Henley, where Haig-Thomas then lived, the First Four reached the final of the University Fours and lost by only 1½ seconds to Univ. In the Long Distance Race, several hard practice courses over the full distance paid off. The First Eight won the race outright, and the 2nd crew composed almost entirely of novices performed well too. Another freshman, Richard Oake recalls: 'He [Haig-Thomas] was controversial, very orthodox - tubbing, mileage, emphasis on the start; he lived with us. Apart from huge experience

Above: D.P. Wells' blades,
Torpids 1953
Head of the River 1953
O.U.B.C. Silver Challenge
Pairs 1953
Visitors Challenge Cup 1953
O.U.B.C. Challenge Fours 1954
Head of the River 1954
equalled only by Sir James
Gobbo, his pairs partner

and knowledge, PH-T had an enormous capacity to inspire self-belief. He produced, made, the 1953 crew. The Eight was in essence demoralised, having dropped two places in Eights 1952, and five in Torpids, which was considered a disgrace. He took us on because he saw a bunch of heavy characters, and told us 'You'll never have style, but I'll make you row'. He was meticulous in dealing with each individual. He inspired us that we would make a crew. The effect of the one win at Henley was enormous, and was built on that ethos of 'could do something'.'

October 1952 brought to Oxford J.A. Gobbo from Melbourne and J.H. Richards from California. Rhodes Scholars and experienced oarsmen, they both won Trial Caps that December along

with R. Van Oss and David Wells. Jack Richards might have won a Blue had he not slipped on a bottle of 1885 Madeira at the Trial Eights' party and broken his wrist. Though in pain, the fracture was not immediately identified, and it was only when Jack mentioned it to David Jamison, by then a lecturer at Corpus Christi College and a demonstrator in the Department of Physiology, that is became clear how serious the matter was. Jamison would have been sympathetic – it was the same fate that had befallen him in 1946. Trial Caps were allowed to row in Torpids then and so the other three helped make a fast First Torpid. On the first afternoon they made history by becoming the first crew to achieve an over-bump in the first division, on St Peter's Hall. They made four more and so ended the week fourth on the river. The Second Torpid made seven bumps and regained its position as the highest second boat on the river; the Third Torpid did well too and the total haul for the week was eighteen bumps. For the first time since 1932 the Boat Club celebrated with a Bumps Supper in Hall. The Captain's Book records that 'The Bump Supper and its consequences unfortunately cost the College a lot of money'. The *Oxford Mail* reported: 'After a hilarious dinner in Hall, certain Magdalen dignitaries were chaired (and cheered) around the Quad. Later in the evening, there was a magnificent bonfire in the meadows behind Addison's Walk, with a firework accompaniment'. The Senior Dean of Arts, Dr Karl Leyser, handed down fines of £1 per culprit except to Thomas Buckley who had to find £5. Richard Van Oss, one of the miscreants attending the decanal summons, recalls Leyser told Buckley this was 'because you can afford it'.

After this Hilary Term success, expectations ran high for great things in Eights Week. Haig-Thomas was joined on the towpath by Gully Nickalls and David Jamison. All three subscribed to the Orthodox Style. Five of the Torpid were available for the Summer Eight and retained their seats: Richard Van Oss at 3, Laurence Shurman at 5, David Wells at 6, Jim Gobbo at 7, Harry Holt at stroke. Peter Fullerton, now Captain of Boats, took the bow seat with Alan Binder at 2, and Jack Richards, whose wrist had barely healed, at 4. Richard Oake was coxswain, he recounts the week: 'The first night we disposed of New College in the Gut. On the second night we had to deal with Merton, the second best crew on the river. They got off to a very fast start, were light, excellent in a following wind, - they were all oarsmen, and had real style. On the second, then the third and the fourth nights Merton had a following wind. We got within a canvas, but couldn't catch them. On the fifth night, morale was high and as luck would have it the weather changed and we got a head wind. Our heavies found a rhythm and real thrust, and we got Merton along the boathouses after a long and hard spurt up the Green Bank. It was an immense relief. We still had Balliol to beat, and only one night to do it, so there was tremendous needle. Fortunately, we again had a head wind, and they were not as good as Merton, so we got them on the Greener. I remember the sky was black with storm clouds, the air electric. Literally at the moment we got the bump on Balliol there was a tremendous crack of thunder and the heavens opened.' And so Magdalen were Head for the first time in twenty one years. Half the College was at the boathouse and the celebrations were given a tremendous start by Komarakul Na Nagara arriving from the Thai Embassy in his Rolls Royce stuffed full with champagne; he had been the coxswain the last time Magdalen had been Head in Eights Week, in 1932. At the ensuing Bumps Supper the President, Tom Boase, was present and clearly delighted. James Griffiths, then Vice-President, also present, spoke and recalled the 1932 dinner which he had helped to earn. A bonfire in the meadow followed and an eight was burned 'to the strains of the Eton Boating Song played on a trumpet'.

College balls, like degree days, are prone to divide a crew on the question of priorities when preparing for Henley. Nowadays, one year in three, Qualifying Races for the Regatta are the same day as the ball and a simple decision has to be made: one cannot do both. In 1953 the Commemoration Ball attracted some of the First Eight while others wanted to concentrate on Henley. Each went their own way and the ball-goers were ostracized. Peter Haig-Thomas moved Jack Richards from four to stroke but the crew did not really come together and in the Ladies' Plate they lost to Eton by eight feet. After Eights' Week Richard Burnell wrote in *The Times*: 'Magdalen could hardly be called a really good crew, for they were inclined to be clumsy, and did not seem to be good stayers'. The need to change the seat order and bring in members of the Second Eight with little time, after the break for Schools, cannot have helped. However two fours were made out of the eight. The Wyfold four had a bye in the first round but were beating easily by Glasgow University. The Visitors' four – Richards, Gobbo, Wells and Fullerton – fared better and worked well as a unit. They first beat Lady Margaret Boat Club, Cambridge by 1½ lengths; First and Third Trinity were thought to be the favourites but they also fell to Magdalen, by 3 lengths. They next beat Trinity College, Oxford by ¾ of a length. In the final they met King's College, Cambridge and, as they had in each heat, Magdalen established a initial lead and held it. King's hit the booms twice before the Barrier and this gave Magdalen a big

margin; they won by 3½ lengths to win the Visitors' Challenge Cup for the fifth time in M.C.B.C.'s history. The season was a triumph at all levels and had been achieved without any Blues, Peter Haig-Thomas was feted as the architect of the success, for his ability to make winners out of a good crew. Jack Richards became Professor of Chemistry at Caltech; Jim Gobbo a Supreme Court Judge in Victoria, for which he was knighted, and later Governor of Victoria; Laurence Shurman became the U.K. Banking Ombudsman; and Alan Binder a director of Shell and other major companies; Peter Fullerton had a career in the diplomatic service and later the home civil service; David Wells joined the medical profession.

The autumn and winter of 1953-54 was difficult. M.C.B.C. struggled in the Long Distance race: though Peter Fullerton and Alan Binder won the O.U.B.C. Double Sculls and Gobbo and Wells won the O.U.B.C. Pairs. Jim Gobbo went on to win his first Blue. This year the Torpids rules were changed to prevent Trial Caps from rowing in the event and thus Richard Van Oss was not able to participate. The notable point of the week was the Third Torpid

Bumping Balliol for the
Headship , 1953.

making five bumps despite hitting the bank. Another major change on the river came into force in 1954 when Eights Week was reduced from six days to four. The argument promulgated was that six nights ruined a good crew and reduced the time available to train for Henley (the four day Torpids experiment, which had been in place for five years, was made permanent). Richard Oake recalled: 'The Eight were less settled, and most had Finals' nerves and worries about what we'd get after spending so much time on the river, and what we'd do afterwards. Therefore, no entries had been undertaken to outside regattas'. Haig-Thomas coached the Eight and Alan Binder the Second Eight, and in addition three other eights were put out. The Eight held onto the Headship despite a strong challenge from Balliol. The Second Eight rose two to reclaim the position of highest second boat. At Henley a Ladies' Plate Eight lost in the semi-final to First and Third Trinity B.C., Cambridge. The same college beat Magdalen in the final of the Visitors'. John Feltham was the coxswain of the Eight; in 1965 he became a Law Tutor at the College and, among other senior posts, was Vice-President 1989-1990. Of his undergraduate time on the river he recalled: 'Fortunately, coxes were not thrown in in those days, and we enjoyed our Bumps Supper in Hall afterwards'. Commenting in the early 1990s on the changes on the river since then, he continued: 'With hindsight, that was the highpoint before Magdalen struggled with the new conditions on the river. The big change is the advent of women's rowing. To this must be added the increasing number of colleges putting more boats afloat so that there are now seven men's and five women's divisions of twelve boats each for Summer Eights after at least a further 18 to 24 have competed for each of the lowest divisions. It became clear that increased competition on the river conflicted with rising academic demands, and to a lesser extent with the ethos of particular colleges'.

The Autumn Fours of 1954 is a story worth telling as a tale of endurance and sportsmanship. Having seen off Oriel and Trinity, Magdalen faced New College in the semi-final and the result was a dead heat. It has already been noted that the accuracy of the judging of the O.U.B.C. small boats events frequently led to such verdicts; on this occasion it was ordained that the re-row be held in the evening and the Captains' Book notes that they finished 'in darkness while the watermen performed miracles of remote control and blind navigation' with another dead heat. A further re-row the following morning produced the same outcome. Richard Van Oss recalled: 'We were threatened with a re-row against New College even as a huge haystack fire near the start covered the river in dense smoke, necessitating rowing for four strokes and then holding the breath for four; not good when rowing hard! In order to avoid the gloomy prospect of rowing forever, I suggested we toss to determine which crew meet Brasenose in the final, and to share the honours if any. There was nothing against that in the Rules. New College won the toss, we got fairly sloshed, and rode shakily down the towpath cheering New College on as they rowed a fine race to beat Brasenose. A great day, and so the Fours Cup is inscribed as shared by New College and Magdalen'. The stern pair of Gobbo and Wells went on to retain the O.U.B.C. Pairs comfortably. Gobbo was elected the next President of O.U.B.C. Flooding prevented the Long Distance Race from being held.

The wartime worry over care of the equipment in the light of the shortage of craftsmen and materials continued, like rationing, for a long time afterwards. By 1954 Magdalen needed a new boat and

## A glass racing eight for an Oxford club

AN Oxford college boat club is hoping to have a crew rowing at Henley this year in a new racing eight made of glass—the first of its kind in the world.

Magdalen College is responsible for what is a revolutionary experiment which, if successful, will have a profound effect on rowing clubs everywhere.

The new eight will be of resin-bonded glass fibre, no heavier, and probably lighter than the conventional cedar-wood shell, tougher, less expensive to maintain and, later on, cheaper to make.

It is being made by a Portsmouth firm which has already made 15ft. sailing boats, a cabin cruiser, an Admiralty barge and now life-boats.

Dr. G F. Paechter, junior treasurer of Magdalen Boat Club, advocated the idea, and the suggestion was made to the builders after he had sailed one of their "Flying Fifteens" last summer.

The boat club was won over, the firm itself was enthusiastic and so was the Oxford boat-building firm which will rig out the shell when it comes out of the mould.

### PROBLEMS TO SOLVE

When the prototype is seen on the Thames depends on whether technical difficulties in constructing the dummy from which the mould will be made, can be overcome in time for the finished article to be seen at Henley.

The Oxford University Boat Club, whose president, Mr. J. A. Gobbo, is an undergraduate at Magdalen, is interested in the experiment.

The fibre glass is stronger than wood, but also denser, so if the boat is flooded it will sink. To overcome this special "buoyancy bags" are being put under the canvases.

The glass fibre can be sawn and drilled but not chiselled. In a collision with the bank or anything in the water it does not split but is holed.

Any hole can be repaired with the aid of special resin and the glass fibre, and in two hours the boat is ready for use again.

The boat will not be transparent—any colour in a wide range is mixed with the resin, and Magdalen's boat will be admiral blue with a red band running along its entire length.

"It was suggested that dark blue would be most appropriate," Dr. Paechter said today, "but we thought that should more properly be left for the University Club, with red for Lady Maggie at Cambridge."

The main advantages of the glass-fibre shell is that it does not need varnishing, thereby reducing maintenance costs, it is stronger than wood, it does not "whip," and in quantity production it will be cheaper than a wooden eight, which costs about £300.

"Of course we can't say what the eventual cost will be and the prototype is bound to cost more," Dr. Paechter explained, "but once the mould is made the cost of which should be written off by the first eight boats produced, it should be good for about 100 shells.

"Good as it is for colleges, it should be invaluable for schools and not only eights but tubs can also be produced in the [...]

### THIN SHELL

The shell is built up by alternate layers of a special resin and the glass fibres which are either woven or "matted." The maximum thickness of the Magdalen shell, which has no ribs, is 3-16th of an inch, and to this will be screwed the keelson and the in-rails will be tacked in.

"We ought to know by the middle of next week whether we shall be able to have our new eight in time for Henley, Dr. Paechter told a reporter.

"The dummy from which the mould is being made has been holding us up, but if the latest effort is not successful the mould will be made from an actual cedarwood shell.

"The whole thing opens up wonderful possibilities and I suppose the next thing will be oars made from the same material.

"We have had one sample section already and that passed all the tests."

The *Oxford Mail* reports the new boat.

was keen to have one to mark the success of the previous year. This was the period when new materials were being experimented with, particularly in Germany where Willy Empacher was making boats in Eberbach, east of Heidelberg, on the banks of the River Neckar. From this yard came, in 1955, the first glass fibre and polyester boats – a launch and a touring boat for two scullers.[1] Through George Paechter, a Magdalen D.Phil graduate who was at the time a university lecturer, the proposal arose – inspired by his experience in glass fibre Flying Fifteen sailing boats - to order a glass fibre eight. A mould was taken from a Tims' boat and eventually the new shell arrived. Tims Senior pronounced: 'Yes, I'll fit it out with all the woodwork, but I won't guarantee she'll be any good'. The boat, which had cost more than the usual £300 for a wooden shell, was named St Mary Magdalen and her maiden voyage was a crew of old heavies: Earl, Gleave, Irvine, Durand, Jamison, Burnell, Gobbo and Garton, with Clapperton to cox. The craft proved to be very heavy indeed and it did not run well. It was quickly moved down the pecking order to be used by lower boats. Partly for its weight and to some extent owing to its matt grey interior it became known as the 'concrete boat'. By the following summer it was relegated to use by the Fourth (Rugby) Eight who managed, nonetheless, to make three bumps and avoided being caught on the final day through the clever steering of their cox, R.O. Havery. In the following day's report in *The Times*, Richard Havery was complimented – flattery indeed for a fourth boat to be mentioned, though Richard Burnell liked to comment on his old College's achievements when the opportunity presented itself. The First Eight were caught along by Balliol along the Green Bank and then two nights later by Merton. Magdalen would not be Head again for fifty years. This mewing of Magdalen only added to the misery the previous term when the First Torpid had crashed four places, though the Second Torpid had made five bumps to regain the position of highest second boat.

This was an era of change off the river as much as on it and new influences on M.C.B.C.

[1] C.Dodd, The Story of World Rowing, Stanley Paul 1992

I.L.Elliott (Keble) and D.C. Rutherford (Magdalen) (nearest camera) coming through R.J. Nicholson and C.L. Marshall (Nottingham Britannia Boat Club) in the final of the Silver Goblets and Nickalls' Challenge Cup, Henley Royal Regatta 1960

# 9 1956-1971

## Challenging Times, Goblets Success, Ethos, the London Rowing Club influence

The second half of the 1950s and the early part of the next decade were a difficult time in the fortunes of M.C.B.C. The Club entered an era of experienced oarsmen departing that were not replaced by the usual intake of those who had rowed at school. In addition, the Captain's book comments that within the University and the College there was a greater emphasis on academic work. One frustrated Captain, who considered the Boat Club's interests as paramount, termed the issue of experienced oarsmen refusing to row in their final year the 'Magdalen Disease'. In fact the situation was not confined to Magdalen. The nature of the University itself was changing: students were be admitted from a wider range of backgrounds and many tutors were properly placing the focus on study but to do so reduced the time available for recreational activities. Some colleges earned a reputation for being averse to giving places to those who had sporting aspirations even if their academic credentials were satisfactory; of course this might be true of individual tutors more than it could be called college policy. Magdalen's President, Tom Boase, talking to Richard Burnell on the raft at the boathouse one afternoon during Eights Week, observed a phenomenon that appeared to buck this trend. Keble was admitting good numbers of Etonian oarsmen creating spectacular success on the river whilst the college's academic results also improved at an astonishing rate. It seemed that their achievements on the river attracted the attention of many applicants who had scarcely heard of the college and thus bright students from leading academic schools were applying in number. Aside from this aberration to the change of climate, there were other aspects affecting the decline in college rowing in the mid 1950s – ones which affected both Universities. Changes in the social and economic conditions began to make themselves felt as Britain moved out of the long post-war recovery and whilst life returned to normal it was not the same as it had been up to 1939. Concerns about post-degree employment also had their influence. Magdalen had a tradition of competing at Henley, and the Boat Club's calendar listed the Royal Regatta as a fixture on an equal footing with Torpids and Summer Eights. Participation was becoming more difficult, partly through the timing of the examination season and to some extent the rise of international entries, especially after 1954, and the position of British club rowing relative to that of Oxbridge colleges.

Writing in the early 1990s, Richard Burnell reflected on the state of rowing in Oxford and on how the sport fitted into college life: 'The Boat Club does not operate in a vacuum. One of the merits of rowing is that it is a true team sport. Each oarsman or woman need the supports of their crew mates and knows that they need his or hers; every crew needs the whole-hearted backing of its club; and every club needs at least the sympathy and support of the community in which it operates'. He went on to observe one of the key principles that makes a college boat club what it is: 'Rowing can be

just a spare time recreation, and it is absolutely right that it should be for so many, perhaps the majority of those who row. But competition at higher levels is a serious business, demanding dedication and sacrifices. You only get to be Head by finding better oarsmen or women, coaching and equipping them better, and working them harder than their rivals.' In support of Burnell's argument Magdalen was well backed by old members coaching for the College. Such volunteer expertise was invaluable to the succeeding generations: Tom Durand, John Gleave, David Jamison and Gully Nickalls all gave liberally of their time; Alexander Lindsay and David Rutherford followed after they had graduated. This assistance was not just in Trinity Term but for Torpids and the small boats events. However there was not sufficient 'heavies' to coach the second crews; these were left in the capable charge of the boatman, Edgar Dickens. Not only a boatman and coach, he also rowed himself, for many years stroking the watermen's crew, Sons of the Isis. 'Dick' was sparing with his advice to captains and would invariably preface any wisdom with: 'Well, Sir, if I was you, Sir,' and then deliver some shrewd judgement on an individual or crew performance. His standard towpath cry was 'Well rowed, Boys'. Away from the river Dick was a

City Councillor, and later as an Alderman he ran for Lord Mayor. Perhaps surprisingly, he was a true blue Tory and this seemed to be difficult for him in the Town Hall where the political complexion of Oxford City Council never had much of that colour in its make-up. Dickens was employed jointly by Magdalen and Trinity on an equal basis. His time was naturally limited and therefore, with a growing Boat Club, not all of Magdalen's lower boats could benefit from his input. These crews sometimes also lost out to coaching by the senior end of the Club as the demands of University rowing, now running a squad system, reduced their time to help their Club mates. In fact this increased pressure also kept the triallists and Blues from M.C.B.C. meetings and the sense of a club as expressed by Burnell was compromised. Against this backdrop Magdalen rowing went into a tough period, one unlike anything hitherto in its history.

A. T. Lindsay

After the results of Summer Eights 1955, the incoming Captain, Ian Anderson, invested in new, shorter yet wider, oars. He also purchased weights equipment 'for the crew to improve themselves with'. Reflecting on the year past he wrote of a 'lack of enthusiasm from the top and a scarcity of coaches at the beginning of the year', when Tom Durand had been unwell. In the Long Distance Race the crew used a clinker boat rather than a shell and dropped from ninth to fourteenth. The First Torpid had a bevy of coaches and made two bumps but failed to catch Merton on the third afternoon. President Boase gave them a dinner in the Lodgings 'which failed to provide the necessary stimulus', they finished fifth on the river. The Second Torpid had formed only ten days before the event and it fell four places. Though Tom Durand was still unable to coach, the First Eight had the benefit of Gully Nickalls' wisdom and they used the new oars and added weight training to the regime. Losing the stroke man to illness, they fell two places to fifth. 1957 was not much fun: the First Boat dropped a net two places during Torpids and the Second Boat four. The next term the First Eight benefited from two weeks each of Durand, Nickalls and Garton; they gained a place to fourth but again the Second Eight fell every evening. A year later, 1958, the First Torpid held its position while the Second Torpid continued its downward trend, notwithstanding a technical bump in its favour after Queen's III failed to get on their station on time. In Eights Week the First Boat slipped another place at the expense of St. Edmund Hall. Alexander Lindsay, in his freshman year, and David Rutherford, now in his second season, had been in the Isis crew and now went on to participate in a Magdalen four for the Empire Games Trials. They then rowed down to Henley. The Captain, Raymond Snow, recalled that on the way 'they rescued a body - alas too late - who appeared to be a certain Mr Harry of no fixed address. Mr Rutherford fully exploited his powers of description to the Daily Express who paid five guineas for the story. The health of Harry was drunk fully and often. At Reading Regatta, the Four was leading in the final when they were rammed by St. Edmund Hall who achieved a disqualification. The words that ensued exceeded the bounds of drawing room conversation. At Henley, the Four beat Corpus Christi, Cambridge and then were beaten by Keble, the winners of the Visitors' Challenge Cup'. This loss to the up-and-coming college had probably been avoidable. The Magdalen crew were divided over whether they should attend the Commemoration Ball; unsurprisingly their coaches forbade

such an interruption but backed down when the vote would have resulted in withdrawing their Henley entry. Rutherford recalls that he 'watched unhappily from the stroke seat the gathering thunder on the face of the umpire, Gully Nickalls, as Magdalen slipped inexorably further and further behind their opponents'. Later in July five Magdalen men – Nickalls, Durand, Irvine, Burnell and Rosser - were involved in running the Empire Games Regatta at Lake Padarn, Wales. 1958 being the College's Quincentenary, they felt moved to send loyal greetings to the President on St. Mary Magdalen Day (22nd July). Their presence and number at this event once again showed the contribution of Magdalen oarsmen to the sport of rowing beyond the immediate environment of the Isis.

October 1958 was encouraging for no fewer that twenty freshmen joined the Boat Club and a

# The Old Waterman

*And so, Eights Week is coming round again.*
*I think I'll take a stroll beside the river,*
*The sky looks all the bluer for the rain.*

*The smell of May hangs heavy by the Plain*
*And sets an old man's memories a-quiver*
*To think Eights Week is coming round again.*

*Time was I knew them all, the rowing men.*
*Boy-like I thought them gods, the great and clever,*
*As skies look all the bluer for the rain.*

*So rowing shows a man his proper grain,*
*Swinging and sweating in a crew together,*
*Ah well – And so Eights Week is round again.*

*Mind you, its naught to what it was. But then*
*What is? Things can't go on the same for ever.*
*The sky looks all the bluer for the rain.*

*Storms pass and men. But the real things remain*
*The shouts, the lungs pumped dry, the gasped endeavour,*
*The bump! And hark! Eights Week is here again.*
*The sky looks all the bluer for the rain.*

Maida Stanier
(wife of R.S. Stanier, Master of Magdalen College School 1944-1967)

new policy was adopted of 'teaching individuals to row properly, rather than to enter as many crews as possible in to as many races as possible at the expense of technique and oarsmanship.' In total four crews were entered for Christ Church Regatta and all won their first rounds; it was hoped the experiment would pay dividends during Torpids. At the same regatta Nicholas Daniloff entered the single sculls but 'was overtaken by disaster when the river bended but his steering was unable to do likewise'. Bad weather affected training for Torpids but the First Boat managed to make two bumps while the Second Boat slid another three places down the division. Lindsay and Rutherford gained their Blues in the 1959 crew which beat Cambridge by six lengths; Ian Baillieu was in the Isis crew which came second in The Tideway Head of the River Race. However, O.U.B.C. kept most of the Blue Boat together, augmenting it from Isis, to enter the Grand at Henley and to visit Japan, and so the Magdalen First Boat was weakened. At the start of Trinity

## The Fourth Eight stirred the Burnell pen at *The Times* with a paragraph

Term David Rutherford was elected President of O.U.B.C. and Alexander Lindsay as Secretary. Lindsay stood down as Captain of M.C.B.C. and Malcolm Barton took on the duties for the term. Nonetheless the First Eight bumped Queen's on the fourth evening to finish fourth on the river. The Second Boat were bumped on the first three days but managed to row over on the fourth 'with the cox consulting his map as to the nature of the upper reaches of the Isis'. The Fourth Eight stirred the Burnell pen at *The Times* with a paragraph on how it had managed to bump St. Catherine's III twice and yet find itself still behind them at the end of the week! The O.U.B.C. venture brought Oxford and Harvard side by side for the first time in a number of years; in the semi-final of the Grand the crimson and white crew from Massachusetts won by half a length. The Oxford crew went on to the All Japan Championships where the heat and humidity were as much the opposition, they lost by six inches in the final.

That autumn the Magdalen Four was strong; Peter Burnell had arrived as a freshman from Eton to become the third generation of his family at Magdalen. He took the bow seat while Lindsay, Baillieu and Rutherford occupied the other positions. In the semi-final they rowed a dead hat against St. Edmund Hall, the eventual winners, and then lost the immediate re-row by a second. During Michaelmas Term M.C.B.C. made some changes to the fleet, disposing of a clinker eight to the College School they forgot to return the exemption plate to the Thames Conservancy and were chastised by the authority. Meanwhile, Rutherford suggested to the O.U.B.C. Special Fund Trustees that practical help for Oxford rowing might be provided by a 50% grant to colleges towards buying new small boats. The Trustees, whose Treasurer was John Garton, agreed and after words with Colin Cooke, Senior Treasurer of M.C.B.C., a successful bid was lodged for half the costs of a £155 pair and a £100 single scull. Rutherford, who had been at Rugby and therefore learnt his rowing at Oxford, was then somewhat surprised to be invited by Ian Elliott of Keble to partner him in the University Pairs. Rutherford pointed out his last of experience in small boats but Elliott, in his usual forthright manner, brushed that aside and then ventured out in a Magdalen boat. They were coached by Dickens. Baillieu provided vocal support from the towpath invariably bellowing 'You are only slightly down and now gaining with every stroke'. In the final they broke the pre-1939 course record by 14 seconds. On the strength of this they decided to prepare for the Goblets and Henley, musing that 'it would not entail much extra effort' to fit this in alongside training for the Boat Race.

The 1960 First and Second Torpids both dropped a place, the following term the Summer Eight held its place and the Second Boat fell once more to finish 32nd.

Rutherford, Elliott and Lindsay rowed in the 1960 Boat Race and won, then went on to train with O.U.B.C. for Henley and, it was hoped, the Olympic Regatta in Rome. Elliott and Rutherford gained the grudging consent of Jumbo Edwards, the O.U.B.C. coach, to enter for the Goblets whilst the Eight entered the Grand. Given that Edwards was the third (and last) oarsman to win the Grand, the Stewards' and the Goblets in the same day, and two Olympic gold medals within three hours of each other at Los Angeles in 1932, one might have thought he would have been more tolerant of their wish to double-up. He did not offer the pair any advice but they had their fair share of coaching when in the eight.

Edgar Dickens coached them and they were careful not to do too much work that might compromise the eight. The new pair which Rutherford had secured a half grant for was built by George Sims at Eel Pie Island; he and Elliott visited Sims and gained his sympathy. The resultant boat was perfectly made for them, matching their heights and weights, it did many years service and when eventually its days were over the bows were mounted in the Old Kitchen Bar. Alongside this new boat, the pair benefitted from a new, much lighter, set of oars from Aylings. Alexander Lindsay had cut an oar in sections and his engineer's mind told him the oval hole running through the centre of the loom was ninety degrees off from the orientation that would give it the maximum possible strength. A trial set was made amid much difficulty, the oars being a quarter lighter than the standard. Rutherford and Elliott took delivery of them just before the Royal Regatta and the difference in feel when rowing with them 'was sensational'. Having been disqualified for their steering at Marlow Regatta, they switched the steering position to Rutherford at stroke and won their first two heats at Henley without being unduly stretched. The O.U.B.C. Eight won its first round of the Grand. For the semi-final, against Caius College, Cambridge, Gully Nickalls was the umpire. Gully prefaced the start by ponderously addressing both crews: 'should I have occasion to warn either crew about their steering, I shall refer to the crew on the Bucks station as 'Caius' and to the crew on the Berks station as 'Keble'.' Rutherford recalls the four oarsmen looked at their opponents in puzzled amazement; eventually one of the Caius crew spoke up 'Gully, would it not be less confusing if you referred to our opponents as Magdalen?' Gully's instant reply was 'Of course, but I did not think it was proper for me to make that suggestion'. Such was the concern at that time for conflicts of interest. The Eight lost to Barn Cottage in the final of the Grand and the Goblets were scheduled for 5.30pm, against a pair from Nottingham and Union R.C. Rutherford and Elliott made a sluggish start and were down by a good length at the end of the Island, this was two lengths by the Barrier and four lengths at Fawley, striking a laboured 32 strokes per minute and wandering erratically back and forth across the course. Earlier in the week the pair had learned that they winners of the Goblets got to keep the solid silver vessels and that they cost the Regatta Stewards £64 each. Rutherford appealed to Elliott's commercial instinct and shouted to him 'Come on Ian! Have you forgotten we are rowing for real money?' The effect was instant, the rate of striking went up and they surged forward, the now enormous deficit was being reeled in. In the Press Box, The Times' Richard Burnell seeing them at the Mile, put away his notebook and said 'they can't do it now; they have left it too late'. The Daily Telegraph correspondent, Tom Durand, had more faith in his old College and replied 'I wouldn't be so sure'. About four lengths at the Mile was reduced to 3 at the Mile and One Eighth signal and 2 lengths by the start of the Enclosure., the rate coming up all the time. Rowing as men possessed, with superlative equipment and supremely fit, the pair were only half a length down on their opponents at the Progress Board, they drove their boat on and passed Nicholson and Marshall to win by two-thirds of a length. It is clear that the Keble and Magdalen pair rowed over the second half of the course faster than the first, a rare achievement, the more so to do it in a final. The umpire, Jack Beresford, went to the dressing tent and exclaimed 'That was the best race I have ever seen' – quite a compliment from a man who had won his third Olympic gold medal, aged 35, from behind at the Berlin Games of 1936. Rutherford's win remains Magdalen's last at Henley; fitting perhaps that it should be the Silver Goblets and Nickalls' Challenge Cup, the event which above all has the closest connections to the College.

The Oxford Eight was selected by the A.R.A. for the Rome Olympic Regatta. Rutherford hurt his back at the last minute and did not go, Alexander Lindsay (and Ian Elliott) rowed for Great Britain on Lake Albano.

Returning to Magdalen and the Isis, there was now a yawning gap between the first and second boats in both Torpids and Summer Eights and this was to be the source of difficulty through the decade that followed. The experience and morale of those migrating from the second boat to the first was not enough to bridge the divide and maintain the general position on the river. 1961 brought a complicated - and short-lived – alteration to Torpids racing whereby crews split into two files on leaving the Gut and into three at the boathouses. A bump was awarded for overlapping or the crew could row on to bump the boat ahead in its own lane as an overbump. Under this system the Second Torpid fell to 41st and thus out of the permanent ladder, whilst the Third Torpid achieved

The 1962 Eight

an overbump and went up five places to finish 39th. The Club was fined £5 for overtaking the second boat. That Easter a training camp was held at Eton and 'much of value' was learned by the two eights. The first mention of an ergometer is to be found in the Captain's entry for April when the Club was given a hydraulic sculling machine. It did not find favour and he 'understood that this was now being used by an elderly female acquaintance of Dick's who was incapable of exercising any other way'. In Summer Eights the last experiment with fixed pins was conducted. The First Eight was bumped by Lincoln and finished sixth, the Second Eight was steady at 32nd. Robin Lewis, who was Captain the following year, recalled that the switch back to fixed pins was primarily due to his influence, and that of Archie Nicholson (co-author with Peter Haig-Thomas of *The English Style of Rowing*) who had coached Lewis at Eton. Peter Burnell, with Ronnie Howard of Christ Church, won the O.U.B.C. Double Sculls. Burnell won his Blue in the Boat Race of 1962. There were low numbers in M.C.B.C. and it was only 'hoped to raise' a Second Torpid. In fact one appeared and fell two places, the First Torpid were bumped to sixth by Oriel. Circuit Training is mentioned for the first time in the Club's records – just a year after the ergometer. Robin Lewis introduced a trialling system for selecting the Summer Eight and there was discussion about moving training to Culham to obtain good water. Gully Nickalls coached the First Eight, assisted by a 21 foot catamaran launch designed by Robin Lewis that was largely constructed on the estate of his father, Lord Merthyr. In *The Sunday Times* of 6th May 1962 this craft was photographed and described. The picture showed Gully sitting in a deck chair with a megaphone, wearing a dinner jacket. With him were Peter Sutherland and Raymond Crawford. The article does not explain Gully's choice of dress but it does make the point that the launch afforded the coach the chance to see the crew from all angles and to conducting timing by arriving at the finishing post before the crew. The Eight ended up ninth, the Second Eight avenged the previous year's loss.

H.R. Gillespie was elected Captain for 1962-63 and then again for 1963-64. Along with A.J. Strong, A.N. Crowther and A.D.J. Nielson, Hugh formed a four that was to enjoy some racing through the year. In the autumn they defeated New College, stroked by the President of O.U.B.C., they also won a round of the Visitors' beating Caius College, Cambridge easily. Their opponents in the next round were the eventual winners, Christ's College, Cambridge. Anthony Strong and Andrew Crowther entered the Pairs and saw off an O.U.B.C. and then an Oriel crew. Half the novices were trained under the new O.U.B.C. scheme in *Leviathan*, a huge barge with eight oarsmen side by side with room for the coach to walk up and down the middle, whilst the M.C.B.C. gradually worked up another eight from the rest. However, the numbers in the Boat Club were small and a meeting was curtailed for lack of attendance, and 'much beer was left unconsumed'. In December 1962 the Senior Treasurer received a letter from John Garton, Treasurer of the O.U.B.C. Trust Fund, seeking contributions from each college in the sum of £7.10.0 per term for four years to enable the work to be undertaken to straighten the Gut. Earlier that year the new Donnington Bridge had been opened providing a means for vehicles to cross the river at that point and replacing the previous foot bridge. Torpids 1963 were cancelled owing to the river being frozen and though the crews trained at Sandford, boating from their periodic base at the King's Arms, they did not enter the Head that was organised at Godstow in seventh week. A training camp preceded Trinity Term, a number of the experienced oarsmen wished to settle for a Schools' Eight rather than commit to a first boat; so the Eight was almost entirely novices. Some old members assisted and there was a two week period training at Henley. The First Eight bumped Merton then rowed over and on the third day were caught by New College in the Gut. The Captain recalls with some frustration: 'We in fact rowed over the fourth night, although a bump which Oriel claimed to have made according to the opinion of an umpire on the bank, was eventually awarded to them. The verdict was accepted by Magdalen with extraordinary magnanimity and intense dissatisfaction'. They finished tenth. The finalists making up the Schools' Eight had a spectacular week of bumping and over-bumping to win their blades, rising from 32nd to 27th. On the Saturday, the 1923 crew returned for a fortieth anniversary celebration of their Headship. This was the last Magdalen crew in which Gully Nickalls had rowed. Reflecting thirty years later on the difficulties being experienced, Robin Lewis felt it was not social conditions: 'but with hindsight one can see that there was a division between University level oarsmen - still dominated by the public schools and thus much influenced by O.U.B.C. coach 'Jumbo' Edwards - and the rest. Oxford college-level rowing in general was much weaker than its Cambridge equivalent. It's always easier to raise enthusiasm in successful times, and the reverse is equally true. I think the 1961 fixed-pins experiment caused some additional unhappiness'. There was commitment to tubbing novices and even during the snow of that Hilary Term they had driven daily to Henley to continue, until the ice also closed that reach.

Michaelmas 1963 started on a sombre note as the Captain had to inform the Club of the death of Mark Hillary who had stroked the First Eight that summer and died whilst climbing Mount Parnassos. His mother generously donated a silver Novice Sculling Cup in his memory. *The Daily Telegraph* described the 1964 Torpid as 'neat and speedy', picking up the 1962 finishing order they rowed over, collided with some swans and bumped Oriel, whose bung line was caught on their rudder and then rowed over to finish fifth. In Summer Eights Merton and Exeter bumped Magdalen to leave them the bottom crew in the division: a position only previously occupied on the first day of the club's racing in its foundation year, 1859. The Second Eight went down to Keble II who had two Blues on board, a situation then allowed by the rules; St John's bumped Magdalen on the last night. The Third Eight, with only two weeks' training, made three bumps.

R.A.D. Freeman matriculated in 1963 as an Academical Clerk, so was not expecting to do much rowing due to his Choir duties of six days each week for practice and a service. Richard Freeman joined Robin Webster to win O.U.B.C. Pairs, and then the Senior Pairs in the Oxford Royal Regatta in the sixth week of Trinity Term. Freeman had stroked the First Torpid, but their collision with the swans had denied them their potential success. 'Hugh Gillespie inveigled me into becoming Captain for 1964-65. ... I resolved to improve the M.C.B.C.'s standard of fitness, so the First Four went to Henley two weeks early to practise. A Boat Club meeting approved a plan to re-introduce the M.C.B.C. scarf, to be given on merit at the Captain's discretion. It would be the pre-war pattern

# I resolved to improve the M.C.B.C.'s standard of fitness, so the First Four went to Henley two weeks early to practise.

and solely confined to members of the Club; 6 feet long, 2 feet 6 inches wide, single stripes of black and white, the black 1 foot and the white 1 foot 6 inches wide; cost 32 shillings and sixpence.

Freeman's younger brother Christopher arrived at Keble and they resumed their partnership in the pair, fostered while at The King's School, Canterbury. Together they won the O.U.B.C. Pairs. A year later they took the University Double Sculls trophy beating Daniel Topolski and Richard Southwood. Magdalen started the academic year with only seventeen oarsmen, including just three freshmen, and had twenty-one available for Torpids. In those years of multi-lane racing the Torpid course after the Gut was divided by buoys into lanes. This year it became clear to everyone that the tow-path side had a disadvantage of a half to one length over the other two lanes. After the Gut, Magdalen lost their lead on Oriel, and so dropped one place. The Second Torpid had to row-on to qualify and made five bumps. A very successful dinner attended by President Boase, and James Griffiths, then once again Senior Dean of Arts, was held to celebrate the Second Torpid's success.

Freeman resolved to improve the standard of Magdalen rowing and so asked David Rutherford to coach the First Eight. A very inexperienced crew became fit and keen under his tutelage. They started heavy training at Henley two weeks before term, and continued it there with evening outings. Rutherford imposed a strict regime and had a great impact. Morale was high, but luck was cruelly against Magdalen. On the first evening St. John's drifted out from the bank having gone aground after bumping New College just beyond the Gut. The cox did not see them; when just about to bump Exeter, Magdalen hit St. John's and two Magdalen men were

# Michaelmas 1966 was perhaps the quietest term Magdalen had ever had on the river

thrown from their seats. Recovery was quick, but water poured in through a six foot crack, and University College finally bumped them. The Eight rowed over on the second night, but on the third were caught by St. Edmund Hall II, a very good crew with the highest number of bumps in the week. St. Edmund Hall I were Head of the River that year, but it was galling for Magdalen to be bumped by a second boat. Magdalen had dropped out of Division I for the first time ever. Generations of Magdalen oarsmen were mortified.

After winning the University Pairs again with his brother, Freeman recalled: 'Chris mentioned to Roger Bray, a former Magdalen Academical Clerk who was just starting his D.Phil., that we both stood a chance of being chosen for the 1966 Blue boat if we did the thrice weekly weight-training sessions at Iffley Road. Roger volunteered to sing in place of me those three times a week to give me the opportunity. Dr Bernard Rose (the *Informator Choristarum*) and President Boase remarkably agreed. I made the Trial Eights but, at the beginning of Hilary Term, was initially only in the potential Isis crew. However, after two weeks of this crew's regularly beating the potential Blue boat, I was moved up to row bow in the other crew. We won the Boat Race. I was the only Academical Clerk ever to get a rowing Blue! Chris was brought into the crew four days before the race, so making the 1966 crew the first Oxford crew to have two brothers since the Edwards brothers rowed in the late 1920s'. The 1965-66 season had started with twenty-two members. The First Torpid dropped three places to ninth. Two boats trained hard for Summer Eights. The First Eight was coached by the Freeman brothers. Richard recalled: 'This was not a pretty crew, but a very satisfying one to coach because all members really tried their hardest and a sense of camaraderie was developed by the strong influence of Philip Halford-MacLeod. We had several novice oarsmen in that crew, one of whom was a Canadian ice hockey player, missing many front teeth!'. They made one bump to regain their position as sandwich boat in Division I. They were also the first Magdalen Eight to finish higher than it had started for several years. The Second Eight dropped two places. Michaelmas 1966 was perhaps the quietest term Magdalen had ever had on the river: for one reason and another various boats did not go out at all and those that did were infrequent. An extraordinary preoccupation with ideas of an appeal to old members for blazer funds faltered with the reflection: 'when one wonders if such an appeal would be looked upon kindly considering the Boat Club performance on the river'. N.D.V. Darlington took over the captaincy at Christmas; he felt exposed being a novice only the year earlier and with such low morale in the Club, but did so to save it from disintegrating altogether. The 1967 First Torpid dived nine places to eighteenth, the Seconds plunged four to thirty fifth. Gathorne Girdlestone recalled they were in part victims of the complex lane system which took some time to clarify the results of each day's racing. It was abandoned after this year. Magdalen perhaps reflected a wider problem: the O.U.B.C. Trust Fund gave a fibreglass sculling boat to each college. Their report commented 'these boats have been received with mixed reactions, it is quite apparent that one of the best ways of developing an oarsman is by putting him in a sculling boat … a squad consisting of good scullers can produce consistently good crews. Both University boat clubs used sculling this year as a basis of their training'. They introduced a sculling competition the 'Trust Fund Sculls' to promote the policy. The boat given to Magdalen was named *Thomas Toothpick*; in 2004 it was donated to the University Sports Department for use in the new Rosenblatt Swimming Pool as a craft for capsize tests. Feeling that burning a boat to mark the

Headship was a Victorian anachronism, the Club decided to make a gift of a boat that could benefit others. With a slow leak and old age against it, the boat went off to fulfil this important if inglorious task.

Nick Darlington declared his strategy for remedial action for Eights Week: outings at 6.30am and rigorous circuits, running for stamina, and training meals to increase protein intake two weeks before Summer Eights. He had persuaded the 1961-62 Captain, Robin Lewis, who had promised to train a First Eight from scratch. The early Trinity meeting of 35 oarsmen recognised that people had to pull their socks up to stop the decline. Everybody was willing to do everything they could to make Eights Week a success. The problem facing Magdalen was not lack of enthusiasm of its members, but the small number of experienced oarsmen. In the whole Club there were only three or four oarsmen who had rowed at school. The Eight was blighted by illness and lack of coaches to work with Robin Lewis. Darlington wrote: 'Morale was good, and there was determination, but we were a bunch of amateurs. When

The 1966 Eight

sickness hit, our numbers were so low that a few people rowed or coxed in more than one eight. It was whilst coaching that spirited but clumsy eight that the Hon. Robin patiently and enthusiastically exhorting us to do better (or less awful) things, complete with megaphone, cap and blazer, cycled slowly off the tow path and disappeared entirely from view under the water for several seconds. He reappeared continuing to instruct us with panache undampened'. However the First Eight dropped four places to seventeenth and the Seconds three to fortieth. At the Michaelmas 1967 meeting, the new Captain, Michael Stocking, outlined his drive for recovery. It was to start with tubbing and three outings a week for the Novice Eight. By the Hilary Term 1968 meeting of only 11 members, work pressure had obliged Stocking to stand down in favour of Paul Isolani, with Girdlestone replacing him as Secretary. Gathorne's father Peter had offered to finish both Torpids for the last fortnight. His father had been in the 1923 Head of the River crew, and in the Magdalen Henley VIII which lost the semi-final of the 1922 Ladies' to Shrewsbury School. He later had no hesitation in sending Gathorne and his brother to that school on the basis that a school crew that could beat Magdalen must be good. The Bursar and Senior Treasurer of M.C.B.C., Dr Colin Cooke, said that a new boat and blades might be considered if the Club could prove itself worthy of such expenditure. By this time Edgar Dickens was showing his years, and had to be approached with some diplomacy regarding the condition of the boathouse, matters of equipment, and coaching. The First Eight rose one place, the Second Eight dropped another three.

The 1968-69 academic year seemed to suffer from problems of attitude within elements of the Club and some strange recruitment tactics, apparently at the hand of some senior members, which shifted the ethos away from the pleasures and challenges of the river to an undemanding social activity. The First Torpid caught Merton despite their amusement at watching the stroke man, Girdlestone, being helped into the boat. He had damaged his ankle four days earlier escaping from the warden of the Waynflete Building via a first floor window trying to avoid being caught after the curfew. Merton were quieter on their return to their boathouse next to Magdalen's. The reinstated original Torpid system remained different from Summer Eights. Division I consisted of six boats, and the remaining five divisions each had nine boats. The rules were then that 'On Thursday and on each successive day the top boat of the previous day's racing in each division automatically joins the bottom of the division above. Thus by Saturday there are nine boats starting in Divisions I to V, and six in VI'. Magdalen made four bumps in all that week and were back in Division II at fifteenth. The bow seats of the 1969 Torpid and Summer Eight were occupied by H.I.H. Prince Tomohito of Mikasa, the nephew of the Japanese Emperor. The Press got hold of this information and descended on the river in search of photographs. Girdlestone recollects: 'We spent a happy afternoon going up and down river avoiding the photographers, moving off as soon as they arrived for a close-up. Then one intelligent man realised that if he stood on Donnington Bridge we had to pass him. He got his photograph.' The First Eight dropped to 20th, the Second Eight to 49th, though nothing is recorded in the Captain's Book.

The 1970 Eight

Notwithstanding the position, Dr Cooke recognised that equipment was essential, and authorised a new boat and oars. David Rendel took on the considerable burden and responsibility of the Captaincy for the 1969-70 season. His assets were his own energy and persuasiveness, the new boat, and not least the prospect of Neil Rosser, an M.C.B.C. wartime member and now international coach from the London R.C., who was persuaded to coach the Summer Eight for 1970. Rosser looked at the two reasonable novice eights entered for Christ Church, and helped pick a crew for Torpids. Before Hilary Term that crew were down at Putney getting blisters, wet from rain and snow, and extraordinarily tired after rowing at least sixteen miles a day. Under Peter Jones, Simon Rippon and Bob Marks of London R.C., who assisted Rosser, they learned what rowing was really about. The Torpid went up to 19th. Thanks to St. Edward's School's waterman, the Summer Eight trained at Godstow, with much encouragement from Bob Marks. The new boat was brought out for the first time, and Dr Cooke's investment was vindicated with bumps on Pembroke, Trinity and Exeter. The rot had been stopped, and the Eight climbed from 20th to 17th. The Secretary wrote: 'The credit for a successful reversal of the trend in Magdalen rowing lies primarily with Captain David Rendel, who dragged us down to the boathouse every day, and to the splendid coaching organised by Neil Rosser'. The successful Rosser, Marks and Rippon triumvirate had been arranged over pints of Pimm's at the previous Henley. Rendel's determination had paid off: he had visited every freshman and persuaded many to at least give the sport a try, this doorstep technique in drumming up support was doubtless invaluable experience when he was canvassing as a Liberal Democrat candidate for the seat of Newbury which he won in a by-election in 1993.

In 1971 the revival developed, A.G. Simpson had been elected Captain in the previous October and his Torpid climbed five places to 14th. The Summer Eight trained from St. Edward's School boathouse, pushed itself hard and made use of the new boat. They went up two places to 15th; being an extremely light crew, averaging under 11 stone; they would have been at an even bigger disadvantage but for excellent four course meals prepared by the Second Chef, Bill Jarvis. Jarvis had been at Magdalen since 1932 and was a keen oarsman himself, as detailed in the chapter on the Servants'

Rowing Club. The era of the early morning outing had arrived and a keen Second Eight went out at 7am to avoid the congestion on the water. J.W.R. Goulding, who was to become Captain that autumn, arranged frequent pre-dinner sherry sessions in his rooms in the New Building. Jeremy Goulding felt this would hep foster a sense of common purpose. Their cox, Robert Gordon, instilled discipline and rigour whilst increasing the commitment of the crew. They made three bumps. The Third Eight was normally a 'Gentlemen's Eight' but this year it became known as the 'J.C.R. President's Eight' for he – Graham Kent – was at stroke. Kent had determined not to row at Oxford after a miserable time on the river at King's College School, Wimbledon; however he had succumbed to David Rendel's call for Summer Eights. They were bumped on the first three days and then with a crew missing behind had to row over on the last day: much further than they had rowed before or bargained on. A crab was caught by someone who had overindulged the night before and they were over-bumped. As Kent recalls of Rendel: 'Ever the gentleman, thanked us for at least being on the river so that we could retain some place for the Third Eight for the following summer'.

After a decade of difficulty, Magdalen's fortunes had started to turn for the good.

[1] R.D. Burnell, Well Rowed Magdalen!, Magdalen College 1993

The First Women's Eight, 1981

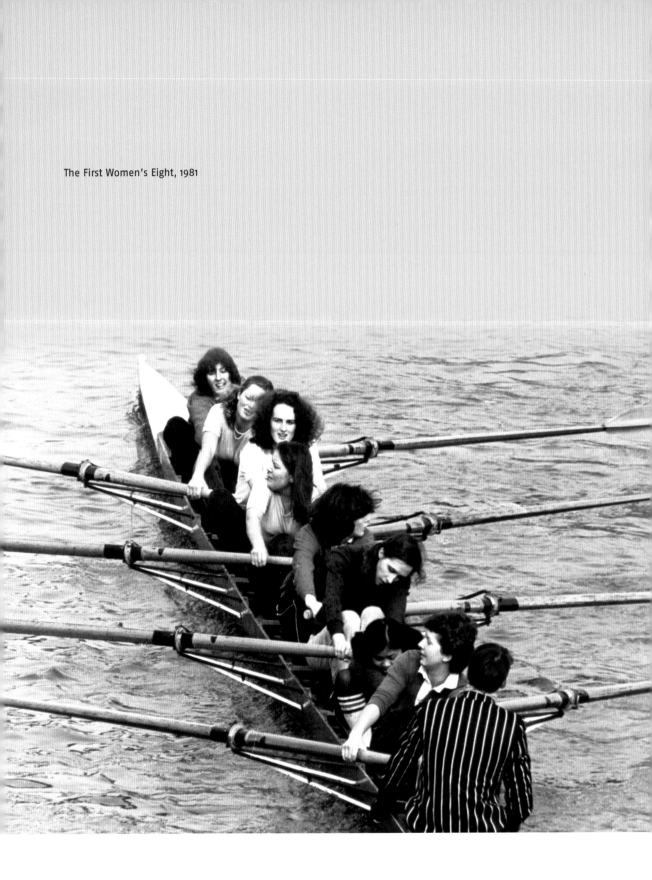

# 10 1972-1988

## Revival, Boat Accidents, the Arrival of Women, Growing Numbers

The change in fortunes which had begun the year before proved to be the start of a real revival that would see Magdalen return to challenge for the Headship once again. The College would soon be debating the question of going mixed and women would be admitted for the first time in 1979; that would very quickly have its own impact on the Boat Club.

Jeremy Goulding was elected Captain for 1971-72 and twenty members came along to the first meeting of the year though a number 'had no intention of rowing because of work'. David Rendel was back to row, as also was Eric Redman, a Rhodes Scholar who had arrived in 1970. This year saw a real breakthrough, Goulding skilfully giving full reign to the talents of Michael Magarey, a Rhodes Scholar from the Adelaide State Sprint crew. Magarey started by doing much to improve the spirits of the Four which he stroked in a hard race in the autumn regatta. Magarey won his first Blue in the 1972 Boat Race. On the first afternoon of Torpids the First boat overtook St. Edmund Hall. After two row-overs, on Friday the river was closed due to high water and two foot waves. On the Monday, in awful conditions, stroke's and five's seats came off completely. Redman, at five, discarded his and rowed with no seat, rubbing his backside raw by the finish. Stroke replaced his seat back-to-front, the boat being stroked by Rendel at seven meantime. Goulding wrote: 'Magdalen were bumped by Exeter who hampered us badly allowing Trinity to overtake. We returned to the boathouse depressed and very cold in the pouring rain. The only bright spot was the College chef Bill [Jarvis], a faithful supporter, who had come down to the boathouse and produced two bottles of rum to revive our spirits'. Eights Week brought great success; Goulding continued: 'Regaining Magarey from the Blue Boat, we were coached at Godstow by Simon Rippon and Peter Jones to a complicated programme of interval training which Magarey had used successfully in Australia. The crew was enthusiastic, strong, and determined to make up for the disappointments. On the first night we bumped Brasenose within two minutes, and on the second night took St. Catherine's with equal ease, leaving us sandwich boat at the bottom of Division I. We bumped Lincoln at the Gut,

but they failed to acknowledge. Though they had escaped to 1.5 lengths we started after them and bumped them very decisively opposite O.U.B.C. We were now back in the First Division. One of the best moments of the week was Friday night. Dick came to the boathouse with a large spray of lilies which, I was given to understand, had always been carried by the cox of Magdalen First Eights - until they dropped out of the First Division. There was a sense in which Dick exuded the feeling that, at last, he was looking after the interests of a 'proper' crew once more.' Goulding became Headmaster of Shrewsbury School and ensured it once again rivalled the other great rowing schools. That night Magdalen bumped Merton without difficulty and on Saturday took St. Edmund Hall coming out of the Gut. At Tims' raft they exchanged the cox for stroke, and returned to the boathouse victorious to the delight of everyone, especially the President. They were awarded their Blades and at a great Bumps Supper that evening, with James Griffiths in his element, the whole crew were riotously applauded, having firmly established Magdalen, once more, as a First Division crew at 10th on the river. Magdalen was on the way back. The social aspect of the Club was an all-important feature, for without the right atmosphere and 'grouping' of attitudes, the revival could not have taken place. 'We all wanted to row well, to row as a crew, and to win'

A meeting on the first Sunday of Michaelmas Term 1972 drew only a dozen freshmen, the new Captain Tim Bunch, and the Secretary David Rendel. Of these freshmen a few had rowed before. The First Four, rowing in the 1st Division for the first time in more than a decade, won their race by six seconds beating a combined Balliol and Keble crew including three Isis men. The freshmen produced a promising, if light, eight, which won two races. The Torpid struggled for want of oarsmen willing to train throughout the term, the compromise was light work until two weeks beforehand when they went out daily; they dropped a net two places into Division III. The Second Torpid qualified, lost five places in two days, but then rowed over. The Captain's book records that their competing 'generated enthusiasm which they sustained through Eights'. The Summer Eight entered Wallingford and Thames Ditton regattas. In Eights Week they bumped St. John's, Queen's, Jesus and Univ. to finish sixth on the river. The Second Eight made four quick bumps. The Secretary pointed to the anomaly: 'It is rare for a crew in the top half of Division I in Eights to be in Division III in Torpids, and future success in Eights week must surely depend on improving the Torpids'. In the 1974 season, the First Torpid bumped up three places to fourteenth. Eights Week was a real success, the culmination of five years revival for the First Eight: David Rendel had been the key contributor to this about-turn. The 2nd VIII won Blades, and the 3rd and 4th VIIIs qualified and raced well. Recognising these efforts, the President, Bursar, and Dr. Bellhouse (Chairman of the Combined Clubs Committee) authorised the Club to order a new Salter's shell to replace the old George Harris boat. The new craft was delivered at Christmas 1974 and was to become named Lucy. For the first time for a few years Magdalen entered a crew for Henley Royal Regatta. The First Eight decided to compete in the Ladies' Plate. The crew changed the order from that published in the official Regatta Records with stroke and six reversed and R. Flemm rowed at seven. In the first round they drew Kirkland House. Kirkland is one of twelve undergraduate colleges at Harvard University; its boat club has a good reputation. Though Magdalen lost to Kirkland by one length the race was hard fought and the Americans only got in front in the last one hundred yards.

# The social aspect of the Club was an all-important feature, for without the right atmosphere and 'grouping' of attitudes, the revival could not have taken place.

In Michaelmas Term, a door knock campaign bought many new faces to the river, though talent was thin. The Torpid was well managed, more impressive than for several years, and made three bumps. Richard Burnell advised on selection of the Eight for 1975, but at Thames Ditton Regatta it succumbed to a Tiffin School crew, and returned to the Isis under Dick's supervision. Their best night was the first, when the blue canvas of a Keble boat with several O.U.B.C. stars on board came within feet of them by the boathouse. However, the cox, S.J.P. Williams, steered a fine course, and Australian stroke Patrick Carroll maintained the pressure; Keble finally crabbed and fell back. Next day, though, their progress was relentless, and Magdalen were bumped by Trinity Barge. They rowed over on the next two nights, never seriously challenged by Univ. The Second Eight was a crew of great spirit and character, they made three quick bumps on successive nights; then, on the last night, they missed Worcester II near the boathouses, but managed to row them down and bump close to the finish. They were rewarded with Blades for the second year running.

The river was frozen in Hilary Term 1976 and training was limited to running; the thaw came in time for Torpids when the First boat went up one and then down to remain eleventh. The Second Boat dropped eight places. The new boat had to go back to Salter's to be re-rigged; Trinity kindly lent another so that the Eight could enter the Reading Head where they rose from 79th to 32nd. When John Sabine took over as Captain for Trinity Term he held the club together, picking up from Larry Botheras' work of recruitment and coaching over the previous two terms. They entered Wallingford Regatta but in the second round several seats came off their slides.

Dick ordered new ones. Though they moved up on a powerful Keble crew on the first evening of Eights Week, they were not able to keep the pressure on and eventually succumbed to Univ. The rest of the week they rowed over each day. That autumn a new set of 12' 5" oars was ordered from Aylings and new shoes for the first boat, the Salter's ones had never been adequate and had become useless.

The 1977 Torpids were cancelled owing to a fast stream and Dr John Rayne took the Torpid to compete against Thames R.C. and then to the Reading Head where they won the novice pennant. Rayne used his connections at University of London to arrange an Easter training camp and they entered the Tideway Head of the River Race, finishing 178th, one of the few Oxbridge colleges represented. J.P.P. Baker was selected to cox the University Lightweight crew which beat Cambridge. This was the third year of a lightweight race, over time Magdalen would provide a number of oarsmen to this event which is raced at Henley over a 2,000 metre course downstream. Summer Eights were, according to the Captain, Stuart Chubb, 'a debacle': the First Eight was bumped every night to end up tenth. David Heath coached the Second Eight, it went down a net two places, the Third – Chemists – Eight went down six places, but the Fourth – Rugby – made four bumps and won Blades. The season ended with an unconventional approach to Henley by submitting an entry for the Prince Philip Challenge Cup, the open coxed fours event at the Royal Regatta. Hardly intended for an unremarkable Oxford college crew, nonetheless the entry was accepted. Dick Dickens was persuaded to coach the crew along with John Rayne, they moved to Henley for two weeks, training twice daily and they worked wonders. They were drawn against Thames Tradesmen's Rowing Club, a crew which had been part of the eight that had won the Olympic silver medal in Montreal the year before. The plan had been to train up the day before the race and then scratch but it emerged that the majority of the crew had no wish to do this. John Baker was not available to cox as he was committed to the Isis crew but City of Oxford R.C. lent two youngsters to cox during training. The other crews in the event were Garda Síochána, Ireland, and the University of California; since the Garda, a national four, had soundly beaten Thames Tradesmen's at Nottingham International Regatta, it was rumoured the latter would scratch leaving Magdalen to face the Irish Police. As it was Thames Tradesmen's raced Magdalen on the Saturday afternoon and beat them easily; the Garda beat California and then won the final. The Captain's book concluded: 'The traditionalists may criticise entering a Henley race above our class; but the pot hunter is ludicrous. Competing is more important than winning'. An excellent dinner concluded the season with President Griffiths in the chair, and Dr Bellhouse, Dr Rayne and Mike Rosewell present. Rosewell was then master in charge of rowing at St Edward's School and had been a big help with allowing training at Godstow and providing some coaching.

The same four entered the O.U.B.C. Fours that autumn and beat the House but lost to Oriel. Three novice eights were entered for Christ Church Regatta, an encouraging number of crews. Alexander Lindsay had returned to work in Oxford, and put a lot of time into coaching the Torpid and the Eight of 1978. The First Torpid dropped five places and the Second fell eight in one day. The O.U.B.C. may have had Magdalen in mind when it commented: 'Alterations to the rules, introducing sandwich boats and a women's division, so bemused the coxes that the first division was declared void after the first afternoon'. In preparation for Summer Eights the first boat had two changes from the previous term and the shell was bow-rigged to be stroked by John Sabine. At Wallingford Regatta they won the President's Cup for Senior 'C' Eights. Nerves, however, took hold during Eights Week and two men came off their seats. Steve Parker had a slipped disc and was in great pain but as there was no replacement he courageously rowed all week; later he took his Finals kneeling on a cushion and was hospitalised for the summer. Despite Parker's valour, they dropped two places to finish at the bottom of Division I.

# For the first time in 521 years, women were admitted and they took to the river soon afterwards

Forty attended the Michaelmas recruitment evening and in addition to the novice eights, a coxed four and two scullers entered Christ Church Regatta. The three eights all reached their semifinals. February 1979 was extremely cold and dulled enthusiasm for Torpids with the result that the second boat failed to qualify. The first boat was coached by Alexander Lindsay and gained four places to finish 12th on the river. R.C. Thomas and F.H.R. Fleming rowed in the University Lightweight Boat, which was again coxed by John Baker; racing in a thunderstorm they lost to Cambridge by half a length. T.J. Carpenter rowed for Isis and also lost. The Summer Eight looked strong with a stern five of University oarsmen and experienced four in the bows, the training was somewhat erratic owing to various hiccups but the last three outings were coached by Magdalen's Cornish firebrand, Larry Botheras, the morale and speed of the crew rose and it looked like the fastest M.C.B.C. crew for five years. First Wadham were disposed of, then Univ., both in the Gut; on a rerow the following day Univ. bump was achieved at Donnington Bridge and Merton were caught that evening. A spirited attempt on Saturday, to catch Exeter, was denied by them first bumping New College. It had been a good week and left Magdalen ninth on the river. Richard Burnell, one of Magdalen's greatest oarsmen, won £50 from 'Ernie', the National Premium Bonds computer, and donated it to the Boat Club to be 'used for something special', it was put towards equipment purchases.

October 1979 was a seminal moment in the life of the College. For the first time in 521 years, women were admitted and they took to the river soon afterwards. The first name to appear in the records of Magdalen women's rowing was Shelagh Scarth, a Canadian Rhodes Scholar, who gained her Blue in the winning Oxford crew of 1980; thus putting the College on the Women's Blues list before a Magdalen women's boat had been formed. The Women's Boat Race had been started in 1927 in the form of a time and style race. It was held on the Isis at lunchtime (to minimise the number of spectators), and Oxford won.[1] From then on the race was held on the Cam or the Isis though it was not a firm annual fixture for some time. For a period from 1953 to 1964 no race was held and in 1978 the Women's Boat Race moved to Henley to join the Lightweight Men.

Few freshers attended the start-of-year meeting but a novice eight reached the semi-finals of Christ Church Regattas, however they did not feel they were up to the task of racing in Torpids. The one boat that did enter contained the Captain, G.P. Robbins and the Secretary, C.B. Farr plus six novices. Despite Alexander Lindsay's coaching they fell six places to sixth in Division II. Trinity Term saw the first Magdalen women taking to the river in a mixed eight being, as the Head Porter, Michael Strutt, put it: 'one of the best initiatives for integration'; from his vantage point in the Lodge he observed the process and his team of porters were very supportive. Wendy Bromidge, Women's Captain in 1982-83 recalled their friendliness in the Lodge 'seeing us off early in the morning cold or wet to row'. The men's Eight contained M.D. Andrews, a Blue that year. Andrews, who had learnt to row at Abingdon School, had matriculated the previous Michaelmas. Mark Andrews' Boat Race was one of the closest, Oxford winning by a canvas. The Magdalen Eight also contained the lightweights, and was coxed by C.E.G. Cozens. They spent the term at Godstow, returning to the Isis ten days before racing when Steve Royle, O.U.B.C.'s coach, took them for their final preparation. The crew were very tense on the first evening but nevertheless caught New College along the Green Bank. It was a short-lived success as they caught Magdalen back the following day after someone came off their seat. The second eight dropped two places and were described as 'a motley crew' with one person coming off his seat sixteen times in one race. The third eight, a Schools crew, were neat and powerful and gained two places, thus rising high enough to secure Magdalen three fixed positions. That year the boathouse was redecorated for the first time since it had been built, but the College was feeling poor and provided only the paint – the club had to provide the labour. A bar was built with the aim of providing a more attractive environment for Eights Week hospitality; the business it generated would help the Club's finances.

Charles Cozens was concerned about the gap between the first and second boat positions – one of forty-four places – and the fact that Magdalen had only one permanent slot in Torpids. There was also the question of accommodating the needs of women's rowing, and so he committed to being Captain for two years; as it was Finals got in the way. Various initiatives brought encouraging responses. The fleet consisted of a 1975 shell, a 1969 boat, and a 1961 craft for the third boat. There were two old coxless fours and a coxed four; the 'concrete' boat and the clinker were not being used, though the latter served the women that autumn and the following year. There was a pair and a few singles. Cozens launched an appeal to old members explaining the position and announcing the establishing of a long term boat fund. The College provisionally agreed to the joint financing of a new Eton shell and a set of oars, at a cost of £5,680, but initially the Bursary did not state the level of support it was willing to give, nor that £2,000 was available as a grant. In a letter to Brian Bellhouse, Treasurer of the Combined Clubs Fund, the Senior Bursar, Bill Johnson, said he did not intend to reveal this sum to Cozens until the student rent strike was over.

Edgar Dickens was due for retirement after a remarkable 44 years service to the College. In the preceding decade he had been increasingly pre-occupied with his duties as an Alderman of the City and there had been concerns over the state of the boathouse and the equipment nevertheless his coaching skills were as good as ever. He was honoured with a retirement dinner which was attended by many senior old members of the Club including Richard Burnell, David Rutherford and Harry Holt. He and his wife were presented with a silver salver. For many years afterwards he continued to coach for the House and he literally died in the saddle, of a heart attack while coaching on his bicycle in 1990. Steve Gaisford was already the New College Boatman and his services were secured for

## Boatie-Speak

*A lexicon of the language only boaties understand*

**Amber/Red flag** - The amber flag causes bitter disappointment amongst all (except 1st VIII) rowers because they are not allowed to row. If the red flag is up the first VIII are disappointed too.

**Bank Tub** - A raft attached to the bank which is set up like a boat. A good way to learn the basics of technique with no danger of falling in.

**Blades** - Crews which bump on each of the four days of Torpids or Eights are awarded blades. There are some old blades hanging in the college bar, or of course you could always ask one of last year's second VIII to show you theirs (blade, that is).

**Blue** - Anyone who rows for the University is awarded a 'Blue'. If you row in the second crew you get a 'Half Blue'. See also ego.

**Boatie** - One of those mighty individuals who rows. Intelligent, athletic, and above all great company, this is what all mothers want their children to be.

**Bump** - The aim in Torpids and Eights is to catch up to the boat in front and touch their boat with yours. This is known as a 'bump', although depending on the cox it can sometimes be more like a ram.

**Catch** - The part of the stroke where you put your oar in the water. Also something you do at Boat Club parties.

**Erg** - Short for Ergometer, a great way to keep fit. Some people unreasonably call it a torture machine.

**Finish** - The part of the stroke where you take your oar out of the water. Also something that Boat Club parties rarely do.

**The Gut** - The section of the Isis where the river bends and becomes very narrow. Also a part of the anatomy that suffers at Boat Club parties.

**Pot** - A trophy. Many of the smaller regattas on the Isis award pots of varying quality. You can also get a pot if you attend too many Boat Club parties.

**Rowing Tank** - Run by the OUBC at the Iffley Rd sports complex. Sort of like a boat set up in a swimming pool. Pretty pointless for speed, but good for technique.

**Summer Eights** - The main competition in Trinity Term (usually just called 'Eights'). THE place to be seen in the summer.

**Torpids** - The main competition in Hilary Term. (except for Boat Club parties...)

### The positions in a boat

Extract from an M.C.B.C. Guide for Freshers

Magdalen, working for both colleges, and later also for Balliol. Steve became Magdalen's fourth Boatman in one hundred and eight years and has now clocked up nearly thirty years service himself. He set about putting his skills to work on the fleet.

Cozens wrote: 'Thus, hopefully, began a new era in the history of the Boat Club', and his view seemed to be supported by the first novice eight winning Christ Church Regatta. However, frustration manifested itself the following term when resident past Captains would not row in the Torpid and as Cozens rued: 'thus giving their successors exactly the same problems which they themselves strove against. The sin this year was compounded by the fact that an

appeal was in progress at the time. It is indeed unpardonable for the Club's current members to appeal to old members and then fail to support the Club themselves'. In the end the 1981 Torpid held its position. Meantime a women's crew had formed, coached by Scarth and Andrews along with Cozens, and it entered Torpids but did not qualify. Summer Eights brought four men's and two women's crews to the river; the men's first boat was, however, mixed as Scarth was at bow. This was a pragmatic decision and caused a furore with the colleges they bumped but was fully accepted by the other members of the crew. Andrews, following his second Blue, was at seven; S.G. Potts and H.E. Clay, who had both rowed for Isis, were also in the crew. High water made the river unusable for the first two days; they made two bumps to rise to fifth on the river. The two women's crews shared the clinker boat. The first of these qualified and started 32nd – 8th in Division III. Rowing over on the third afternoon, they dropped one place on the last day. The men's third boat was steered by Magdalen's first female coxswain, Katy Ling. Cozens noted there were now more people rowing for M.C.B.C. than at any time since 1963. The proportion of women in the College was then around a third and so they were well represented in the Boat Club. A sponsored row to the Palace of Westminster furthered the fund-raising campaign.

The autumn of 1981 began with high morale and a novice men's eight went five rounds before losing in the final of Christ Church Regatta. The 1982 Torpid made a net gain of one place but the second boat managed to write off their shell by hitting a cruiser, Isis Quintet, twelve strokes into their race on the first day. Using another boat for the rest of the week, things did not improve. Cozens kept a low profile having resigned from the choir on the grounds of too much work. He had enjoyed the support of Bernard Rose, the *Informator Choristarum*, but Dr Rose's retirement brought a less flexible climate. Indeed, Rose used to take Eights Week off and leave services in the care of the Senior Organ Scholar while he and his wife Molly went to the river. Guy Philipps agreed to share the

Captaincy but the benefits of autocratic and strong leadership led to Cozens resignation though he continued to cox and play a significant part running the Club without an official post. Trinity Term started with a shortage of equipment and coaches but three men's and two women's eights were boated. Hopes were high of taking the Headship but the first eight was not as strong as it might have been had other priorities not intervened. There were two Blues, Andrews and Clay, and Potts at stroke, from Isis, on board; training from Wallingford four times a week they were coached by Alexander Lindsay and John Pilgrim-Morris. In the last ten days they were rowing with great length and determination. They bumped Lincoln on the first day but were caught by them on the second evening through that now perennial problem of someone coming off their seat, in fact someone who had suffered that fate the year before. Things were a bit tetchy in the crew, especially between the University oarsmen and the others. Cozens reflected on the position: 'When it became known that I was intending to row I was summoned before the College President and Vice-President and asked to explain my behaviour. I had prepared a detailed time-table showing that even spending 2-3 hours a day coaching or rowing, I

A sunken 2nd Torpid 1982, by the Isis pub

still had at least 10-12 hours available for academic work. I argued that this alternative activity stopped me from going stale, and gave focal points to the day. Moreover, it also gave an element of pressurised stimulus with a rigorous timetable to work to. The College authorities fully agreed with this, accepting the argument that a healthy body supports a healthy mind. The point is that able people who recognise their responsibility to the Club interest can find a way to meet it'. The 1982 Second Eight was stroked by P.L.M. Beckwith and coached by Mark Andrews. Paul Beckwith was a Commonwealth Scholar from Australia and is now a Waynflete Fellow of the College. The crew achieved six bumps, including an overbump and moving up a division. Beckwith did much to engender a crew spirit, helped by them being allowed to join the late crew table in Hall. Dominique Jackson captained the women's section of M.C.B.C. and, as her successor Wendy Bromidge recalled, 'It was

The Women's Eight 1984

her amazing enthusiasm which inspired me to take up the sport'. If there were less men coming from rowing schools, there were virtually no women who had had an opportunity before Oxford. The women's boat finished Eights Week at 36th.

D.H.R. Matthews took on the mantle of Captain of Boats for 1982-83 and was noted for his great support of the women's side of the club. Wendy Bromidge, who shared the captaincy of the women with Emma Burnett, in commenting on the purchase of the first boat specifically for their use: 'Emma was going out with the Captain, Duncan Matthews, and that helped, though he was a good ally anyway, a joint approach to Dr Bellhouse was successful'. He also encouraged the women's first boat to join the men at the Trinity Term crew table which meant 'we could pay for steak and better food a few times a week'. Men's training was almost entirely on the river, ergometers were still a novelty: there was one at Iffley Road, mainly for use by O.U.B.C. The autumn of 1982 heralded the first win for the women, taking the novice eights trophy at Christ Church Regatta. Torpids 1983 saw five men's and two women's boats afloat which produced a combined total of thirteen bumps. The women's first boat made three of those and thus took them to 24th on the river and into the permanent positions; Wendy Bromidge noted: 'I felt like we'd arrived'. J.L. Brod, who was to be Captain the following year recorded that 'we desperately tried to stop Danny Barnett from smoking during Torpids, but on the last day he insisted on paddling in with a lit cigarette in his mouth'. H.E. Clay and W.J. Lang won Blues. The men's Summer Eight psyched itself up to go Head, coached by John Pilgrim-Morris and Mark Andrews it undertook seat-racing to finalise the make-up. L.E. Foyster, who had taken on the captaincy at Easter, was challenged for his seat but survived. They caught New College just up the Green Bank and then Keble in the Gut the next day. On Friday they gave chase to Christ Church but missed the bump by about a canvas; the following day was uneventful, the House going flat out for Oriel whom they missed by the narrowest of margins. The Daily Telegraph noted that 'It now appears Magdalen are the fastest boat on the river'. So Magdalen finished third on the river, had they caught Christ Church they would certainly have got Oriel and taken the Headship. The women had their new shell from Salter's, named Lady Windermere, and they rose to 31st by the end of the week. That summer saw one of the first Magdalen marriages, certainly the first all-M.C.B.C., when Mark Andrews and Shelagh Scarth wed.

Four men joined O.U.B.C. in autumn 1983; Jan Brod made it to Trial Eights but was then dropped and resolved not to row again but was persuaded to carry on by Foyster. Bill Lang won his second Blue in the 1984 Boat Race and Seth Lesser was selected to cox the Oxford Boat. Alison Bonner, who had come to Magdalen in 1981 from Putney High School, won her Blue. Back on the Isis, the women's Torpid had a difficult time and dropped seven places to finish 30th, the men gained two places, the seconds rose one. The Summer Eight missed a few oarsmen, including Bill Lang who was seeking Olympic selection, and was bumped down two places but left the following year with the Headship still achievable. The women's Eight had some experience on board in the form of Dee Jackson, Emma Burnett and Eve Kemsley, and there was real competition for seats. They bumped Balliol to gain promotion as bottom boat of Division III which was the first year that became a fixed division in response to the growth of women's collegiate rowing.

The shortage of boats was becoming acute and a debate ensued about how to increase the fleet. John Pilgrim-Morris advised that the only make worth buying would be Empacher, the well known Bavarian boat-builder, but the College advised it did not have £10,000 available to spend. In the end Jan Brod raised a large sum from an appeal to old members and the College found the balance. The new boat was delivered at Easter 1985. A new coaching launch and outboard motor were also obtained. Unfortunately the new eight suffered a hole on the first evening of Eights Week after some appalling coxing by Oriel; some riggers and oars came off badly in the debacle. Steve Gaisford was kept busy with repairs, so often the Boatman's fate during the bumps season in order to have a boat ready for the following day. The boat maintained its position throughout the week. The men's second boat made two bumps. The women were coached by Ali Bonner, Seth Lesser, Jan Brod, Mike Hughes and Steve Potts – plenty of attention from Magdalen's Blues. They went up on the first three days and needed to catch St. Catherine's on Saturday in order to win their Blades. The S.C.R. showed its support at the boathouse but the

2nd Torpid 1987

fourth bump was not to be.

The Captain's log for Michaelmas Term 1985 notes that for the first time the Club used a video camera to assist with training. There were no experienced oarsmen among the freshmen but Michael Danziger arrived from Yale and at 6' 3" was encouraged to join the Boat Club. Owing to ice Torpids 1986 were reduced to three days, the men were bumped twice but gained once place back. The women had a dramatic first afternoon when they clashed with Merton's men's boat while spinning at Iffley Lock and suffered a hole through the side of the shell at stroke, just by Carol Giblin's feet. It became a race against the leak as the cox, Sally Hinds, stuffed spare clothing into the breach as the water gushed in. Once again the Boatman had to spend the evening making repairs. They gained two places. Alison Bonner took her second Blue in the winning Oxford crew; she went on to row in the Great Britain eight which came sixth at the World Championships. A year earlier she had been in the coxed four which had come eighth.

The science of modern boat design is fascinating and little more so than the physics of a three or four inch square rudder being capable of steering an eight of about sixty five feet long and a gross laden weight of over three-quarters of a tonne. Magdalen went to Evesham Regatta and had the misfortune to lose their rudder during a race. For the first two evenings of Eights Week they made life very hard for St. Edmund Hall whom they were chasing, even overlapping past the boathouses. On the third day the rudder failed again and the men were bumped by Worcester. P.N.E. Bradbury, the Captain, recorded: 'Since 1983 there has been a steady but inevitable decline in the Eight's position in Division I. The main reason has been the loss of almost all the talented oarsmen who maintained our high position at the beginning of the decade. Although a dearth of really first-class oarsmen can be tolerated for a couple of years, a consolidation on the organisational side has been necessary in order to be able to maintain the standard of rowing and maintain position on the River. The training was hard enough, and the coaching by John Pilgrim-Morris and Jan Brod excellent. They have boosted the crew to a 1st Eight standard.' Reflecting on his final year's rowing, Jan Brod wrote that the dearth of schoolboy oarsmen was biting deep into the life of the Boat Club. This was exacerbated by the fact that other colleges seemed to be

ALISON C. BONNER
1981-1985
WITH STROKE KIM THOMAS (HAMPTON R.C.) PRACTICING FOR OLYMPICS
1981 NOVICE OAR
1983-84 JOINT CAPTAIN MCWBC
1984, '85 AND '86 BLUE
1985 1ST LIT. HUM.
1986 NATIONAL CHAMPIONSHIPS - PAIRS GOLD
1988 SEOUL OLYMPICS - COXLESS PAIR, EIGHTH.

recruiting specifically in this area, albeit without compromise to academic requirements. Taken over time there is an ebb and flow in the fortunes of colleges as moods vary and as applicants are influenced by records of success as much as by encouragement to apply to one college or another.

The women's first boat made three bumps for the second year running and finished 30th. The women's novice eight failed to qualify but entered Oriel Regatta with unremarkable result. Not wishing to miss out on the camaraderie of rowing they held a 'Tail of the River' party: the fact that two other crews in the getting-on race had been slower than them was a mere detail.

Both novice men's eights reached the semi-finals of the 1986 Christ Church Regatta but both ended in disaster, with the bow man coming off his seat in one boat while the other crew crashed into the bank. The women also entered two boats for this regatta but, whilst they were both knocked out in the first round, the first women's novice eight had a very lucky escape the week beforehand. Training on the Isis with the red flag flying, to indicate the river is in full spate, then meant that all crews were required to spin at haystacks corner. The coach did not arrive and Louise Garcia, who had just returned with another boat, her first time coaching, offered to take them. Both she and the cox forgot the rule and went on down towards Iffley Lock. Garcia wrote of the incident: 'the girls could do nothing to prevent the ferocious current carrying them inexorably nearer the weir. The boat was cross-ways on to the weir when the bow began to be drawn under. The girls had to get their feet out - luckily the boat was so old that one wore trainers and laced the feet into clogs. The girls at the stem could walk up the now inclined boat and be helped onto land with only their feet wet. The bow three were not so fortunate. As the boat went literally over the weir they - including two non-swimmers - were thrown into the water. I vividly remember Maya de Souza struggling to keep her head above water, with her long hair swirling around her in the current. Vanessa Graham and Cathra Horrobin got a good wetting too, and it was a freezing day'. All managed to get back to College and recover. Steve Gaisford was not too bothered about the loss of the craft as it was well past its prime. The insurance money paid for two second-hand boats from St. Edward's School for £500. Paul Bradbury retired as Captain at Christmas and recorded that he felt that M.C.B.C. was looking 'healthier than it has for years'. He had introduced the expansion of the number of Club Officers to share the increasing workload, making each role manageable within the time available to students. He complimented Jo Spreadbury, the retiring Women's Captain, noting that she had made their section of the Club 'as important as the men's'. This view was not entirely supported elsewhere as two internal newsletters were published that autumn and the following spring 'to improve communications'.

Hilary Term 1987 had a frozen start with the Isis solid for 0th and 1st weeks but the men's first Torpid put the new Empacher to good use by bumping Univ. and then Wadham to finish fifth in Division II. The second men's Torpid broke the record for the getting-on race and was nine seconds faster than it nearest rival; they bumped Brasenose before the commentary had got started. An argument and appeal ensued but the bump was upheld: Brasenose should not have still been spinning when the gun went off. Bumps on Merton II, Trinity III, St. Catherine's III, Lady Margaret Hall II, and then New College III secured Blades for the crew, most of the bumps occurring in a very few strokes from the start. Magdalen had not had a second Torpid in the fixed divisions since 1957; this success was the first set of Torpids Blades since 1971. Several of the crew went on to row the following term and the next year, rising through the boats. There was tension within the Club with the first boat split in its loyalty to the Captain, some feeling that the selection for the boats was not right. The women boated two crews, the first was stroked by the Women's Captain, Laura Buckley and achieved two overbumps, quite a feat when half the crew plus the coxswain were only in their second term of rowing. The week was hard though and the vagaries of Torpids racing left them only up one net place. The second boat missed qualifying by two seconds; Meir Hakkak wrote that it was: 'nothing short of a disaster, with the boat thrashing about like an epileptic octopus. Returning to the raft they sang beautifully though, their drop in concentration on the rowing having a marvellous effect upon technique'. The co-operation between the two halves of the Club improved enormously during this season with Matt Robinson and Simon Howarth coaching and coxing the women and the production of three mixed eights for Cherwell Regatta. Laura Buckley and Liz Robinson made Magdalen's debut in the Women's Lightweight Squad but their reserve four was disbanded in January. This event had started in 1984, racing at Henley in March, it would be 1990 before the College was represented in the race.

Seven men's and four women's boats prepared for Summer Eights; much boat sharing was required and therefore a careful schedule of outings was necessary. The men's first eight dropped four places. The Captain, R.G. Hitchcock, felt that there were men rowing in the Schools eight who could and should have been rowing in the boat suited to their ability rather than the one they were willing to give time to. From striking distance for the Headship four years earlier Magdalen were now languishing at the bottom of the first division. His frustration was compounded by the fact that Magdalen had no University oarsmen while colleges around them in the division did, the need for Club loyalty, he felt, was as great as ever. Others noted that off the water the land training had been devoid of peer pressure and did not include any weights. The second eight managed to beat the firsts in training but went on to suffer from illnesses and complacency and though it bumped Wadham II it then rowed over for the rest of the week. Howarth noted that the Club had changed: the Magdalen crews for Trinity Term 1987 had no schoolboy oarsmen among them and yet the numbers participating had risen from the beginning of the decade. The Club was struggling to cope with organising so many novices, to find coaches and boats but rejoiced in the enthusiasm. The women's fist boat had four from the previous summer but had a difficult Friday and was caught by St. John's in the Gut. The following afternoon they held off a fast St. Peter's crew finishing on distance [a length and a half] having had them as close as two feet away at one stage: an epic bumps race. For the first time the women qualified a second boat for Eights Week and they bumped twice before crashing into the bank on the third day. The coxswain was Sue Hincks, she recalls that the accident happened owing to: 'bad advice from the tow-path in the form of a roared imperative to 'steer left''.

The 1987-88 season was to be a fight-back for the men. A good start to the year led to a successful Torpids week, the men's first boat climbed five places and thus back into the Division I, Queen's, Exeter, Worcester, Lincoln and finally Trinity all suffered for the Magdalen cause. This had been achieved on a strict diet of land training, high rate work and timed pieces under the supervision of their outside coach, Simon Mills. The second men's boat made four bumps before being driven up the bank by a fast New College crew, however the bow pair jumped out and they managed to re-launch and get back in and get away before another crew closed on them. The third men's Torpid failed to qualify. The women's boat made three bumps to finish 27th. In Summer Eights they made three more. The men trained at Abingdon, coached once again by John Pilgrim-Morris who was a part of the O.U.B.C. coaching team. They were a good fast crew which included two fourth year students, however, caught by St. John's and then Hertford they fell to second in Division II but the following day a bump on Lincoln gave them the sandwich boat position. Hertford and St. John's were both fast crews with a number of University oarsmen onboard. Oriel was Head and Hertford challenged them to a side by side race after the final division on Saturday. The landlord of the Isis pub put up a £100 prize but Oriel 'chickened out of that one'. After the success in Torpids, the result in Eights Week was a disappointment to finish back in Division II for the first time since 1973. That summer Alison Bonner was selected to row for Great Britain at the Seoul Olympic Regatta in the coxless pair, with Kim Thomas of Hampton Rowing Club; they came eighth. Bonner remains Magdalen's most recent Olympic rower.

1989 was to be a year in which two new dimensions came into play in the fortunes of M.C.B.C.

[1] I.W. Preston, From Newnham College Boat Club to C.U.W.B.C., 1992

Cres - cant Mag - da - le - nae na - ti,

peat $p$        $p$

lau - stra tu - ta sint por - ta - rum

# 11    1989-2008

# Graduates, Progress, a Captain's Room, the Headships Recovered

The number of graduate students in the University rose steeply during the 1980s and increased the total number of students in Oxford thereby shifting the proportion of students between the J.C.R. and the M.C.R. Magdalen experienced this change and by the end of the decade had over two hundred graduates, many, if not the majority, from overseas. The social side of the M.C.R. operates very distinctly and differently from its undergraduate counterpart; sometimes including separate involvement in sport caused in part by being in residence for much longer periods. When this sport takes place outside University terms and the regular cycle of competition it is very much for the good. In term time, separate activities can be divisive. The need to have a Boat Club which benefits from the best people available at all levels in order to achieve the best results, has already been noted. Between 1989 and 1992 an M.C.R. eight took to the water at various times and with limited, if sometimes dramatic results: it enjoyed itself but caused friction with the rest of the Club though some of its number coached for other crews and played their part in the general effort.

In autumn 1988 the feeling among the Club Officers was that the senior crews had been neglecting work on technique and so it was decided to put out two men's crews to train and enter the senior category of Christ Church Regatta. Late in the term a heavy fog descended over Oxford and the visibility was reduced to less than twenty feet on the Isis. After a collision between two crews at firm pressure the river was closed. The regatta was cancelled but the enthusiasm in the five novice and senior crews carried over to January 1989. For Torpids Magdalen boated four men's eights; the First obtained a technical bump on Hertford but made little impression on a good Balliol crew. The Second Boat was fast, indeed possibly faster than the First Torpid, and won their Blades with five bumps. Owing to the times in the getting-on race, the Third Boat was obliged to take Magdalen's fourth slot, the third going to the M.C.R. crew – which promptly disbanded at the end of Hilary Term. The top two crews entered the Kingston Head of the River Race and finished about

30 seconds apart. The women had two crews in Torpids, the first of which trained at Godstow but suffered a disaster when it hit the bank and were bumped by the whole of the division. The Second Boat qualified for the first time and made two bumps. For the first time for three years, Magdalen was represented in the University crews with Hon. C.W. Lewis rowing in Isis. Kit Lewis was a freshman who had arrived from Eton where he had stroked the Eight in the Princess Elizabeth Cup at Henley for two years, losing narrowly in the final in 1988. A revival in enthusiasm for fours saw Magdalen enter the Nephthys Regatta Lightweight Fours event. They beat Queen's and St. Hugh's to win. In Summer Eights 1990 the women's First Boat made four bumps and so was up into Division II. They had missed Blades through a crab and lack of visibility

The 1990 Eight

in foul weather obscuring the spectacles of the cox, J. Kittmer. The Third Eight, which like the Second Eight, had not qualified, won Oriel Regatta. The men's First Boat rowed over at the head of Division II, as sandwich boat they got close to Wadham but a fast Brasenose crew caught them and thy finished second in Division II. The Second Boat slipped two places but the Thirds made four bumps though the last one was officially discounted. Two novice men's fours entered Reading Amateur Regatta and a selection of small boats, both men and women, entered Horseferry Regatta at Kew.

Tony Smith had become Magdalen's President in October 1988 and quickly lent his support to the Boat Club. Over the course of his presidency he was to be a tireless enthusiast, providing moral support, helping with fundraising, entertaining the crews and cheering the crews at the boathouse. As the new decade began the fortunes of M.C.B.C. were to begin a build on the recent consolidation of spirit and approach of its members. Flood water caused Torpids to be restricted to the men's first boats; the decision taken at an O.U.B.C. Captains' Meeting nonetheless caused fury within Magdalen, one of whose women remarked: 'It's a ludicrous decision to prevent women's first boats rowing when they permit all the men's first eights to do so'. As it was the event was curtailed after three men's eights, including Magdalen's, were swept on to the weir. The two days' racing that had taken place were not counted towards the start order for 1991. Kit Lewis was in the Isis crew while Victoria Wild opened Magdalen's account coxing the Women's Lightweight crew. The Magdalen women had a big boost for Eights Week by the arrival of a new boat built by Aylings, funded through the generosity of the American Friends of Magdalen, marshalled by S.J.R. Cass. Steve Cass who came from (and had returned to) California, had been Captain in 1989-90. The boat was named The President to recognise Tony Smith's support. This was one of the first non-wooden boats Magdalen bought. Though the Club's encounter with the very first glass fibre craft has already been told, modern materials were now standard and colleges were beginning to adopt them as the need to replace trusty wooden boats became necessary. This change was to herald a change in the role of the Boatman – for generations someone who may have been apprenticed to a boat-builder, and who would certainly need skill to repair wooden craft and oars, often at very short notice. They now became

experts at handling carbon fibre and modern plastics. It was immediately successful as the First Boat made three bumps to finish 21st at tenth place in Division II. The men meanwhile were bumped on the second day by a fast and loaded Jesus College crew, they rowed over for the rest of the week.

Hilary Term 1991 witnessed a women's boat that was determined to be the first Magdalen women's crew to win blades. Training at Godstow was combined with serious land training. A nervous crew bumped Osler House II after a minute, then Queen's and, on the third day, Corpus Christi. Nerves rose with the prospect of blades and thought that they should catch St. Hugh's II easily. By the time they got to within a canvas the Women's Captain, Sharon Heath caught a crab. After recovering the situation they caught up the lost length only for Vicky Reynolds to catch a crab; finally they caught their quarry before

*The Women record their success*

the Gut. For the first time in ten years of women's rowing at Magdalen a crew had won their Blades. President Smith gave a celebratory dinner in the Lodgings. The men's Torpid went up one and down one while the Second Boat made three bumps but at 56th on the river were well below a number of third boats. A large number of M.C.B.C. members trialled for the University crews but only S.A. Kenyon was selected, rowing for the Lightweight men. Simon Kenyon achieved this while captaining the College and organising the redecoration of the boathouse; new flags were bought to replace those 'lost'. The missing Captains' Books were recovered (from the periods 1935-39 and 1945-83) and a new one begun. Eights Week saw one sixth of the student population on the river and thus tremendous pressure was placed on the equipment. The men's First Eight rowed over every day behind Hertford and though a technically good crew, Magdalen seemed to lack spirit. The Second Boat similarly remained as it started. The Third Eight started 10th in Division VII and were bumped down two - the second one became known as 'The Infamous Bump' by Magdalen Fourth Boat – the M.C.R. crew - who bumped up four places to be placed one ahead of the Third Eight at the bottom of Division VII. The consequences of division in the club by to common rooms was made manifest in this result, which led to the Club being fined by O.U.B.C.: boats should be in their correct order of speed, thus a

# For the first time in ten years of women's rowing at Magdalen a crew had won their Blades.

Fourth Boat should not be fast enough to catch a third boat from the same college during a bumps race. Sharon Heath persuaded Peter Fullerton to coach the women's First Boat and he concentrated on technique and rhythm. They had a frustrating week gaining a place and then losing it. The Second, Third and Fourth women's crews all failed to qualify; their Captain noted the need for commitment in training if success was to be achieved. In an endeavour to heal the rift with the M.C.R., and to further the interests of the Club as a whole, Kenyon asked Tim Doyle, to coach a novice graduate boat over the long vacation.

B.J.A. Dalton was elected Captain of Boats for 1991-92, with J.S. Cashmore as Vice-Captain and Helena Cook as Captain of the Women; Cindy McCreery, a graduate student from Yale, was made Vice-Captain. Barney Dalton had arrived at Magdalen as an experienced oarsman from Radley; he proved to be an excellent Captain, beginning his reign with an intensive autumn programme which included four men's eights each with two coaches. The novice first crew went out six times a week and did circuit training as well. The women boated three crews and did well in Christ Church Regatta; a coxed four out of the Second Boat entered the Novice Fours event and won. For Torpids 1992 there was a shortage of coaches and so training began before term and with six outings plus two or three land training sessions per week the crews were fit. Dalton noted: 'We had rather a short stroke, and the power in the water seemed somewhat lacking, but quite a good catch and finish kept us going'. An eventful visit to Cambridge to compete in Pembroke Regatta resulted in being losing finalists but they brought away the benefit of experience. They went on to make three bumps and finish seventh in Division I. The Second Boat won blades after a tense final day when they were overlapped on Regent's Park College in the Gut only to miss making contact but caught them at the end of the boathouses. The women had a somewhat disrupted time with debates about outing times and frequency and their captain also training for the University Lightweight crew and yet there was great camaraderie in the crew and commitment to the task. They joined with Dalton's vision for the Club and made two bumps only to be triple bumped to conclude with a net loss of one place. Helena Cook was selected for the Lightweight crew to race Cambridge, as was Viva Bartkus, the O.U.W.L.R.C. President, also racing for the first time, having been a spare the year before. S.D. Grant was selected for the Lightweight men's crew. Stephen Grant was in his first year and brought with him his rowing experience from Winchester. All three won there races, for the men it was the first time in fourteen years. Over the Easter vacation Magdalen took part in a colleges' sponsored row to London, emulating the endeavour of the 1981 expedition. About fifty members of the Club took part with three eights and a four taking part and members rowing in shifts with a coach to move to those not on the water to the next changeover point. A variety of dramas occurred along the way but they reached London and raised £4,600 for multiple sclerosis research in the process. For Summer Eights the men were coached by Kit Lewis who felt he would rather assist than row. It proved to be an excellent arrangement, Dalton recalled that: 'Kit worked us hard, but always knew exactly what was wrong, and soon became highly respected by the crew. He worked mainly on the catch, which combined with Steve Grant's experience at stroke, transformed our rhythm beyond anything we had achieved in the previous term'. Of their performance at Wallingford Regatta, Dalton noted: 'our times in the heats worried the other colleges'. A trip to Thames Ditton Regatta led to a clash with Winchester and they lost after the restart. As Dalton wisely noted: 'as important to lose some races as to practice and win'. When Eights Week arrived hopes were high for blades, after two bumps they were sandwich boat and then caught Keble in front of the boathouse. Being back in the First Division, and through the generosity of an old member, the crew walked down to the river the following day in red blazers and bow ties. Blades were not to be: Worcester caught Brasenose before Magdalen could catch them. The Second Eight won their blades. The women's First Boat was coached by Adrian Smith, the O.U.W.L.R.C. coach, and Stephen Grant, who set a regime that Cindy McCreery considered 'without which, they stood no chance'. Two bumps and two days rowing over were there reward. The Second Boat worked hard to qualify and then made two bumps. A new Boat Club constitution, reviewed to bring it up to date and to reflect the changes since the College went mixed, was passed at the Annual General Meeting but not without creating the impression of two clubs – one for the men and one for the women. A few years later this unintended consequence would be put right.

Magdalen then received an invitation that connected the Club with its earliest history. Reading Amateur Regatta had reached its sesquicentenary and wanted to recreate some of the races of 1842. Once again Magdalen beat St. John's and Wadham. M.C.B.C. then formed a crew with Christ Church to enter the newly created Temple Challenge Cup at Henley Royal Regatta; they were beaten by Worcester College in the first round. 1992 was the year the new asymmetric – cleaver – oars became the latest innovation to make a mark on the rowing world. Magdalen was keen to get a set and President Smith started to raise the funds for a set. However, Professor John Stein, the Treasurer of Combined Clubs, wrote to the new Captain, D.A. Valder, to warn him the Boat Club's two accounts had a combined deficit of £1,500 but he would assist from the C.C.F. surplus. He added that the cost of the new multi-gym would be borne this way and therefore not technically the Boat Club's property. The old Empacher eight was sold to New College for £5,500 but for some reason only £1,500 was paid; Stein offered to intervene with his old college.

River closures dogged the Michaelmas Term 1992 but Magdalen went to the Cambridge Winter Head of the River Race and won, beating a large number of clubs and other Oxbridge colleges. 1993 started with more difficult weather and only the more senior divisions of Torpids were run. The highlight was an overbump on New College at the end of the boathouses – an almost unprecedented event in the First division, a bump on Christ Church on the last day left them fifth in Division I – within striking distance for the Headship. The women made three bumps and finished at their highest position. Women's rowing in Oxford was now very competitive and Sharon Heath, the Women's Captain of 1990-91 recorded the need for a committed group that would want to take on the best of the other colleges. The entered the Women's Head of the River Race and, without any A.R.A. points, were able to compete as novices. They finished a respectable 89th. Along with some of the men, they went to an invitation regatta in Paris over the Easter Vacation. The men won the Plate competition. Exams and injuries plagued the men's preparations for Summer Eights and it was third week before a settled crew took to the water. Once again there was drama with New College who refused to concede a bump despite an overlap for ten strokes afterwards and so the Magdalen cox, Tim Slater, called out 'We'll come and get you then'. He forced them into the bank and Magdalen finished tenth. The women's First Boat made two bumps and finished sixth in Division II. In early December the Club took delivery of a new eight built by Janousek and named it Friends of M.C.B.C. in honour of its generous donors, a group founded by Peter Fullerton which has gone on to become the backbone of support for Magdalen rowing. A new coaching launch The Dink, named in honour of 'Dink' Horsfall one of Magdalen great oarsmen, was completed and put to use at Godstow. Roger Hutchins' book *Well Rowed Magdalen!*, a first work on the history of M.C.B.C., was published in December. This original work, compiled with Peter Fullerton and with a chapter from Richard Burnell, was compiled from Captains' Books and O.U.B.C. records.

The 1993-94 season opened with P.A. Henry as Captain and he endorsed the view of Pat Johnson, Captain in 1926-27 and one of Magdalen's coaches until after the Second World War. Johnson was clear that attention should be given to the whole club and not just to the First Boat. Paul Henry also introduced a minor revolution by switching Magdalen's blades from a plain varnish finish to black with the white lily motif. This was a natural progression given that the carbon fibre blade had become the norm and hardly suited to the traditional appearance. The asymmetric shape lent itself well to the positioning of the lily. Another big change for the Club was the allocation of a permanent Captain of Boats' room in College. After much debate and process through various committees, St. Swithun's I.10 was set aside for this purpose and provided a home for the Horsfall Library, kindly donated by Mrs Betty Horsfall in her late husband's memory, and a collection of oars and pictures owned by the Club, whilst also providing a residence for the Captain of the day. Torpids 1994 were cancelled after the first day; once again the elements were against the aspirations of the crews. Magdalen had

six crews racing in Summer Eights in addition to three more which did not qualify – perhaps the greatest number of members the Club had ever had. The men's Third Boat was fortunate to be able to row on Friday after being caught by the Police, trying to paint Donnington Bridge. The men's First Boat made one bump while the Women's Boat, having gone up one place and then been bumped, stayed put on the table. The men's Second Boat made six bumps thereby surpassing even the record of the 1926 Second Boat. Over the season, the Club had been to a wide range of domestic regattas and gained much from the experience. A dinner was held

St Swithun's I.10
The Captain of Boats' Room

in College, preceded by a photograph of the whole Club on Cloisters Lawn. A plan to enter Henley with an all-Magdalen eight, coached by John Hill, ran into complications of the old chestnut of whether to attend the Commemoration Ball or not. Hill had joined the coaching team that year though without any experience. The Regatta's Qualifying Race for the Temple Cup was a direct clash. As it was there was a major thunderstorm just before the start and the crew returned to Oxford to go to the Ball. The retimed qualifying race the following morning was a challenge to sleep patterns and yet the crew missed qualifying by just one place. Henry concluded his notes on the year: 'It is Magdalen's club spirit that keeps us where we are today, the spirit that gets everyone out coaching novices and that induces freshers to take up rowing'.

During the following year Magdalen Boat Club lost one of its greatest sons with the death of Richard Burnell. Alexander Lindsay took over the position of President of the Friends of the Boat Club. T.N. Flemming and J.S. Cashmore rowed in the Isis boat, making them the first Magdalen representatives in University boats for three years. A year later Denny Levett was in the Women's Blue Boat, P.L. Bollyky rowed in the Lightweight crew, and Flemming was again in Isis, this time with D.P. Forward - a duo they would repeat in 1997 when Diana Sabot and Lisa Walker rowed in Osiris. Torpids 1995 were washed out for the first two days and only the senior boats were allowed to row for the rest of the week: Magdalen's position remained unchanged. At the Tideway Head of the River Race they temporarily won the Novice Pennant following an investigation into the status of the crews that were faster than Magdalen but turned out not to be of novice status. However, Magdalen had changed their status to Open and this seemed not to have been recorded by the organisers, so in the end it was a pennant that wasn't! At Eights Week, three bumps for the men's First Eight took them to sixth on the river, the best position for ten years. Dan Topolski came down to the river twice to provide some wisdom. The women, having lost a number of Finalists, had a difficult term.

There are only limited records for some of the next few years, leaving a less than complete picture of the Club's activities and the experiences and thoughts of its Captains. Newsletters came and went. These are vital tasks as a matter of creating an archive and a record for those who follow to consult and learn from. One of the reasons for this situation may be the rise of email and the use of computers; perhaps it is ironic that with these powerful tools increasingly available, less is committed to pen and long term records are not kept. Where written notes might find their way into a file, an email is not retained to the Club's detriment.

Coxswains who refuse to acknowledge a bump do little more than risk injury and boat damage for the umpire or marshal will not have missed clear contact when there is sufficient overlap for the bowman the chasing boat to shake hands with the stroke of the other. In 1996 the Magdalen men had just such a situation with St Edmund Hall. They bumped in front of the boathouses but they did not yield. Alex Hartemink, the bow man, recalled that this incident: 'left our cox no choice but to ram them. The resulting bump was quite an intermingling of oars all akimbo'. This crew finished 2nd on the river, Magdalen's highest position for a generation. The crew had been coached by David Rachel who had been brought in at the start of Trinity Term to join John Hill. That autumn the new Captain, Marcus Jones, with the help of the Friends of M.C.B.C., extended the facilities of the Waynflete gym adding free weights, squat stands and mats. David Rachel provided a programme for the year, this was made possible through a sponsorship deal brokered by President Smith with Oxford Molecular. This involved trips to Molesey Boat Club where he was based; otherwise Godstow remained a good stretch for the fours away from the bustle of the Isis. Successes at Tiffin Small Boats Head and Wallingford Head of the River Race followed. Jones's notes claim that: 'even Christmas Day was a training day and across the country, just before Christmas Dinner, twelve lycra-clad M.C.B.C. rowers set off for a three mile run'.

If New College seems to have been Magdalen's greatest rival over

## Easy-Oar!

Information for those new to the Magdalen College Boat Club, October 1994

For many people, rowing is the quintessential Oxford sport, steeped in tradition and prestige. For others, it's just a way of having a lot of fun. The fact that you are reading this indicates that you have an interest in rowing, and I hope that during your time at Magdalen you will take the opportunity to give it a go in some form. The Magdalen College Boat Club (MCBC) has a history going back over 150 years. Indeed, this summer marks the 150th Anniversary of Magdalen's first appearance at Summer Eights. In the early part of this century we were the dominant force in Oxford (and indeed British) rowing, and in 1912 a Magdalen VIII won the gold medal at the Stockholm Olympic Games. Even today we can still claim to have achieved more University rowing Blues than any other Oxford college. We are also fortunate in that we have possibly the best set of archives of any boat club in Oxford, and in recent years these have been revitalised. Perhaps the best place to start learning is Roger Hutchins' book *Well Rowed Magdalen*, which chronicles the history of the MCBC from its earliest days right up to the present. It's available at very low cost from the JCR shop and is well worth a look.

Recent times have also seen somewhat of a renaissance in Magdalen's performance on the river, so that last year we got more bumps than any other college at Torpids and Eights, and won three of the four novice events on the Isis. Last year also saw the first VIII narrowly miss out on Henley, and attend numerous external regattas. So there are plenty of opportunities for rowing at all levels within the Boat Club, and you are sure to find one you like. Of course, the Boat Club is also a great way to meet people, and it is well known that boat club parties are the best in college. We run a regular programme of social events all through the year, which makes rowing more than just a sport, and also a great place to make friends. So if you want to be a part of the club, get in touch with a member of the committee (their names are included in this sheet) and before you know it you'll be officially christened a 'Boatie'.

M.C.B.C. Dinner 1996

the years, in more recent times the rise and rise of Oriel has led to needle with them. Seemingly actively recruiting oarsmen, and graduate entry medical students in particular, they have dominated the top of Division I of both Torpids and Eights Week for longer than any other college would care to remember. For all four days of Summer Eights 1997 Magdalen challenged Oriel for the Headship but it was not to be. Jones wrote: 'we gave Oriel a fright and something to remember for next year. Each day we got faster until the Saturday saw us less than a quarter of a length behind with hundreds of people on the Magdalen raft cheering us on'. Meanwhile Jenny Cooper, the Women's Captain, secured the services of Charlie Day (Captain 1994-95) to coach at Godstow, trials were held at the start of Hilary Term 'This resulted in some squad members being replaced by novices'. Two crews emerged but not quite enough for a third; the First Boat won Blades in Division III. The Second Boat had less luck and ultimately dropped out of the fixed divisions. A new boat The *Dawn Treader* arrived in time for Eights Week and as Jenny Cooper records: 'we stormed to victory in our lovely new boat, bumping Worcester, Keble, St John's and Christ Church', making this crew the first M.C.B.C. women's crew to win

Blades in Summer Eights. The Second Eight made two bumps.

October 1997 began with a greatly reduced men's section as, despite the general success of the previous season, none of the previous year's novices continued to row. However, the new intake 'saw frantic activity throughout the College and not least in the Boat Club', recorded Andrew Loveridge, the newly-elected Captain. Christ Church Regatta succumbed to the elements and was cancelled after the first day; Loveridge organised an impromptu fours race at Godstow for the novices with crews named Mr White, Mr Blonde, Mr Pink and Mr Orange. After the racing they 'retired to the Trout Inn for a few beers'. A dinner was held in Hall with College Port consumed afterwards in the J.C.R. 'in quantity'. An innovation in the training regime took the Club to an early January 1998 training camp at Lake Banyoles in northern Spain. This expedition was subsidised by the generosity of the Friends and seventeen oarsmen and women and two coxes went for a week to enjoy the good weather and excellent facilities. On their return the men

The 1997 Women's Eight

moved to Wallingford to enjoy good water, it paid off at Burway Head of the River where they were fastest college crew, easily winning their division. In Torpids the Second Boat moved up a division taking four bumps including one hard-fought one on Univ. II. The final day's racing was cancelled due to the stream but the crew were awarded discretionary blades. The First Eight denied New College a crack at the Headship by delaying their passage by a day through some expert coxing of Brian Altenburg, who was to become Captain the following year. Jacqui Potts won her Blue coxing the Women's Boat while Janet Lucke and Lisa Walker represented the College in Osiris. Trinity Term began with some of the worst flooding Oxford had experienced in the twentieth century. The closure of the river fore-shortened the preparation time available. An afternoon's racing against a crew of recently retired [from rowing] old members, including 3 Captains, the current crew managed to win all three of these hotly contested races. The races were umpired from *Dink II* by stalwarts Peter Fullerton and Alexander Lindsay. Eights Week started with disappointment as Pembroke bumped Magdalen on the first evening, the rest of the week was spent rowing over third in front of a fast New College crew. The women, coached by Matt Stephens, again won Blades in Torpids with an overbump every day, in fact a double overbump on the first day, finishing in Division II. Sophia Turner, Women's Captain, notes that they spent the year borrowing things.

# The women, coached by Matt Stephens, again won Blades in Torpids with an overbump every day, in fact a double overbump on the first day

The rapid expansion of the Club has been noted and it seems that things such as trestles, cox-boxes, life jackets (now compulsory for coxes to wear) had not kept pace with this growth. It is possible to sense a tension between the men's and women's halves of the Club, perhaps a reaction to trying to create separate entities yet with shared resources. Sophia Turner comments that this year saw the first set of women's blazers: they were black with black embroidery and certainly didn't seem to be much liked as they were not in evidence a couple of years later. Perhaps the choice of colour exacerbated the perceived division, had they been red with blue trim they would have been equal with the men. Happily, just such a set was generously provided by Paul Beckwith in 2006.

There are no reports for the next three years, October 1998 to June 2001, and yet it is a period in which the fortunes of the Club were not idle. During Brian Altenburg's reign as Captain the first moves were made to set up a Boat Club Endowment Fund. The plan was to create a sufficiently large capital base so that, in the long term, the Boat Club could be self-sufficient. The alms provided by generous old members would be channelled into this fund rather than continue to appeal each time a new boat was needed. With Tony Smith's ever-present support from the President's Lodgings, the fund was started.

Summer 1999 saw the women gain two places and the men lose one. This took Magdalen women into the Division I for the first time, a great achievement after less than twenty years on the river having started in 32nd at 8th in Division III. A year later, in 2000, Becky Hastings rowed for the Lightweight Women's Boat. In Summer Eights the men rowed over while the women's First Boat made an overbump on the first afternoon to be followed by a further two bumps. For 2001, the men's Torpid maintained its position at 7th on the river while the women's boat made four bumps and were awarded their Blades. There was a total of eight crews for Summer Eights of which seven qualified. The men were coached by Francisco Mascaro' at his new Oxford and District Sculling Centre at Culham. The women consolidated their position by rowing over all week, the men lost two places. A coxed four was entered for the Britannia Challenge Cup at Henley but it failed to qualify. However, Magdalen was represented by S.J. Hermes stroking a composite quad (with Oxford and District S.C.) and it was drawn against a boat from Icena – the Old Wykehamists' Club (in a composite with Falcon R.C.) – stroked by N. McSloy who was at the end of his first year in Magdalen. Two weeks earlier these crews had met at Marlow Regatta and the honours had gone to Icena, the fortunes switched at Henley. Nick McSloy had rowed in the University Lightweight crew in the spring; Joanne Telford had been in the Osiris boat.

H.J.U. Ashton was elected Captain for 2001-02 and Nicola Thompson of the women's boats. The women had plenty of willing male coaches from within the Club, one novice crew made the final of Christ Church Regatta. The men's novice crews did well. Weather conditions again affected training in early Hilary Term; the women trained at Godstow under international oarsman Matt Langridge's supervision. Torpids were cancelled through flooding. Over Easter H.J.R. Morris, a freshman from Radley, rowed in Isis while E.S. Davis and E.W.H. Biden rowed in the Lightweight Boat. Early in Trinity Term Magdalen men entered the Oxford City Bumping Races (for fours) and bumped in all four races to be awarded miniature blades. At Bedford Amateur Regatta there was a fiasco when the judges gave a verdict to Pembroke College, Cambridge. The appeal by Magdalen was turned down, Pembroke had been sure they had lost and had gone home. In Eights Week

2002 the men dropped one place while the women slid four positions: they had had a difficult term with a change of Captain and this must have unsettled the preparation.

In order to safeguard against similar problems arising in future the Club took on a refinement of its officer structure in readiness for Michaelmas Term 2002 by electing, a Captain of Boats and then a Women's Captain and a Men's Captain. This has greatly clarified the hierarchy and worked well since, though in two later years the Captain of Boats has doubled as Men's Captain through pragmatism as much as availability of willing volunteers. More surprisingly, perhaps, in the first year of this new structure, the Women's Captain was a man: Chris Kimber. After many years away, Magdalen senior men's boats returned to Radley as a quiet base with excellent water. Ronan Cantwell and Ed Green replaced John Hill as coaches. The Radley reach is sufficiently wide to allow two eights to train side by side and this proved to be a big benefit. Charlie Ogilvie, Captain of Boats, who had switched from Chemistry to Fine Art, recalled that: 'Bright red leggings appeared when a kit order was placed by some less than aesthetically astute oarsmen'. In Torpids 2003 the women's Second Boat rose seven places. Henry Morris became the first Magdalen Blue for 18 years, Sam Parker and Matt Daggett were in Isis, Joanne Telford won her second Blue and was joined in the boat by Karlee Silver, Davis and Biden made the Lightweight Boat for the second year. In Trinity Term Donald Legget did some guest coaching of the men's First Boat at Radley. Donald, a Cambridge Blue and an Old Radleian, has a distinguished coaching record with Cambridge and Radley over many years. The men rose three places leaving them in striking distance of the Headship once again. The women were less fortunate and dropped a similar number. At the Club's Annual General Meeting, held shortly after Eights Week, R.J. Mawdsley was elected Captain of Boats for 2003-04 and Hannah Felgate as Women's Captain. The author was elected Senior Treasurer in succession to Roger Hutchins. Richard Mawdsley had rowed a little at home in Maidenhead but had essentially learnt his rowing at Magdalen. Torpids 2004 gave the women's First Boat five bumps in four days and therefore Blades. At Bedford Amateur Regatta the women won the novice eights event while the men won the Senior 2 event beating Star Club by 6 inches. At Summer Eights the women's First Boat made two bumps to finish third in Division II. The Second Boat had a tougher time and we awarded spoons having gone down each day.

A new Empacher eight *William of Waynflete* had been delivered just before Christmas 2003. At Easter 2004 Henry Morris and Ewan Davies both represented the University for a second time while Nicola Fawcett took her first Blue. Sam Parker, a second year Chemist from Radley, won his second seat in the Isis boat, James Strong became the first Magdalen man to row in Nephthys, the

# A new Empacher eight *William of Waynflete* had been delivered just before Christmas 2003

Lightweight reserve crew. Perhaps being named after the College's founder the new boat's destiny was to put Magdalen back at Head of the River for the first time in precisely fifty years. Angus McChesney, a member of the Radley staff, coached the men's First Boat, occasionally boating the crew at the same time as Donald Legget was taking the school crew for an outing, thus providing some side-by-side opportunities. McChesney calculated what he believed to be the distance needed to bump each day: and got it spot on. The first evening saw Exeter dispatched along the Green Bank. Overnight people started to talk and say Magdalen could go Head. It is always interesting to see how a buzz like that can go round and so often be right – the collective observation of a crew at racing pace for the first time. However the most important thing is to take each day as it comes and Pembroke were known to be a harder prospect even though they had been knocked off Head by Oriel the evening before. In just over three minutes they were bumped through some expert steering by Heather Chapman in front of Magdalen's boathouse. Friday was set to be the hardest day of all – bumping Oriel off Head. Angus McChesney could not come to the river that afternoon but Steve Hermes came down. Hermes would have been at Magdalen had he been able to stay to take the P.G.C.E. but the forces at work seemed less than pleased that he had already secured a teaching position at The King's School, Canterbury. He would undoubtedly have been a member of the crew. There was not a little drama when Oriel were late at the start and a technical bump against them was announced. The last thing Magdalen wanted was to recover the Headship in such a manner; as it was they were eventually allowed to race, perhaps because a member of the Magdalen boat was heard to say 'let them race, we're going to bump them anyway' – confidence and inspiration at just the right moment, rather than arrogance. Like Pembroke before them, Oriel crossed the stream early, as Magdalen closed on them coming out of the Green Bank the first sound of success was the thwack of the bow man's oar on their stern canvas, right in front of the boathouse. The river bank went wild – not just at Magdalen but at other boathouses. The following, last, day required Magdalen to row over Head to have title to the prized position. As they sat on the start Henry Morris gently reminded the crew of the need for a perfect row – they had the benefit of the clean water but an angry crew seeking to avenge their situation behind. A poor start, a crab, a misplaced tweak of the rudder and it could all end in tears. Thus it was that the gun went and Oriel flew off the start and stayed on distance through the Gut, but through the Green Bank Magdalen's pushes put a greater stretch of water between the crews. Then *William of Waynflete*, with the traditional bunch of lilies on the bows, ran into the wall of noise that was coming from the boathouses. By the time the boat crossed the line it was three lengths clear of Oriel. Every other crew cheered them as they too came to the end of the course. When the crew arrived back at the boathouse to scenes of jubilation one crew member was generous enough to comment that it had felt as if every Magdalen supporter had rowed in the boat that day. That evening Pembroke Lodge rang the Magdalen porters and invited the crew to collect the Head of the River Trophy. It adorned the dinner table on the first floor of The Mitre and somehow later got back to College.

This restoration to Magdalen of the Headship was to lead to an unexpected turn of fortune for the Boat Club. On the last Friday of term, Tony Smith was entertaining at high table a major benefactor of Oxford music. The guest enquired after the red blazers the crew were wearing at the tables below, taking their part in the summer sports formal hall. Zvi Meitar's imagination was captured and shortly afterwards the President told the Senior Treasurer that Meitar wished to support the Club over the next five years with a donation that would be the largest single gift the M.C.B.C. had ever received, to be spent on new boats and professional coaching. This would give the Club a real chance to consolidate on success and allow the Endowment Fund capital, which had been generously augmented with some legacies, including that of the late Deputy Head Porter, Tony Wickson, to grow. The difference this support has made has transformed the Club which has met the changing times of less volunteer coaching and the need to not only improve for its own sake but to keep up with rivals by having professional coaching.

That October a Headship dinner was held in Hall, timed to allow orderly planning and the attendance of many old members including the 1954 crew and Peter Hewison, the Captain from 1932-33. Before dinner the Choir sang Sir John Stainer's *Floreat Magdalena*. This rousing short piece had almost certainly been written for the same occasion in 1888 when his son was cox of the Head crew. It had spent decades buried and came to light in 2003. It is now sung as a grace at each Boat Club official dinner. At the end of the meal and the speeches, the President presented the Eight with the blades and the cox's rudder. The trophy was displayed on a table in front of the fireplace, newly restored and updated after years of neglect.

A.K. Allouni was elected Captain to take Magdalen through 2004-05. He decided on placing emphasis on novice coaching particularly in the light of losing virtually all the experienced oarsmen. Ably managed by Mark Haden, a campaign was launched and brought success in Christ Church Regatta. An arrangement with the manager of the LA Fitness gym in the centre of town provided the senior squad with access to good equipment and expert instruction for strength training. A number of small boats were bought from Empacher. At Wycliffe Head of the River in February the men won the Senior 1 category and went on to dispatch New College on the first day of Torpids. Exeter failed to turn up on the Thursday and so the technical bump was awarded. However it was to be a frustrating end to the week with two days overlapping yet not bumping Oriel of Head. The men's Second Boat made five bumps to become the highest second boat on the river. The women's First Boat, coached by Buffy Williams, wife of the O.U.B.C. President and an international oarswoman, made three bumps to achieve the highest position they had yet occupied in Torpids. The 2005 Boat Race season was represented by Magdalen with Henry Morris in Isis, a very noble post to

Above: Headship Dinner menu

Right: 16th October 2004 –
Headship Dinner

Below: London 2012 Olympic
Bid flag flies over
the Boathouse

hold for one who had been a Blue the two previous years, Nicola Fawcett, as President of O.U.W.B.C. was similarly in Osiris, along with Marianne Perrott. When Summer Eights arrived the women's First Boat made three bumps to put them back it the First division. The men, coached for the first time officially by Donald Legget, rowed over Head with no serious threat from Oriel who burned out after the Gut. Even subbing in Peter Reed, who had won a gold medal that morning at the Rowing World Cup at Dorney Lake, did not give them enough extra speed. The men's Second Boat made three bumps including the scalps of two first boats and Oriel II. This boat was stroked by Ewan Davis, who had stroked the First Boat the previous year but accepted the decision to replace him with the relatively inexperienced Phil Killicoat. Trinity Term 2005 was Tony Smith's last as President, his contribution to the fortunes of the Boat Club over his seventeen years in office is immeasurable. The Headship Dinner was held in Leander Club that October and the new President, Professor David Clary took the chair, Tony Smith and Zvi and Ofra Meitar were guests of honour. The new era in the President's Lodgings was to quickly prove to be to M.C.B.C.'s benefit as David and Heather Clary showed the same interest and enthusiasm for rowing as they did for all other aspects of College life.

For several months a London 2012 Olympic Bid flag has been flying from the boathouse. M.C.B.C. had responded to the request to have at least one in every city in the country. With its distinguished record in the Olympic Games, including both the previous London Games of 1908 and 1948, it seemed the right thing to do. With the bid won, all that remains is to ensure a Magdalen oarsman or women wins a medal and thereby maintains the Club's record.

R.D. Johnson took on his second Captaincy when he was elected for 2005-06; he had already been Captain of Glasgow University Boat Club in his days as a medical student. Coming to Oxford after a few years in practice as a surgeon, Reuben Johnson brought experience and maturity to the task of defending the Headship and ensuring the rest of the Club grew and thrived. Radley had recently

# Floreat Magdalena

Sir John Stainer

Sic - ut li - li - um be - a - ti, Cres - cant Mag - da - le - nae na - ti, Far a -

bun - det hor - re - is: Clau - stra tu - ta sint por - ta - rum, Pax ae - ter - na

cus - tos ha - rum, Mag - da - le - na flo - re - at, Mag - da - le - na flo - re - at,

Mag - da - le - na flo - re - at, Mag - da - le - na flo - re - at.

had a new Boatman in Andy Thomas, an accomplished oarsman who brought experience and good humour to the long winter training. A men's quad entered various events including the Tideway Fours Head of the River where is finished 30th overall, the highest place achieved by an Oxbridge college crew in many years. A coxed four also did well, rising fifty places, and the following day won the autumn fours back on the Isis. The women's novices, coached by a charismatic women's vice-captain Mark Haden, were the first success of the year when they won Christ Church Regatta in style. After Christmas Nic Thomas, Andy's wife, joined the coaching team and took the women's First Boat. A new Empacher eight for the

The Tideway Head of the River Quad

The Women's Eight prepares to race

women was delivered in January and at a ceremony at the boathouse, Zvi Meitar named it *Meitar II*. Short of returning oarswomen, Torpids 2006 saw them drop one place. The men set off second in hot pursuit of Oriel but over four days never quite made it, even though they overlapped on the last day. Of the Easter vacation, Johnson noted: 'a good M.C.B.C. presence in Blues Rowing. Deborah Turner, and Marrianne Perrott, and Rose Bosnell formed the stern for Osiris and were victorious over Cambridge. Phil Killicoat, who started rowing at Magdalen in 2005 made it into Isis – a testament to his physical stamina and mental determination. Gareth Jones, Lightweight Men, and James Solly and Adam Nelson, Nephthys, were in winning boats at the Henley Boat Races.' Donald Legget and Andy Thomas coached the men at Radley and they held once again the Summer Headship. On the last evening there was a clear five lengths of water to Pembroke who had earlier bumped Oriel and Balliol. Coached by Nic Thomas in

their new boat, the women climbed three places. The President and
Mrs Clary were as delighted as the rest that the Headship had been
retained in their first year in the Lodgings and gave a dinner for the
men's and women's First Boats in the week after Eights. For the first
time in many years Magdalen qualified for Henley Royal Regatta.
A combined Magdalen-Exeter coxed four was entered into the
Prince Albert Challenge cup. The crew consisted of four Magdalen
oarsmen: Phil Killicoat, Samuel Parker, Reuben Johnson, and
Magdalen cox Al Stewart. The crew were stroked by Exeter man,
Jake Sattelmair. Jake was previously in the Harvard Lightweight
crew and was bow 2005 Isis crew. On the Wednesday of Henley the
Magdalen-Exeter crew were drawn against Dutch crew G.S.R.
Gyas. After a blistering start, Magdalen-Exeter went off at a stroke
rate of 50 and took a length from G.S.R. Gyas by the end of the
island. Settling down to a rate of 37 they held this margin to the

Barrier. The Dutch crew put in a big push and managed to squeeze back half a length. Passing the Enclosures the Dutch continued to close but Magdalen/Exeter held on to win by a mere third of a length. Jack Richards, from the victorious Magdalen Visitors' four in 1953, was there to greet the crew back into the boat tents. On the Thursday the Magdalen crew faced favourites, University of London who went on to become the losing finalists. During the World Championships at Dorney Lake another new men's boat was delivered from Germany to replace the Second Boat which had been rowed straight into a steamer pile near Folly Bridge. Insuring on 'new for old' has its compensations and the craft went in at the top of the fleet and restored the name *De Profundis* to a Magdalen boat, the title of Oscar Wilde's letter from Reading Gaol, also the opening line of Psalm 130.

J.H. Northern took on the mantle of Captain for 2006-07, an experienced oarsman from Bedford School he had Lauren Adair as Women's Captain and L.J.A. Rooney as Men's Captain. Louis Rooney was another of the Radley diaspora and a veteran of the three Headship crews. Though plenty of training and recruiting took place the year was dogged by bad weather and both Christ Church Regatta and Torpids had to be cancelled; leaving the men in particular frustrated that they could not have another crack at the winter Headship. The Thomas's and Donald Legget continued to

Architects of Success: Nic Thomas, Donald Legget, Andy Thomas. Dinner in the President's Lodgings

lead the senior coaching team and training continued at Radley. The women slipped two places in Summer Eights, amid some concern there was no women's Second Boat. The men's First Boat rowed over Head once again to make a fourth year at top spot. In the following week the President and Mrs Clary once again kindly entertained the top crews to dinner in the Lodgings. The men's Second Boat made three bumps while the Third Boat bumped and then overbumped as sandwich boat all on the second day, they then bumped both of the following days to end up highest third boat on the river. It was in fact Magdalen's Fourth Boat but took the third position when the actual Third Boat

failed to qualify. The summer ended with a revival of S.C.R. rowing. A challenge was made for a fours race against the M.C.R. and on a Sunday afternoon at the end of September a roughly 500 metre sprint was held ending at the boathouse. Varying degrees of seriousness were attached to the event which the M.C.R. won by about half a length. A good number of Fellows came down to the river to watch. The Fellows' four contained Professors Dreyfus and Turberfield and Doctors Gilbert, Stargardt and Moreno, who coxed. They entertained the graduate boat of Mark Haden, Gijs van Boxel, Matthew Werley, Markus Schwarzlander and coxswain Alastair Stewart to dinner in the S.C.R. afterwards. Talk of a rematch has not yet resulted in anything being arranged but a number of the Fellowship took to the main boats during 2008.

The One Hundred and Fiftieth year of Magdalen College Boat Club began with yet another cancellation of Christ Church Regatta leaving seven frustrated crews. Mark Haden was elected Captain, a man of considerable experience built up as a Vice-Captain, Social Secretary and coach of innumerable novice crews. He took on the role of Men's Captain as well and sought out the services of the profession- als who had helped so much in Magdalen's recent success. Hilary Term 2008 brought better weather and when Torpids arrived the Magdalen men were ready for Oriel. They didn't manage it on the first day but had the measure of their quarry and took the Headship on Thursday afternoon. Magdalen had not held this position since, almost unbelievably, 1937. The following afternoon Jock Fletcher-Campbell, veteran of the 1932-33-34 Torpid Head crews came down to the river to watch them row over and to meet the crew. Dee Jackson provided yet more tireless support and coached the women's crews again. They shared the men's success by both the women's First and Second Boats achieving Blades.

To have held the Double Headship would have been to equal only the 1932 record but sadly it was not to be. The men's First Boat held off Pembroke's challenge on the first day through a mishap in their boat and they were caught by Balliol. The following day they caught Magdalen and then Oriel and Christ Church took them down to fourth spot. Still in a position to strike at the Headship in 2009. The rest of the Club enjoyed success, the women's First Boat making a bump while the seconds made two. The men's Fourth Boat had rather more success than the Thirds and seconds and made three bumps, three Fellows were members of the crew.

The year ended with another row to London, this time to raise money of the C.L.I.C. Sargent children's cancer charity. A mixed squad set off with Dee Jackson as the hard-working land support and made the Palace of Westminster in three days. The 2008-09 season will open as every year does; recruiting novices from among the freshers and seeking to retain the Torpids Headship and regain it in Summer Eights. The women are well placed to continue their rise to their first Headship very soon. University representation will continue to be important and Ben Harrop-Griffiths is the President of O.U.L.R.C. for the coming year's challenge. Zvi Meitar has generously offered to revive the M.C.B.C. medals and new dies have been sunk, silver for Head crews, bronze for Blues, a magnificent way to record achievement and to revive a tradition dormant since the 1930s. Magdalen Boat Club is the largest single group within the College, attracting as it does so many to the joys of the river, along with its scores of loyal and enthusiastic old members, it will celebrate its 150th year with an anniversary dinner to be held on the River Thames in London on 1st November. Some might feel the College Hall is the right place but when it cannot accommodate the numbers, where better to be than afloat upon the Elysian stream?

# *Floreat Magdalena*

The 1887 Barge, with the Boatman R.A. Talboys coaching a Four

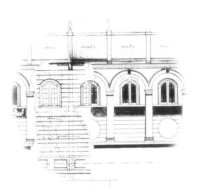

# 12

## Barges and Boathouse

### The Barges

An Oxford college boat club barge had two main functions: it was a changing room and clubhouse, and a grandstand for viewing the bumping races, Torpids and Summer Eights. The deck and upper deck of the barge were designed for this purpose and for entertaining visitors and guests. They were a colourful sight in Oxford for over one hundred years. The basic design for the college barges was taken from several London Guild barges which were brought to Oxford in the mid-nineteenth century as part of the process of the Lord Mayor of London's survey of the river.[1] Such barges were used in the seventeenth and eighteenth centuries by the London Livery Companies for ceremonial occasions on the river, including the Lord Mayor's Show. In 1846 O.U.B.C. bought a barge from the Merchant Taylors' Company, and Balliol and Exeter followed suit acquiring craft from the Skinners' and Stationers' Companies respectively. The idea of using barges for college boat clubs took hold, and most of the later barges were built in Oxford by Salter's to individual designs chosen by the colleges.

Being a relatively late foundation, Magdalen College Boat Club did not acquire a barge of its own until the late nineteenth century. In the early years from 1859, M.C.B.C. hired a room in Salter's barge and shared this accommodation with the University and several other Colleges. The hull of this large barge, or houseboat, was originally constructed for carrying timber. The superstructure or 'house' was later built onto it and used for Salter's boat letting business at Folly Bridge. It used to be moored along Christ Church Meadow during the summer and was taken up to the wharf near Folly Bridge for the winter. In this barge the boating men all used to change up to the time of the formation of the O.U.B.C. and the gradual introduction of College barges. Magdalen was the last to make use of Salter's barge, using the little room on the meadow side as a dressing room up to 1873'.[2] The room in Salter's barge was 'so extremely small as to make a change very desirable as soon as the number of men frequenting the river began to increase. But though with the revival of College rowing in 1871 proposals for hiring a barge were begun, it was not till 1873 that this step was actually made'.[3] There are no College records or photographs of this first Magdalen barge, but there are a few references to it. President Warren noted in his diary in 1886: 'The College this day became Head of the River. They overlapped their rivals before the gut and finally bumped them just before passing the College barge.' Sherwood relates that after the new Magdalen barge was commissioned in 1887 'Wadham took possession of their old one'. Jesus College had looked at it but decided it was too expensive to repair. The barge hired by Magdalen was probably moored downstream of the old mouth of the Cherwell, at the end of the growing line of College barges.

In 1885 the College decided to raise a fund for the building of their own barge. A circular letter in Magdalen Archives of January 1886 suggested that 'a memorial ought to be raised to the late Senior Tutor and Estates Bursar, T.H.T. Hopkins.' Hopkins had been one of the founders of the Boat Club in 1859, and had been until the time of his death in 1885 a keen supporter of its interests. A further circular letter of 18 February 1886 mentions that 'the Committee have resolved to consult an architect to obtain designs and tenders.' Funds raised rose to £700 against an original estimate of £600. In November 1886 the Committee requested Mr E.P. Warren to prepare designs for a barge and to arrange tenders for carrying them out, his first commission in Oxford. Edward Prioleau Warren was the President's younger brother; the plans were duly approved. It has been suggested that Sir Edward Lutyens had a hand in the design but there is no evidence for this, as he would have been only eighteen at the time. The lowest tender, of £800 from Salter's, was accepted and it was decided not to sacrifice certain parts of the design in the interests of economy. The upper deck could accommodate about one hundred and fifty people, some on tiered benches. The top-heavy load caused the barge to list during the races, and to reduce the amount of freeboard considerably.

After Eights Week, some Oxford colleges used to send their barges down river to Henley Royal Regatta. Towing a 60-foot barge with ornamental superstructure through dozens of bridges and locks with minimum clearance and without damage was a considerable feat of watermanship. The barges were towed by two horses and took several days to cover the sixty miles. At Henley the barges were moored on the Bucks side of the river and used as grandstands for college members and their guests to watch the races. Lunch tents were sometimes provided alongside. At the height of their popularity in the 1890s the college barges and other houseboats stretched in an almost unbroken line along the regatta course from the finishing post to Fawley, the halfway mark. This practice seems to have ended in 1914 with the outbreak of World War One. After the war, in 1919, the Henley Stewards' Enclosure was opened and the need for the barges as grandstands came to an end. The initiative for this Members' Enclosure to fund the cost of the regatta came from Sir

Harcourt Gold who rowed for Magdalen and Oxford between 1896 and 1899, he had been elected a Steward of the Regatta in 1909.

The 1927 Barge moored at the Swan Hotel, Streatley-on-Thames, 2008

By the early 1920s the Magdalen barge of 1887 was beyond repair. The superstructure was sound, but the hull was almost certainly the problem. Most college barges had hulls of oak or elm timber; they took in water and had to be pumped out regularly by the boatmen. The fact that there is no record of anyone buying the old Magdalen barge suggests that it had to be scrapped. A letter from S.G. Lee to the President described the barge as 'going out of existence' and deplored the fact that the boatman had failed to salvage the brass plate on the barge commemorating Toovey Hopkins, one of the founders of the M.C.B.C.

Main: Interior of the 1927
Barge. The Boatman, Jack
May, is in the doorway

Inset: A 1920s Barge Party

When the College ordered their new barge in 1927 they decided on completely new technology, a ferroconcrete hull. It is not known who in the Governing Body had this innovative idea, but they approved £500 towards the cost.[4] The consulting architect commissioned to design the barge was George Drinkwater. He was a graduate of Wadham, had rowed for the O.U.B.C. in the Boat Races of 1902 and 1903, and, with T.R.B. Saunders, was the author of the *Official Centenary History of the Boat Race 1829-1929*, and *The Boat Race*, published by Blacke in 1939. To add to his credentials he had coached Magdalen in 1911. It was probably he who decided to ask L.G. Mouchel and Partners of London to design the concrete hull, and worked with them on the design of the superstructure. Mouchel were pioneers in the construction of ferroconcrete floating buildings and vessels at that time. The S.S. *Armistice*, designed by Mouchel, was the first British-built seagoing concrete ship of 1918. Its advantages were seen to be reliability, strength and satisfactory behaviour. Lack of good quality timber after the war had forced manufacturers to look to innovative construction methods. The Mouchel archivist, George Crabb maintained that the low centre of gravity of the ferroconcrete construction eliminated the chance of the barge tipping over. The hull weighed forty-two tons, was seventy feet in length and had walls forty-two inches thick. The hull of the Magdalen barge was built on the slipway of the British Motor Boat Club at Chiswick by Messrs Holloway, and launched on 7 March 1927 on a flood tide. The wooden superstructure was also built at Chiswick by Holloway who had a fine joinery works. The barge was to be fitted out at Salter's in Oxford, but the Thames locks were closed over the winter delaying the journey until the spring, leaving Salter's only one month to fit her out before Eights' Week. There was also a problem in the barge clearing Abingdon Bridge; her overall height would not clear the arch and the bargee did not want to risk taking in water into the concrete hull to improve the headroom. Ken Irvine, who had rowed for the College before the First World War, cleared the nearby pub by offering free beer onboard. There were quickly enough people on the barge to clear the arch.[5]

'This was a particularly ornate barge with Romanesque feel, her elegantly raised stern being glamorously decorated with strong rounded arches supported by columns, into which were fashioned, with elaborate decoration, round but slightly arched casements. Intricate roundels sporting the initial "W", paying reverence to the founder of the College, William Waynflete, were set out below a dado of foliate relief. A door and five wide arched sashes carry the programme to the bow of the craft, linked by a soft wave-like cornice and intersected by bosses finishing at a slightly raised portico. A turned set of railings provides a finishing touch to the elaborate decorative programme below'.[6] The M.C.B.C. scarlet flag with lilies flew from the masthead during the races. The interior of the new

Drinkwater's drawings
for the 1927 Barge

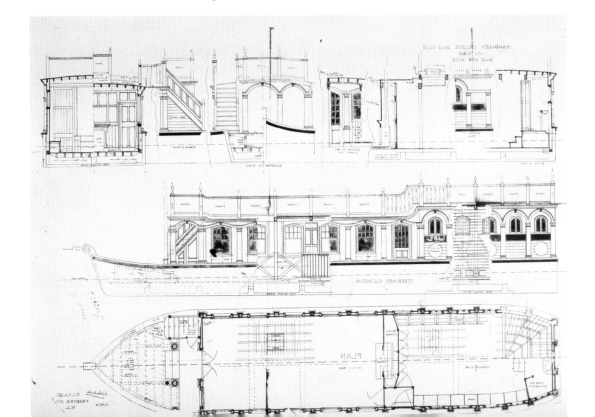

barge was similar in design to the old one. The club room took up two thirds of the length and had six large windows on either side. There were leather-covered benches under the windows running the length of the room on which the crews could sit and chat while changing or listening to the coach or Captain. There was a coal-burning stove at one end of the room with a mantelpiece, above which hung the portrait of Hugh Benjamin Cotton, stroke of the Magdalen crew and bow in the OUBC crew from 1892-95. Every inch of wall space was hung with framed photographs of Magdalen crews. There was a writing table in the middle of the saloon, and cupboards in which the Boat Club Records were kept. There was a small library of rowing books and bound copies of Punch, to while away the time spent waiting for outings. An Avery bench-type weighing machine which told undeniable truth was in daily use. The rest of the barge was taken up with the Boatman's cabin, the galley for tea making, a shower room with a lavatory, both of which

The 1927 Barge loaded with Eights Week spectators

operated on river water, and a pump for the bilge. The oars were racked overhead in the club room, not kept in a boathouse. This was because the boats used to be towed down to the barges in a string every day from Salter's by the College boatmen, and moored alongside the rafts attached to the barges. They were then towed back up to Salter's in the evening where they were stored. A 'Fixed Tub' (a single seat practice boat) was also moored against the barge to coach novices and demonstrate the correct rowing cycle.

Hubert Betteridge, who rowed in the 1937 crew wrote: 'My memories of the barge are of everyday sounds and tastes — the clanking of the pump as the redoubtable Jack May (the Boatman) filled the tank for our icy showers; the thump of the fixed pins from the training tub outside; and the well-buttered teacakes and strawberry jam as a reward for our labours'. Peter Hewison, Captain in 1932-33 recalled that 'the new barge was the largest and most beautiful, most expensive, on the river. The changing room was restricted to the First Boat but this was not much of a privilege as the cold shower was pumped straight from the Isis'.

The era of College barges was, however, drawing to an end. The Magdalen barge of 1927 was the last but one to be built. Several Colleges were by then already considering the construction of their own boathouses. Indeed, the Magdalen Governing body had discussed that possibility in 1922.[7] By the late 1930s the needs of the Boat Club were outgrowing the barge. The Magdalen Barge continued to be used until 1946. She was then sold to Talboys, the Oxford boatbuilders, who used her as a store. There is no record of what happened to the contents of the barge when it was decommissioned. The barge was later used as a houseboat on the Thames near Oxford. Eventually, she was bought in 1979 by Mr Newling Ward, Managing Director of Gulliver Hotels. After thirty years of neglect she was in very poor condition and the bilge was full of water. She was painstakingly restored, thanks to Gulliver Hotels, by the Pangbourne firm of Champions and converted for use as a floating annexe to the Swan Diplomat Hotel at Streatley. (formerly the Swan Inn, a famous old Thameside watering hole mentioned in *Three Men in a Boat*). There she is used for parties, weddings and conferences. The barge is well preserved in its new colours of blue and white instead of the original black and white Magdalen livery. The Swan Hotel is now owned by Nike hotels. In April 2008 an excellent dinner was held on board, attended by a number of past Captains of M.C.B.C., as well as the current officers; a plaque recounting the barge's history was presented to the hotel's General Manager.

## The Boathouse

In April 1938 its was decided to seek to build a boathouse and twelve months later Trinity College had agreed to share the costs and have ownership and use of just under half the building. Christ Church had decided to build for their own boat club's needs, on their meadow, and were willing to grant leases to other colleges to follow suit subject to there being a minimum of seven colleges. In October 1937 C.E. Tinné, Hon. Treasurer of O.U.B.C. sent a cir-

cular letter to all college boat clubs asking them if they objected to moving their barges from in front of the proposed building plots. Each would be allocated a width of 87 feet 4 inches of riverbank by 110 feet deep, beginning from the downstream end by the new Cherwell cut and allocated in the order the requests came in. Thus Magdalen and Trinity were the first to build, next to Christ Church's own boathouse. Merton and Worcester were next. These colleges had noted that the costs of repairs to their various barges were likely to exceed the cost of building a permanent boathouse; since Christ Church were offering 99 year leases at a ground rent of £10 per annum this was clearly an attractive proposal. It would also negate the costs of boat storage at Salter's and the other yards on the Isis. The five colleges saw the wisdom of building together and thus sharing costs. George Drinkwater was appointed architect for all three buildings and a draft builder's agreement from Christ Church was prepared in May 1939 and signed on 28th August 1939. G.C. Pipkin & Sons, the builder from Warwick Street, tendered at a total of £9,100 for the combined Magdalen and Trinity boathouse and a similar building for Merton and Worcester. Magdalen and Trinity signed an agreement in October that year with Magdalen paying 5/9ths and Trinity 4/9ths. If Trinity were

unable to pay Magdalen would loan to them at 4% p.a.

Stephen 'Luggins' Lee, now a Fellow of Magdalen, was the point of contact for this project with Trinity's Bursar, P.A. Langdon. He had taken this on during his period as acting Home Bursar, Harry Weldon having gone off to the war and passing Lee the duties of Treasurer of the Combined Clubs' Fund. The funding of the building was to be shared between the C.C.F. and the J.C.R. The architect's fees were paid in September 1939 and the builder was to be remunerated in monthly instalments from November that year to completion in April 1940. Construction was, however, hampered by the start of World War II and the College had to decide (in conjunction with Trinity's Governing Body) whether or not to continue – Drinkwater wrote pointing out that to curtail the project would simply put the builder's men on the dole. Work might as well continue at least until conscription. The two colleges decided to take advantage of the tender price and get started, no one knew how long the war might last or what the costs would be once it was over. By the time it was completed it had cost £4,811.17.7 including architect's fees. Trinity's share of this left Magdalen with a cost of £2,583.7.7 against a budgeted £3,000. At this point the building had no heating, electricity or plumbing.

In spring 1943 the Admiralty inspected the boathouse with a view to Naval occupation – there was to be a University Royal Naval Unit and a base was required. In a letter to Magdalen and Trinity the Admiralty proposes terms for occupation for 'the period of hostilities'. The installation of electricity had been deemed unnecessary by the colleges and so this a cable was laid from Iffley Road and down Jackdaw Lane and across the new cut. The drainage came by the same route. The colleges obtained a War Damage assessment on the rates and obtained a reduction from 2/- in the pound to 6d. Once the War was over, the Admiralty sought to terminate the arrangement on 24 June 1946, claiming that they had vacated and the colleges had taken back practical possession during Eights' Week. The colleges exchanged correspondence to see if they could formulate a claim for damages but did not pursue this. Magdalen replied pointing out that the Naval Unit had not in fact moved out of the first floor, and that they had been permitted to access the boat bays, and so the terms of the agreement should remain in place until this was done; it took until July 1947 until the colleges had vacant possession and they could return to the question of completing the building work. The raft was added a year later. The O.U. Royal Naval Division expressed their gratitude to the College for the use of the boathouse by presenting the Fellowship with a porcelain bowl with silver embellishments.

One of the complications of the disrupted construction was that the roof was not well done and over the years it has had several

Porcelain Bowl with Silver Mount – a Gift for the use of the Boathouse during the War

ADMIRALTY,

2, PORTLAND PLACE,

BATH.

/o June 1943.

Sir,

## Magdalen and Trinity College Boathouse, Christchurch Meadow, Oxford.

With reference to my Surveyor, Mr. Hancock's recent interview with you in company with Mr. Denholm Young, I confirm that I am prepared to recommend for Admiralty acceptance the following terms in respect of the Naval occupation of the Magdalen and Trinity College Boathouse.

(a) The Admiralty to pay £40 per annum exclusive of outgoings for the period of hostilities.

(b) The Owners to bear the cost of completing the structural work to the property and the Admiralty to pay for the installation of the heating, lighting and sanitary arrangements as required for Naval purposes.

(c) The Admiralty only to be liable for damages to the premises taken over in excess of normal wear and tear.

(d) The Owners to retain the use of half the Ground Floor as now occupied for the storage of College Boats.

(e) The arrangement to commence as from 29th September, 1942, and may be determined by the Admiralty giving three months' notice to expire on any quarter day.

2. If you will let me have your confirmation of these

/terms

AH.

major repairs. A fire in 1961 led to a refurbishment. In 1999 the first floor was refitted and improvements to the changing facilities were made. The floor of the first floor had always been under supported, this was highlighted by the bounce caused when women's crews warm up; in 2006 the joist were doubled to accommodate this need. The embankment was rebuilt in 2005. In its 150th year, M.C.B.C. has a large enough fleet of boats and numbers of crews to make a bigger boathouse desirable but the meadow is now full and only a project undertaken with Trinity, and Lady Margaret Hall who have been their tenants since 1980, would make it feasible. For much of the year Magdalen racks senior boats at Radley College boathouse and they train on that reach: it is a huge advantage and a privilege to be able to do so, the river there is quiet and provides a good long stretch. It is quite clear why, over the decades, Magdalen has boated there for large periods of time, indeed the record of the Demies and Commoners Fours race in 1859 is on that reach.

[1] Kenneth Nicholls Palmer, Ceremonial Barges on the River Thames, Unicorn Press 1997

[2] W.E. Sherwood, Oxford Rowing, Henry Frowde 1900

[3] H.A. Wilson, Oxford University College Histories: Magdalen College, Robinson & Co. 1899

[4] College Acta 1927, Magdalen College Archive

[5] Sir Roderick Sarell letter, Magdalen College Archive

[6] Clare Sherriff, The Oxford College Barges: Their History and Architecture, Unicorn Press 2003

[7] College Acta 1922, Magdalen College Archive

Winners of the Servants' Fours 1946 & 1947

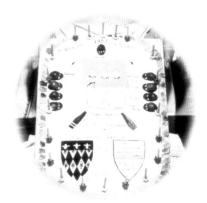

# 13

## Magdalen College Servants' Rowing Club

Over the course of time there has been a number of reasons for the loyalty and longevity of service that people give an employer. Today such qualities are much less common than even it was thirty years ago, as many influences come to bear on individuals' choice of career and employer, though many College staff still buck the trend.

In the days when someone would join a College straight from school, or from vocational training, and stay there until retirement, one of the aspects of their career which would cement this unswerving loyalty would be the camaraderie among the staff. Most commonly this took the form of social activities out of working hours and sport was a natural draw for recreation and a competitive spirit.

Until the mid 1950s the domestic staff of Oxbridge Colleges were known collectively as servants; perhaps now seen as a derogatory term but before that time it was perhaps more reflective of the range of duties performed as much as of social structure and the generations of local families that became dynasties in the service of colleges.

The earliest record of organised college servants' rowing is 1850 with the formation of the 'Oxford University and College Servants' Rowing Club'. This club served two principal purposes: firstly it created a structure under which individual college servants' clubs would compete against each other and the best would form a crew to compete biennially against their opposite numbers from Cambridge. Secondly it gave a home to those employees whose own college club had foundered as cricket and other sports drew people away from the river to college servants' clubs on the games field. An Easter-tide regatta for four-oared boats was established in 1874, held over three days in clinker boats it was called the 'Oxford University Servants' Four Oar Challenge Cup'. Later there were Challenge Pairs and Challenge Whiffs. Club Open Fours and Open Gig Pairs were also part of the programme these two events were not subject to college affiliation. On the August Bank Holiday weekend the servants' rowing clubs would enter the City of Oxford Royal Regatta which was founded in 1858. The City Bumps Races began in September 1889 and the O.U.& C.S.R.C. competed from the first year. Starting behind Hinksey, they took the Headship in 1891, though it contained no Magdalen personnel. Latterly college servants'

The President

# MAGDALEN COLLEGE
# SERVANTS R.C.

Winners of Grand Challenge Cup
The Challenge Pairs
The Challenge Whiffs
Private Fire Brigade Challenge Cup
Finalists College Cricket Club

FRIDAY, SEPT. 30th, 1927.

---

A Celebration Dinner
held in Hall

Philip Bennett
A Chamberlain
[signatures]
J A Smith
[signatures]
G M Driver
P C Hosier

F E Brightman
G. H. Clapton
H J Quelch
E. Hope.

A A Miller

E Craig
F Robins
E J Kelly
A E Papier

*Menu*

———

Purée Americaine

———

Fried Fillets Sole

———

Roast Sirloin Beef
Roast Sparerib Pork
Vegetables

———

Apple Tart and Cream
Meringues à la Chantilly

crews entered in their own right and competed against the local clubs in clinker fours.

Magdalen's servants do not appear to have been on the river representing their College in the beginning however they won the Fours for the first time in 1886; they also had a run of success in the 1920s. Whilst those that made up the crews were drawn from a variety of departments across the College, scouts, who were then always male, made up the largest constituency, perhaps not surprisingly as they were the most numerous group of employees. Chefs, porters, gardeners and works tradesmen took part at various times. Typically boats were rented and College colours adopted, entries fees were paid – in 1908 these were 7/6 per crew. The course for the Fours was from Long Bridges to Folly Bridge. The O.U.&C.S.R.C. wore dark blue and white jerseys but the crew that was formed to compete against the Cambridge Servants R.C. was allowed the initials C.S.R.C. and crossed oars on a blue cap. For this race and the other events in the season three rules applied: the coxswain should weigh no less than 7 stone; all competitors must have been employed by the college he represented in the previous term; and the boatmen could not be a member of a crew as this was considered to be using professionals. This last regulation came about after a fuss in 1882 when a New College Servants' Four entered for the City Bumps with a waterman onboard. A letter from the City Rowing Club set out the objection but New College were unrepentant and so all the crews except Queen's and New Colleges withdrew. As already noted, this was the period when the amateur debate was raging at national level. Initially it meant that the working classes could not row with such as undergraduates but as the argument moved on and the definitions were refined this was narrowed to those who made their living on the river and hence college boatmen and local watermen were the only working men proscribed from collegiate servants' crews, though they were often officers of the local rowing clubs.

# they 'went into training' and forewent smoking and all but a little beer

Only pockets of information exist on the servants' activities on the river. In 1927 the M.C.S.R.C. swept the board and the College gave them a dinner in Hall on 30th September, 85 people were present, and the President, Sir Herbert Warren, was in the chair. Though Warren was an enthusiastic supporter of rowing the staging of this dinner was quite an innovation in terms of servants and Fellows mingling socially. They had won the City Regatta Grand Challenge Cup, the Servants' Challenge Pairs, the Servants' Challenge Whiffs, the Private Fire Brigade Challenge Cup, and were Finalists in the College Servants' Cricket Cup.[1]

Bill Jarvis was Second Chef at Magdalen for 46 years from 1932 to 1978 and a key member of the Magdalen College Servants' Rowing Club and the O.U.&C.S.R.C. The biennial Oxbridge match was a three day affair that included cricket and bowls; in 1934 Jarvis stroked the Oxford Servants' crew that beat their Cambridge counterparts on their home water of the River Cam, and then the Senior Eights at the August City Regatta. E. Dyer was the bow man in the Second Boat. Jarvis repeated this double in 1936 when the Fenland crew visited the Isis and then once more at that summer's local regatta. Jarvis again stroked the boat in 1948 when no less than four other Magdalen personnel were in this Oxford boat. Coxed by P. Wright, the others were B. Castle (7), G. Willis (5), T.G. Charlett (2) and they beat Cambridge on the Cam; they were awarded 'Blues'. These took the form of crossed oars on the blue O.U.&C.S.R.C. blazers and caps. These men were the core of the Magdalen Servants' Four which won in 1946 and 1948 and 1949. The river was in full spate in 1947 and no racing was held. Tom Charlett was Head Scout for 50 years, and George Willis, Pat Wright and Bryn Castle were all scouts. Castle had survived internment in a Japanese prisoner of war camp.

In 1950 the O.U.&C.S.R.C. reached its centenary and a short history was produced by a Bert Piper. Magdalen was well represented that year: B. Castle was the Captain and T.G. Charlett was Vice-Captain, on the committee were W. Jarvis and G. Willis.[2] At a dinner and smoking concert to mark the centenary, held in the Victoria

Arms Hotel in Walton Street at the end of the three day Easter regatta, S. Cleverly was the oldest member present. By this time Magdalen's record put it third on the river with nine wins in the Fours. Christ Church servants had clocked up twenty-two, Brasenose thirteen.

In retirement, Bill Jarvis recalled life in the College Kitchen and the Servants Rowing Club. The M.C.S.R.C. started the year with practice once or twice a week until the end of Hilary Term when they 'went into training' and forewent smoking and all but a little beer, until the Easter inter-collegiate Fours. One or two colleges, like Magdalen, put on two boats under their own colours, so altogether 12 or 13 would race. 'We copied the undergraduate life style as much as possible. For instance, we finished the Easter Regattas with a Smoking Concert at the Druid's Head. Some undergraduates coached us - I remember [Jock] Fletcher-Campbell in particular. It was great. Hard work, long hours, but with many advantages. That's why people stayed so long and identified with such pride in their colleges. It's a way of life that's over now.'[3] Bill Jarvis was a Territorial Army volunteer in the Oxford Royal Artillery battery commanded by Magdalen Fellow and M.C.B.C. coach Lt. Colonel Pat Johnson. In 1940 they were mobilised together directly from summer camp. Bill came back after the war to his old work and rowing, whilst Magdalen and the M.C.B.C. lost Pat Johnson to a new career in military circles (first as Director of Studies at the R.A.F. College, Cranwell). Of the training for the varsity servants' race, which had to be undertaken at the same time as preparing for the Oxford City bumps, Jarvis noted: 'In the year of the Cambridge contest we had to keep up training in a shell eight until about a week before the bumps; a bit like track training in light running shoes, then racing on the day in army boots.' Referring to the Challenge Fours he commented that: 'because they were timed

Bill Jarvis with the cake he made for the 20th anniversary dinner of the 1953 Headship

O.U.&.C.S.R.C.
1926.

Bow. E.A. DYER. (MAGD) 9-7.
2. J. WILKINS (UNIV.) 10-1
3. W.J.S.TURGES (QUEENS) 11-1.
4. P.R.GRIFFEN (QUEENS) 10-8.

WON 2 LENGTHS.

Cox.S. BOSSOM. (CH.CH.) 7-7.

5. J.E.K.KIRKBY. (MAGD) 11-9.
6. W.J.CROZIER. (BALIOL) 12-4.
7. M.BASKERVILLE. (MERTON) 11
STR. R.W. LEE. (CH.CH.) (CAPT.) 10

Blade recording the Oxford Servants beating their Cambridge counterparts

races they were always hard. You had to row yourselves out.' Of his duties in the College Kitchen, Jarvis recollected that, until the Second World War, they produced family lunches, picnic baskets and teas for Eights' Week. These were taken down to the College Barge by the J.C.R. Staff by river: the food was passed from the kitchen terrace straight into waiting punts.

By the early 1950s women were replacing men as scouts and by 1952 many colleges could only manage combined crews. Magdalen's last success was in a composite four with University College in 1955. Soon after this the smaller clubs merged with the City club, enticed by the prospect of racing at Henley and at other regattas away from the Isis. By 1956 O.U.&C.S.R.C. operated only on a social basis; its demise was also blamed on the rise of 'big money' at the Cowley factories. In particular the quality and range of the social facilities at the Morris works, which were available to family members of workers, had the effect of drawing brothers and friends from the river and cricket pitch.

In 1973 the M.C.B.C. crew which had taken the Headship of Summer Eights twenty years earlier, had a reunion dinner in the New Room. Bill Jarvis baked and decorated a commemorative cake. In 1993, and now fifteen years into retirement, he joined them as a guest for their fortieth anniversary dinner, wearing with pride his blue O.U.&C.S.R.C. blazer.

## Wins in The Clinker Fours

1886: Bow: G. Medcraft, 2: W. Williams, 3: J. Shillingford,
   Stroke: E. Hawtin, Cox: E. Birmingham.

1924: Bow: J.R. Ing, 2: E. Dyer, 3: S.W. Cleverly,
   Stroke: W. Jeffs, Cox: G. Hawley.

1925: Bow: W.A. Spindler, 2: E.A. Dyer, 3: J.R. Ing,
   Stroke: S.W. Cleverly, Cox: W.H. Spindler.

1927: Bow: W.A. Spindler, 2: E.A. Dyer, 3: J.E. Kirkby,
   Stroke: S.W. Cleverly, Cox: S. Robinson.

1928: as 1927 but Coxswain changed to P. Wright.

1930: Bow: W.A. Spindler, 2: R.G. Francis, 3: J. Davie,
   Stroke: S.W. Cleverly, Cox: P. Wright.

1946: Bow: D. Gray, 2: T.G. Charlett, 3: B. Castle,
   Stroke: W. Jarvis, Cox: D. Brookes.

(1947 river flooded, no racing)

1948: as 1946 but Bow changed to G. Willis.

1949: as 1948.

1951: Bow: W. J. Pacey, 2: D. Cozier, 3: R. Feary,
   Stroke: D. Bestley, Cox: A. Lyford (Keble).

1955: University College and Magdalen composite, Bow: R. Webster (Magdalen).

## Wins in The Challenge Pairs

1927: Bow: J.E. Kirby, Str: S.W. Cleverly, Cox: S. Robinson.

1928: as 1927 but coxswain: P Wright.

1946: Bow: B. Castle, Str: W. Jarvis, Cox: D. Brookes.

## Wins in The Challenge Whiffs

1927: E.A. Dyer

1928: E.A. Dyer; spare man: J. Ing.

[1] President's Notebook, Magdalen College Archive PR/2/21
[2] Oxfordshire County Record Office Ox CRO O1/MS/2
[3] William Jarvis, 'Magdalen Memories I', Magdalen College Record 1991

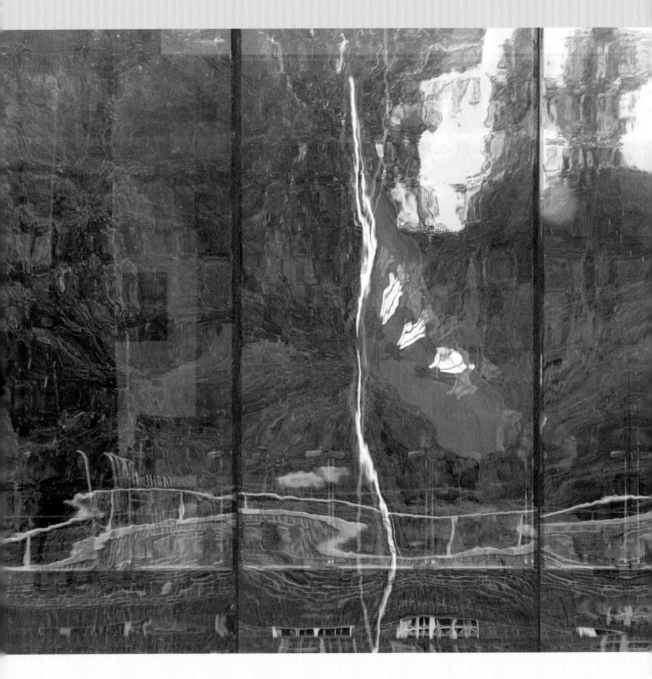

# 14

# Aristotle on Rowing

A.D. Godley was a Fellow of Magdalen from 1883 to 1912 when he was elected to an Honorary Fellowship; he was a classical scholar and author of humorous poems. From 1910 to 1920 he held the post of University Orator; he was awarded an honorary D.Litt in 1919. One of his publications, *Reliquiae*, was a collection of poems and other works some of which had appeared either in the *Oxford Magazine* or the *Classical Review*. One piece, that appeared in Oxford xxii, volume xvi, 1897-8, page 374 on 25th May, was a light-hearted take on rowing in the style of the philosopher Aristotle's writings, particularly on his works *Nicomachean Ethics*, *Physics* and *Metaphysics*, and had references to Aristophanes' comedy *Knights*. Thus Alfred Godley's title was '*Aristotle on the Eights*'. *Reliquiae* was edited by C.R.L. Fletcher who had been an undergraduate at Magdalen 1876-1881; he was a contemporary of Godley who was an undergraduate at Balliol. Charles Fletcher was subsequently a Fellow of All Souls College and later of Magdalen. Fletcher was a keen oarsman and won the O.U.B.C. Fours in 1878 and 1880 and the Pairs in 1879; he therefore doubtless had a particular affinity for this piece. He was in the bow seat of the 1879 Eight and rowed in that crew in the Ladies' Plate at Henley that year and in the four derived from it which competed in the Visitors' Challenge Cup. There is no record of Godley having rowed during his time at Magdalen, but he may have done. At the time this piece was published in 1898 the Boat Club was making no particular mark on the river: it was two years since they were last Head.

## Aristotle on the Eights

'Every Fellow and every undergraduate, and in the same way every Proctor and Vice-Chancellor, aims at the good. But it is a question whether rowing be a good in itself and apart from its accidents, such as breaking of stretchers and the like. In the first place, then, they endure pain because of what I have elsewhere called ἡ ὑποκειμένη ὕλη: [the underlying matter] and this is that to which Aristophanes refers when he speaks in the *Knights* of those who fought at Salamis. Secondly, if contemplation be the chief good, no one rows for the sake of contemplation: for he goes rather in a punt, where one may slumber though life, having virtue. But the rower is not allowed to contemplate, at least the things which are out-

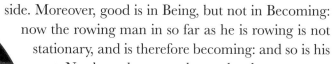

side. Moreover, good is in Being, but not in Becoming: now the rowing man in so far as he is rowing is not stationary, and is therefore becoming: and so is his art. Not but what even those who do not row, at least as is necessary, are also not stationary: but the cause is outside themselves: according to the words of Telemachus in the *Odyssey*,

*I will go as a passenger.*

But some way that Being in a boat is not Becoming, but the reverse: and perhaps it is, relatively. Again, to the philosopher the good is an end, and not a beginning: but the man in a boat aims at the Beginning rather than the end: and this is absurd. Again, the magnanimous man does not seem to be such an one as to row, except slowly and solemnly, and being bumped: which indeed will perhaps deprive him of magnanimity: for he cannot be the object of compassion. Perhaps it is here as with bicycling, of which one of the cyclic poets says,

*No Megalopsyke*
*Would ride on a Bike*

except provided sufficiently with externals, such as a tall hat. Now the rowing man is not sufficiently provided with externals.

There being also an art of steering, and it being acknowledged that the work of the steersman is to steer and not to row, he will aim generally at the middle, being a mean: yet the middle of the stream is not always a good absolutely, nor yet for him. For with regard to the For Which it is sometimes a defect. There are also many topics of persuasion which he may employ in addressing his crew, such as recollections of ancestors and the like; or he may recall the saying of Odysseus,

*Endure, my heart: yet worse thou hast endured.*

as for instance, when they were sandwich boat in the Torpids. But to go through the ship encouraging each man by name belongs rather to the rash man than to the truly courageous. And above all things it is necessary that he should remember what Plato says in the *Gorgias* about the steersman, that he is not proud, because he does not really know which of his crew he has benefited and which he has injured by not allowing them to be bumped, and that they are in all probability no better with regard to virtue when he lands them

A.D. Godley

than when he first set sail. Concerning the coxswain let so much have been said.

Next to this it would seem to be necessary to discuss the question whether the spectator is a good: but it is difficult: for the fact that the Relative is Absolute throws everything into confusion. This then we will leave for the present, and say concerning number and entertainment of kinsfolk that it is better here also to preserve the mean: for to have no people up is perhaps like Diogenes, but to have too many recalls that which was said of Danaus when he went to the Olympic Games with his daughters, himself the fifty-first. Also it is truly observed, that the man who put ten cousins into one Canadian canoe was as justly blamed as he was who hired the University barge for the entertainment of one uncle. Yet it is a difficulty,

*Endure, my heart: yet worse thou hast endured.* as for instance, when they were sandwich boat in the Torpids.

whether or not at these times a man is responsible for his actions: for at any rate they say things to their teachers for the sake of their relations, which no one would maintain unless he were defending a paradox: as for instance, that poetry is more philosophic than history: or, that no one expects probability from a mathematical lecturer: or, that young men are not yet fit to hear Moral Philosophy. Now if this were said for the sake of pleasure, it would be blameworthy: but as it is, all these things will probably come under the head of the Involuntary, or Mixed. And the same applies also to many things which are drunk.'

ἡ ὑποκειμένη ὕλη: the underlying matter (a technical term in the *Physics* and *Metaphysics*), here referring to the rower's bottom; in Aristophanes' *Knights* the Sausage-Seller gives Demos a cushion. Demos: the people or commons of an ancient Greek state, especially a democratic state such as Athens; hence the populace, the common people: he is throughout personified as in this comedy by an old man. The Battle of Salamis was a decisive naval battle between the Greek city-states and Persia in 480 B.C., in which the Persians failed to conquer the Peloponnese. Oscar Wilde made connections

The View from the Magdalen
Boathouse

Left: The O.U.B.C. Boathouse
in 1953, destroyed by fire 1999

Inset: The University College
Boathouse 2008

between the Greeks' style of rowing at Salamis and his own technique (see Chapter 2).

**Gorgias**: is an important Socratic Dialogue in which Plato sets the rhetorician, whose specialty is persuasion, in opposition to the philosopher, whose specialty is dissuasion, or refutation.

**Diogenes**: a Greek Philosopher, born in Sinope around 412 B.C. and known as 'The Cynic'.

**Danaus**: a Greek mythological character married to Pieria with whom he had fifty daughters.

In the opening sentences  is following *Aristotle's Nicomachean* Ethics 'every art and every enquiry, and in the same way every action and every choice, is thought to aim at some good; and for this reason the good has rightly been declared to be that at which all things aim'. He distinguishes things good in themselves from things that are good in a derivative way: in the language of the *Metaphysics* this could be, at least roughly, equated with things essentially good and things accidentally good: in the case of things accidentally good their goodness would be one of their accidents, i.e. non-essential properties.

Aristotle argues that contemplation is the chief good. The argument for this is that goodness must be self-sufficient and lacking in nothing, and Aristotle recognizes that a life of pure contemplation would be too high for a man, being properly the life of the gods. God, the prime mover, is himself unmoved and incapable of change (i.e. of becoming); he is therefore pure Being. When anything changes there must be a cause for the change, and in a sense this cause must lie outside itself and ultimately in the unmoved mover. However in another and more familiar sense, considering human action, we can say that if an action is voluntary the cause of the action is in the agent. But of course Godley isn't implying that those who don't row as much as they should are not acting voluntary, just that they are being carried along. Virtue, according to Aristotle, lies in feeling and acting in accordance with a mean, but not a mean absolutely (as 6 is the arithmetical mean between 2 and 10) but a mean relative to the agent and the circumstances. Those who do not hit the mean may err on the side of excess or of defect. Thus for courage the excess is over-boldness and the defect cowardice; for magnanimity the excess is vanity, the defect undue humility. The reference to 'the fact that the Relative is Absolute' is not to Aristotle but may be a light nod at Francis Bradley's views on truth. Bradley was a Fellow of Merton College and fashionable at the time Godley was writing. The examples in the last paragraph vaguely recall some of Aristotle's examples, which often have to do with the Olympic Games. Aristotle held that young men are not yet fit to hear Moral Philosophy. Mixed actions are actions that the agent would not normally do but does under force of circumstance: they 'are voluntary, but in the abstract perhaps involuntary; for no one would choose any such act in itself'.

It may be that Oscar Wilde's observation on rowing is the most succinct philosophical point and perhaps the one many oarsmen and women contemplate, sometimes without even realising it, on cold winter outings in particular: 'I don't see the use of going down backwards to Iffley every evening'.

MAGDALEN COLLEGE
BOAT CLUB
—
CREWS AND BLUES

# Appendices

# Captains of Boats

| | | | |
|---|---|---|---|
| 1859 | T H T Hopkins | 1896/97 | H Graham |
| 1859/60 | G Norsworthy | 1897/98 | C D Burnell |
| 1860/61 | T H T Hopkins | 1898/99 | H G Gold |
| 1861/62 | G Norsworthy | 1899/00 | C P Rowley |
| 1862/63 | T H T Hopkins | 1900/01 | Hon H E S Lambart |
| 1863/64 | E B Michell | 1901/02 | H H Dutton |
| 1864/65 | M G Knight | 1902/03 | C A Willis |
| 1865/66 | no eights entered | 1903/04 | V Fleming |
| 1866/67 | M G Knight | 1904/05 | J H Morrell |
| 1867/68 | T H T Hopkins | 1905/06 | L R A Gatehouse |
| 1868/69 | W A Clarke | 1906/07 | C L Garton |
| 1869/70 | W A Clarke | 1907/08 | E H L Southwell (MT & HT), |
| 1870/71 | A du B Hill | | A G Kirby (TT) |
| 1871/72 | A du B Hill | 1908/09 | J A Gillan |
| 1872/73 | A du B Hill | 1909/10 | R E Burgess |
| 1873/74 | H J Blagrove | 1910/11 | A S Garton |
| 1874/75 | S T H Burne | 1911/12 | E J H V Millington-Drake |
| 1875/76 | J Moore | 1912/13 | W L Vince |
| 1876/77 | J Moore | 1913/14 | E R Burgess |
| 1877/78 | F P Bulley | | |
| 1878/79 | F P Bulley | | |
| 1879/80 | A H Higgins | 1919/20 | S Earl |
| 1880/81 | A H Higgins | 1920/21 | S Earl |
| 1881/82 | A H Higgins | 1921/22 | G O Nickalls |
| 1882/83 | A H Higgins | 1922/23 | Hon W B Lewis (later Lord Merthyr) |
| 1883/84 | W S Unwin | 1923/24 | P C Girdlestone |
| 1884/85 | H Girdlestone | 1924/25 | C Horsfall |
| 1885/86 | H Girdlestone | 1925/26 | G Jansen |
| 1886/87 | J H W Pilcher | 1926/27 | P Johnson |
| 1887/88 | A C Maclachlan | 1927/28 | M C Graham |
| 1888/89 | G Nickalls | 1928/29 | J M Macdonald |
| 1889/90 | A P Parker (MT), | 1929/30 | A D Dodds-Parker |
| | A Inman (HT &TT) | 1930/31 | T F Whitley |
| 1890/91 | R P P Rowe | 1931/32 | T E E Warren-Swettenham |
| 1891/92 | A H P Clarke | 1932/33 | P G Hewison |
| 1892/93 | V Nickalls | 1933/34 | R F G Sarell |
| 1893/94 | H B Cotton | 1934/35 | M J Morris |
| 1894/95 | H B Cotton | 1935/36 | J D Sturrock |
| 1895/96 | E C Sherwood | 1936/37 | W L Baillieu |

*In the period before 1887 there is no record of the officers but it was usual for the stroke to assume the captaincy. Where there is no record the name of the stroke man has been put in italics.*

| | | | |
|---|---|---|---|
| 1937/38 | J L Garton | 1979/80 | G P Robbins |
| 1938/39 | R D Burnell | 1980/81 | C E G Cozens |
| 1939/40 | R Somervell & L G Thirkell | 1981/82 | G W Philipps (later Lord Milford) |
| 1940/41 | J R A Brocklebank | 1982/83 | D H R Matthews & L E Foyster |
| 1941/42 | G G Freeman | 1983/84 | J E M Cross & J L Brod |
| 1942/43 | L H Truelove | 1984/85 | J L Brod & M C Hughes |
| 1943/44 | D G Jamison | 1985/86 | P N E Bradbury |
| 1944/45 | N K G Rosser | 1986/88 | R G Hitchcock |
| 1945/46 | D G R Campbell | 1987/88 | M J Robinson |
| 1946/47 | J R W Gleave & E Gutt | 1988/89 | N J H Batchelor |
| 1947/48 | R J D McC Kinsman | 1989/90 | S J R Cass |
| 1948/49 | J M G Andrews | 1990/91 | S A Kenyon |
| | & A J McM Cavenagh | 1991/92 | B J A Dalton |
| 1949/50 | A J McM Cavenagh | 1992/93 | D A Valder |
| 1950/51 | J M Clay | 1993/94 | P A Henry |
| 1951/52 | T C Moon & D G Penington | 1994/95 | C R B Day |
| 1952/53 | P G P D Fullerton | 1995/96 | F Kruse-Fautsch |
| 1953/54 | H B Holt | 1996/97 | M Jones |
| 1954/55 | D P Wells | 1997/98 | A J Loveridge |
| 1955/56 | I R Anderson | 1998/99 | B M Altenburg |
| 1956/57 | M T Day | 1999/00 | M E Brelen |
| 1957/58 | R W Snow | 2000/01 | A H M Loveridge |
| 1958/59 | A T Lindsay & M P S Barton | 2001/02 | H J U Ashton |
| 1959/60 | I A K Baillieu & G R Pickett | 2002/03 | C A H Ogilvie |
| 1960/61 | K H Wells | 2003/04 | R J Mawdsley |
| 1961/62 | Hon R W Lewis | 2004/05 | A K Allouni |
| 1962/63 | H R Gillespie | 2005/06 | R D Johnson |
| 1963/64 | H R Gillespie | 2006/07 | J H Northern |
| 1964/65 | R A D Freeman | 2007/08 | M H Haden |
| 1965/66 | R H Vickers | 2008/09 | J A Abdalla |
| 1966/67 | P D Dodds-Parker | | |
| | & N D V Darlington | | |
| 1967/68 | P H C T Isolani-Smyth | | |
| 1968/69 | M A Stocking & D J Saunders | | |
| 1969/70 | D D Rendel | | |
| 1970/71 | A G Simpson | | |
| 1971/72 | J W R Goulding | | |
| 1972/73 | T S Bunch | | |
| 1973/74 | J M H Jackson | | |
| 1974/75 | D H Craig | | |
| 1975/76 | R A Scott & J A Sabine | | |
| 1976/77 | A E Weld Forester & C S Chubb | | |
| 1977/78 | M R Mussared | | |
| 1978/79 | J P P Baker | | |

# Captains of Boats (continued)

| Women's Captains | | Men's Captains |
|---|---|---|
| 1980/81 | Shelagh Scarth | |
| 1981/82 | Dominique Jackson | |
| 1982/83 | Emma Burnett & Wendy Bromidge | |
| 1983/84 | Alison Bonner & Eve Kemsley | |
| 1984/85 | Carol Giblin | |
| 1985/86 | Carol Giblin | |
| 1986/88 | Jo Spreadbury | |
| 1987/88 | Laura Buckley | |
| 1988/89 | Stephanie Panting | |
| 1989/90 | Lindsay Hawarden | |
| 1990/91 | Sharon Heath | |
| 1991/92 | Helena Cook | |
| 1992/93 | Jo Walker | |
| 1993/94 | Jo Dicks | |
| 1994/95 | Ruth Dooley (MT & HT), Shelley Wilson-Webb (TT) | |
| 1995/96 | Claire Murakami | |
| 1996/97 | Jenny Cooper | |
| 1997/98 | Sophia Turner | |
| 1998/99 | Joanne Telford & Mark Carter | |
| 1999/00 | Becky Hastings | |
| 2000/01 | Katharine Radice | |
| 2001/02 | Nicola Thompson | |
| 2002/03 | Christopher Kimber | D R W Payne |
| 2003/04 | Hannah Felgate | |
| 2004/05 | Karlee Silver | D L Cox |
| 2005/06 | Lucy Miller | S C R Dixon |
| 2006/07 | Lauren Adair | L J A Rooney |
| 2007/08 | Chloe Strevens | |
| 2008/09 | Hannah Caldwell | J H Northern |

# The Roll of those who have raced against Cambridge

## Blues & *Isis*

*Note: Owing to incomplete records before the start of the Reserves race in 1965 only those who are recorded as having raced for Isis against Goldie are listed here.*

|  | | | | | | |
|------|---|---|---|---|---|---|
| 1836 | T Harris | | | | | |
| 1858 | W G G Austin | | | | | |
| 1860 | G Norsworthy | | | | | |
| 1872 | C C Knollys | A W Nicholson | | | | |
| 1873 | C C Knollys | A W Nicholson | | | | |
| 1874 | A W Nicholson | | | | | |
| 1877 | H Pelham | | | | | |
| 1878 | H Pelham | | | | | |
| 1879 | J H T Wharton | | | | | |
| 1880 | J H T Wharton | | | | | |
| 1881 | J H T Wharton | | | | | |
| 1882 | A H Higgins | | | | | |
| 1885 | W S Unwin | H Girdlestone | | | | |
| 1886 | W S Unwin | H Girdlestone | | | | |
| 1887 | G Nickalls | | | | | |
| 1888 | G Nickalls | A P Parker | | | | |
| 1889 | G Nickalls | R P P Rowe | | | | |
| 1890 | G Nickalls | R P P Rowe | | | | |
| 1891 | G Nickalls | R P P Rowe | V Nickalls | W M Poole | | |
| 1892 | R P P Rowe | V Nickalls | H B Cotton | | | |
| 1893 | V Nickalls | H B Cotton | M C Pilkington | | | |
| 1894 | H B Cotton | M C Pilkington | E G Tew | | | |
| 1895 | H B Cotton | M C Pilkington | C D Burnell | | | |
| 1896 | E C Sherwood | C D Burnell | R Carr | H G Gold | | |
| 1897 | C D Burnell | R Carr | H G Gold | | | |
| 1898 | C D Burnell | R Carr | H G Gold | | | |
| 1899 | H G Gold | G S Maclagan | | | | |
| 1900 | H H Dutton | C P Rowley | G S Maclagan | | | |
| 1901 | G S Maclagan | | | | | |
| 1902 | G S Maclagan | | | | | |
| 1903 | C A Willis | | | | | |
| 1906 | A G Kirby | | | | | |
| 1907 | A G Kirby | E H L Southwell | J A Gillan | A W F Donkin | | |
| 1908 | Hon R P Stanhope | C R Cudmore | E H L Southwell | A W F Donkin | A G Kirby | |
| 1909 | C R Cudmore | A S Garton | D Mackinnon | J A Gillian | A G Kirby | A W F Donkin |
| 1910 | D Mackinnon | A S Garton | P Fleming | A W F Donkin | | |
| 1911 | L G Wormald | R E Burgess | E J H V Millington-Drake | D Mackinnon | A S Garton | H B Wells |
| 1912 | L G Wormald | E D Horsfall | H B Wells | | | |
| 1913 | L G Wormald | R E Burgess | C L Baillieu | E D Horsfall | H B Wells | |

| 1914 | E D Horsfall | H B Wells | | |
|------|--------------|-----------|---|---|
| 1920 | S Earl | A T M Durand | W E C James | W H Porritt |
| 1921 | S Earl | W E C James | R S C Lucas | G O Nickalls | W H Porritt |
| 1922 | S Earl | G O Nickalls | W H Porritt | |
| 1923 | G O Nickalls | G D Clapperton | | |
| 1924 | G D Clapperton | | | |
| 1927 | P Johnson | | | |
| 1928 | M C Graham | | | |
| 1929 | J M Macdonald | J A Ingles | | |
| 1933 | C Komarakul Na Nagara | | | |
| 1936 | J D Sturrock | | | |
| 1937 | R R Stewart | J D Sturrock | | |
| 1938 | J L Garton | R R Stewart | H A W Forbes | |
| 1939 | J L Garton | R R Stewart | R D Burnell | H A W Forbes |
| 1946 | J R W Gleave | R Ebsworth Snow | | |
| 1947 | D G Jamison | J R W Gleave | | |
| 1948 | J R W Gleave | | | |
| 1949 | A J M Cavenagh | J M Clay | | |
| 1950 | H J Renton | J M Clay | A J M Cavenagh | |
| 1951 | H J Renton | | | |
| 1954 | J A Gobbo | | | |
| 1955 | J A Gobbo | D P Wells | | |
| 1959 | A T Lindsay | D C Rutherford | | |
| 1960 | A T Lindsay | D C Rutherford | | |
| 1962 | P C D Burnell | | | |
| 1966 | R A D Freeman | | | |
| 1971 | | | *D D Rendel* | |
| 1972 | M R Magarey | | | |
| 1973 | M R Magarey | | | |
| 1974 | D D Rendel | | | |
| 1975 | | | *D H Craig* | |
| 1979 | | | *T J Carpenter* | |
| 1980 | M D Andrews | | | |
| 1981 | M D Andrews | | *S G Potts* | *H E Clay* |
| 1982 | H E Clay | | | |
| 1983 | H E Clay | W J Lang | | |
| 1984 | W J Lang | S R Lesser | | |
| 1985 | W J Lang | S R Lesser | | |
| 1989 | | | *C W Lewis* | |
| 1990 | | | *C W Lewis* | |
| 1995 | | | *J S Cashmore* | |
| 1996 | | | *T N Flemming* | *D P Forward* |
| 1997 | | | *T N Flemming* | *D P Forward* |
| 2002 | | | *H J R Morris* | |
| 2003 | H J R Morris | | *S G Parker* | *M Daggett* |
| 2004 | H J R Morris | | *S G Parker* | |
| 2005 | | | *H J R Morris* | |
| 2006 | | | *P Killicoat* | |

> *Note: Owing to incomplete records before the start of the Reserves race in 1965 only those who are recorded as having raced for Isis against Goldie are listed here.*

# The Roll of those who have raced against Cambridge

## Women's Blues & *Osiris* *

| | | | | |
|---|---|---|---|---|
| 1980 | Shelagh Scarth | | | |
| 1984 | Alison Bonner | | | |
| 1986 | Alison Bonner | | | |
| 1996 | Denny Levett | | | |
| 1997 | | *Diana Sabot* | *Lisa Walker* | |
| 1998 | Jacqui Petts | *Janet Lucke* | *Lisa Walker* | |
| 1999 | Joanne Telford | | | |
| 2001 | | *Joanne Telford* | | |
| 2002 | Joanne Telford | | | |
| 2003 | Joanne Telford | Karlee Silver | | |
| 2004 | Nicola Fawcett | | | |
| 2005 | | *Marianne Perrott* | *Nicola Fawcett* | *Deborah Turner* |
| 2006 | | *Rose Bosnell* | *Marianne Perrott* | |
| 2007 | Rose Bosnell | Deborah Turner | | |
| 2008 | | *Rose Bosnell* | | |

## Lightweight Men & *Nephthys*

| | | | |
|---|---|---|---|
| 1977 | J P P Baker | | |
| 1979 | F H R Fleming | R C Thomas | J P P Baker |
| 1991 | S A Kenyon | | |
| 1992 | S D Grant | | |
| 1996 | P L Bollyky | | |
| 2001 | N McSloy | | |
| 2002 | E S Davis | E W H Biden | |
| 2003 | E S Davis | E W H Biden | |
| 2004 | E S Davis | *J R Strong* | |
| 2006 | G M Jones | *J J Solly* | *A C Nelson* |
| 2007 | J J Solly | L J A Rooney | |
| 2008 | B H Harrop-Griffiths | | |

## Lightweight Women

| | | | |
|---|---|---|---|
| 1990 | Victoria Wild | | |
| 1992 | Viva Bartkus | Helena Cook | |
| 1999 | Ruth Dooley | Debbie Benson | Anna Herrhausen |
| 2000 | Becky Hastings | | |
| 2002 | Kelly Perkins | | |

## Leander Club Captains

| | |
|---|---|
| 1892 | G Nickalls |
| 1897 | G Nickalls |
| 1898-1900 | H G Gold |
| 1901-1902 | C D Burnell |
| 1909-1912 | A G Kirby |
| 1913-1914 | A S Garton |
| 1922 | E D Horsfall |
| 1923-1927 | G O Nickalls |
| 1937 | J D Sturrock |
| 1946 | G O Nickalls |
| 1948 | G O Nickalls |
| 1949-1950 | R D Burnell |
| 1957-1958 | A T M Durand |
| 1965 | R D Burnell |

## Presidents

| | |
|---|---|
| 1952-1956 | C D Burnell |
| 1962-1966 | G O Nickalls |
| 1980-1983 | J L Garton |
| 1988-1993 | R D Burnell |

## Hon Treasurers

| | |
|---|---|
| 1934-1948 | A S Garton |

## Hon Secretaries

| | |
|---|---|
| 1921 | E D Horsfall |
| 1946-1950 | G D Clapperton |
| 1951-1956 | A T M Durand |
| 1966-1967 | R D Burnell |

## Chairmen of the Amateur Rowing Association

| | |
|---|---|
| 1947-1952 | Sir Harcourt Gold |
| 1952-1968 | G O Nickalls |

## Presidents of the Amateur Rowing Association

| | |
|---|---|
| 1949-1952 | Sir Harcourt Gold |
| 1969-1976 | J L Garton |

## Hon. Secretaries of the Amateur Rowing Association

| | |
|---|---|
| 1910-1914 | G S Maclagan |
| 1924-1930 | H B Wells |
| 1948-1953 | G O Nickalls |

## Vincent's Club Presidents

| | |
|---|---|
| 1890 | G Nickalls |
| 1894 | H B Cotton |
| 1909 | A G Kirby |
| 1919 | E D Horsfall |
| 1947 | D G Jamison |

## Presidents of OUBC

| | |
|---|---|
| 1873-74 | A W Nicholson |
| 1889-90 | G Nickalls |
| 1891-92 | R P P Rowe |
| 1893-94 | H B Cotton |
| 1895 | M C Pilkington |
| 1898-99 | H G Gold |
| 1904 | C A Willis |
| 1907-09 | A G Kirby |
| 1909-10 | D Mackinnon |
| 1912-13 | L G Wormald |
| 1913-14 | E D Horsfall |
| 1920-21 | W E C James |
| 1922-23 | G O Nickalls |
| 1938-39 | J L Garton |
| 1946-47 | D G Jamison |
| 1954-55 | J A Gobbo |
| 1959-60 | D C Rutherford |

## Presidents of OUWBC

| | |
|---|---|
| 2004-05 | Nicola Fawcett |

## Presidents of OULRC

| | |
|---|---|
| 2002-03 | E W H Biden |
| 2008-09 | B H Harrop-Griffiths |

## Presidents of OUWLRC

| | |
|---|---|
| 1991-92 | Viva Bartkus |

## Stewards of Henley Royal Regatta

| | |
|---|---|
| 1909-1952 | H G Gold |
| 1914-1914 | G S Maclagan |
| 1919-1969 | C D Burnell |
| 1926-1948 | A S Garton |
| 1935-1973 | G O Nickalls |
| 1945-1966 | Sir Clive Baillieu |
| 1947-1973 | E D Horsfall |
| 1953-1971 | G D Clapperton |
| 1959-2002 | J L Garton |
| 1965-1995 | R D Burnell |

## Boatmen

| | |
|---|---|
| 1872-1911 | Richard Talboys |
| 1911-1936 | Jack May |
| 1936-1980 | Edgar Dickens |
| 1980- | Steve Gaisford |

| | 1880 | 1886 | 1888 |
|---|---|---|---|
| **Bow** | H W Boustead | W D Lindley | R duF Bryans |
| **2** | W E P Austin | H G O Kendall | R P P Rowe |
| **3** | G D Dakyns | A C Maclachlan | W G Young |
| **4** | A E Staniland | J B Lloyd | H G O Kendall |
| **5** | J E Ivor Yale | N C W Radcliffe | G Slade |
| **6** | A C Wells | G S Bazley | A P Parker |
| **7** | J H T Wharton | W S Unwin | G Nickalls |
| **Stroke** | A H Higgins* | H Girdlestone* | A C Maclachlan* |
| **Cox** | A E Norman | H E U Bull | J F R Stainer |
| | Bumped Balliol | Bumped Corpus Christi | Bumped New College |

| | 1892 | 1893 | 1894 |
|---|---|---|---|
| **Bow** | W M Poole | H B Cotton | P M Bowman |
| **2** | R S Medlicott | T Royden | G H Foster |
| **3** | T Royden | L L Dobson | E C Sherwood |
| **4** | G H Foster | G H Foster | L L Dobson |
| **5** | A H P Clarke* | E G Tew | E G Tew |
| **6** | V Nickalls | V Nickalls* | W M Poole |
| **7** | R P P Rowe | W M Poole | M C Pilkington |
| **Stroke** | H B Cotton | M C Pilkington | H B Cotton* |
| **Cox** | G B H Fell | G B H Fell | H C Middleton |
| | Bumped New College and Brasenose | Rowed Over Head | Rowed Over Head |

| | 1895 | 1900 | 1905 |
|---|---|---|---|
| **Bow** | P M Bowman | N G Frank | J D Stobart |
| **2** | J M Steward | H H Dutton | G C James |
| **3** | E C Sherwood | Lord Mahon | C L Garton |
| **4** | G H Foster | E D F Kelly | L R A Gatehouse |
| **5** | E G Tew | J M Blair | H F Macgeach |
| **6** | C D Burnell | C P Rowley* | C P Ackers |
| **7** | H Graham | M C Thornhill | J H Morrell* |
| **Stroke** | M C Pilkington | H G Gold | E H L Southwell |
| **Cox** | G B H Fell | G S Maclagan | A C Clarke |
| | Rowed Over Head | Bumped New College | Bumped New College |

| 1906 | 1910 | 1919 | 1920 |
|---|---|---|---|
| Hon R P Stanhope | M M Cudmore | H C Irvine | H C Irvine |
| C L Garton | L G Wormald | J C P Proby | J C P Proby |
| J A Gillan | E J H V Millington–Drake | S Earl* | G O Nickalls |
| J L Johnston | W D Nicholson | R S C Lucas | R S C Lucas |
| A G Kirby | D Mackinnon | F H Lovejoy | S Earl* |
| L R A Gatehouse* | A S Garton | A T M Durand | A T M Durand |
| C R Cudmore | R E Burgess* | W E C James | W E C James |
| E H L Southwell | P Fleming | E D Horsfall | Hon B L Bathurst |
| A C Clarke | A W F Donkin | W H Porritt | W H Porritt |
| | | | |
| Rowed Over Head | Bumped Christ Church | Bumped Christ Church and New College | Bumped Christ Church, Univ. and New College |

| 1923 | 1932 | 1941 (Joint Crew with New Coll) | 1953 |
|---|---|---|---|
| C Horsfall | R F G Sarell | L G Thirkell | P G P D Fullerton* |
| Hon B L Bathurst | P G Hewison | P A M Gell | A N Binder |
| G K Hampshire | P M Bristow | J R A Brocklebank* | R M Van Oss |
| J M Buckley | A Smithies | R Southey | J H Richards |
| G O Nickalls | F D Barmby | | L P Shurman |
| P C Girdlestone | A S Irvine | | D P Wells |
| Hon W B Lewis* | G F C Hawkins | | J A Gobbo |
| G W G Fox | J G Bond | | H B Holt |
| G D Clapperton | C Komarakul na Nagara | | R H Oake |
| | | | |
| Bumped New College | Bumped Univ. and Brasenose | War Time Bumps, bumped 'Trinity and Balliol' | Bumped New College, Merton and Balliol |

| 1954 | 2004 | 2005 | 2006 |
|---|---|---|---|
| G Sargood | R J Mawdsley* | S C R Dixon | L J A Rooney |
| J M Croome | L J A Rooney | R D Johnson | G M Jones |
| W B Patterson | D W Gregory | D L Cox* | S C R Dixon |
| Q S Earl | R D Johnson | P Killicoat | R D Johnson* |
| R M Van Oss | D L Cox | S G Parker | S G Parker |
| D P Wells | H J R Morris | E M Archibald | E M Archibald |
| J A Gobbo | S G Parker | L J A Rooney | P Killicoat |
| H B Holt* | E S Davis | H J R Morris | E S Davis |
| J D Feltham | H A Chapman | A J Stewart | A J Stewart |
| | | | |
| Rowed Over Head | Bumped Exeter, Pembroke and Oriel | Rowed Over Head | Rowed Over Head |

| | 2007 |
|---|---|
| **Bow** | M H Haden |
| **2** | A T J Shutter |
| **3** | M M Werley |
| **4** | A W J Cameron |
| **5** | H J Northern* |
| **6** | M Schwarzlander |
| **7** | L J A Rooney |
| **Stroke** | B H Harrop-Grifiths |
| **Cox** | E C Mayhew |

Rowed Over Head

**HEAD OF THE RIVER:** *Torpids*

| | 1912 | 1913 | 1923 |
|---|---|---|---|
| **Bow** | J B Cavenagh | W L Vince* | C Horsfall |
| **2** | L L B Angas | J B Scott | E C Garton |
| **3** | R Congreve-Pridgeon | R Congreve-Pridgeon | G K Hampshire |
| **4** | G H Leigh | M C Blake | A K Warren |
| **5** | A T A Ritchie | W L F Browne | F R Scott |
| **6** | M K Johnson | L L B Angas | J M Buckley |
| **7** | A C Hobson | J B Cavenagh | Hon W B Lewis* |
| **Stroke** | F H B Sandford | K J Campbell | G W G Fox |
| **Cox** | J D B Fergusson | M E Park | A W Whitfield |
| | Bumped Trinity, Christ Church, New College and Balliol | Rowed Over Head | Bumped New College |

| | 1932 | 1933 | 1934 |
|---|---|---|---|
| **Bow** | C F G Sarell | R W J Fletcher-Campbell | L H P van der Goes |
| **2** | W J Fletcher-Campbell | W Whipple | A K Sibley |
| **3** | W McK Wright | J M McC Fisher | W J Fletcher-Campbell |
| **4** | W Hughes | C A Macdonald | J H Townsend |
| **5** | G A Lincoln | R D Black | M J Morris |
| **6** | A S Irvine | L B Sackville-West | G H D Greene |
| **7** | G F C Hawkins | T T Irvine | B Alexander |
| **Stroke** | J G Bond | W Hughes | J D Sturrock |
| **Cox** | C Komarakul Na Nagara | H J Haldane | J A Watt |

*(This crew also won 1st Clinker pennant in the HORR)

*Bumped Wadham and Corpus Christi

Rowed Over Head

Rowed Over Head

|  | 1936 | 1937 | 2008 |
|---|---|---|---|
| **Bow** | F M Macdonald | S F M Macdonald | G I van Boxel |
| **2** | A M Webb | M Wagner | S J Wall |
| **3** | H Betteridge | J C Long | I A Hunyor |
| **4** | W L Baillieu | F A Willan | B H van Duren |
| **5** | P B Spilsbury | G Milroy | H J Northern |
| **6** | F A Willan | A R Smith | A Janssen |
| **7** | A R Jackson | H Betteridge | M H Haden* |
| **Stroke** | J L Garton | T L Page | J A B Abdalla |
| **Cox** | F C Williams | P H Philip | C J S Young |
|  |  |  |  |
|  | Bumped St Edmund Hall, Balliol and New College | Rowed Over Head | Bumped Oriel |

## *Winners of the OUBC Fours*

|  | 1878 | 1880 | 1884 |
|---|---|---|---|
| **Bow** | C R L Fletcher | C R L Fletcher (steers) | N C W Radcliffe (steers) |
| **2** | A C Wells | W E P Austin | G S Bazley |
| **3** | J H T Wharton (steers) | A E Staniland | H Girdlestone |
| **Stroke** | F P Bulley | A H Higgins | W S Unwin |
|  |  |  |  |
|  | Beat Univ. by 3 sec., time 7 min. 30sec | Beat Brasenose 'Easily' | Beat New College by 3 lengths |

|  | 1885 | 1886 | 1889 |
|---|---|---|---|
| **Bow** | W S Unwin (steers) | W D Lindley (steers) | A W Mahaffy |
| **2** | G S Bazley | G Nickalls | A P Parker |
| **3** | N C W Radcliffe | N C W Radcliffe | R P P Rowe |
| **Stroke** | H Girdlestone | A C Maclachlan | G Nickalls (steers) |
|  |  |  |  |
|  | Beat New Collge by 'about a length' | Beat New Collge 'Not Rowed Out' | Beat Brasenose by a length, 6 min.32 sec. |

|  | 1893 | 1899 | 1905 |
|---|---|---|---|
| **Bow** | H B Cotton (steers) | Hon H E S S Lambart | C R Garton (steers) |
| **2** | L L Dobson | H H Dutton | L R A Gatehouse |
| **3** | M C Pilkington | M C McC Thornhill | A G Kirby |
| **Stroke** | W M Poole | C P Rowley (steers) | E H L Southwell |
|  |  |  |  |
|  | Beat Brasenose by a length | Beat Corpus Christi |  |

# *Winners of the OUBC Fours (continued)*

| | 1906 (2nd boat) | 1907 | 1908 |
|---|---|---|---|
| **Bow** | Hon R P Stanhope (steers) | R Somers-Smith (steers) | W G Forest |
| **2** | C R Cudmore | J A Gillan | J A Gillan |
| **3** | J A Gillan | A G Kirby | A G Kirby |
| **Stroke** | J R Somers-Smith | E H L Southwell | J R Somers-Smith (steers) |

| | 1909 | 1910 | 1912 |
|---|---|---|---|
| **Bow** | E J H V Millington-Drake (steers) | L G Wormald (steers) | E R Burgess |
| **2** | A S Garton | E J H V Millington-Drake | C L Baillieu |
| **3** | D Mackinnon | R E Burgess | L G Wormald (steers) |
| **Stroke** | P Fleming | A S Garton | E D Horsfall |
| | | Beat Trinity by 3/4 lengths | Beat Christ Church |

| | 1919 | 1920 | 1921 |
|---|---|---|---|
| **Bow** | S Earl (steers) | S Earl (steers) | P C Girdlestone |
| **2** | R S C Lucas | R S C Lucas | G O Nickalls (steers) |
| **3** | A T M Durand | W E C James | A T M Durand |
| **Stroke** | W E C James | G O Nickalls | M E Olmsted |

| | 1927 | 1938 | 1940) |
|---|---|---|---|
| **Bow** | M L Formby | J L Garton | L J Thirkell |
| **2** | J M Macdonald | H A W Forbes | P A M Gell |
| **3** | K N Irvine (steers) | R D Burnell (steers) | J R A Brocklebank |
| **Stroke** | M C Graham | R R Stewart | G R Holmes (steers) |

| | 1954 (dead heat) |
|---|---|
| **Bow** | R M Van Oss |
| **2** | T G M Buckley |
| **3** | J A Gobbo |
| **Stroke** | D P Wells (steers) |

# *Winners of the OUBC Pairs*

| | 1879 | 1880 | 1884 |
|---|---|---|---|
| **Bow** | C R L Fletcher | L R West (Ch Ch) | W S Unwin |
| **Stroke** | F P Bulley | A E Staniland | J Reade (Brasenose) |
| | 'Beat Hertford by about 2 lengths' | Beat Worcester by 3 sec | Beat Brasenose & Corpus 'Not Rowed Out' |

*Winners of the OUBC Pairs (continued)*

| | 1888 | 1889 | 1890 |
|---|---|---|---|
| **Bow** | G Nickalls | G Nickalls | Lord Ampthill (New Coll.) |
| **Stroke** | W F D Smith (New Coll.) | Lord Ampthill (New Coll.) | G Nickalls |
| | Beat Brasenose 'Easily' 7 min. 16 sec. | Beat Magdalen and Brasenose by 'about 40 yards', 7min. 37&3/5 sec. | Beat Brasenose and Christ Church by 4 feet |

| | 1891 | 1892 | 1893 |
|---|---|---|---|
| **Bow** | H B Cotton | V Nickalls | H L Puxley (Queen's) |
| **Stroke** | V Nickalls | W A L Fletcher (Ch Ch) | V Nickalls |
| | Beat Brasenose and Christ Church by 3 lengths | Beat Brasenose 'Not Rowed Out' 7 min. 25 sec. | Beat New College by 10 sec. |

| | 1897 | 1910 | 1911 |
|---|---|---|---|
| **Bow** | R Carr | A S Garton | A S Garton |
| **Stroke** | H G Gold | P Fleming | D Mackinnon |
| | Beat Univ. and Trinity | Beat New College and Christ Church | |

| | 1914 | 1920 | 1921 |
|---|---|---|---|
| **Bow** | | G O Nickalls (steers) | A T M Durand |
| **Stroke** | (no detail, except that bow man was from Magdalen) | R S C Lucas | S Earl (steers) |

| | 1922 | 1946 | 1950 |
|---|---|---|---|
| **Bow** | G O Nickalls (steers) | J R W Gleave | J M Clay |
| **Stroke** | M E Olmsted | R M A Bourne (New Coll.) | H J Renton |

| | 1953 | 1954 | 1959 |
|---|---|---|---|
| **Bow** | J A Gobbo | J A Gobbo | I L Elliott (Keble) |
| **Stroke** | D P Wells | D P Wells | D C Rutherford (steers) |

# Winners of the OUBC Pairs (continued)

|  | 1964 | 1965 | 1984 |
|---|---|---|---|
| **Bow** | C Freeman (Keble) | C Freeman (Keble) | M Taylor (New Coll.) |
| **Stroke** | R A D Freeman | R A D Freeman | J L Brod |

# Winners of the OUBC Double Sculls

|  | 1953 | 1960 | 1965 |
|---|---|---|---|
| **Bow** | P G P D Fullerton | P C D Burnell | C Freeman (Keble) |
| **Stroke** | A N Binder | R Howard (Ch Ch) | R A D Freeman |

# Winners of the OUBC Sculls

| 1846 | 1864 | 1872 | 1875 |
|---|---|---|---|
| E G Moon | E B Michell | C C Knollys | L C Cholmeley |
| Beat W Wilberforce, St Mary Hall on a foul | Beat C Y Fell, St John's, by 35 sec. | Beat J B Little, Christ Church 'Easily' | Beat A T Michell, Oriel by 4 sec. |

| 1883 | 1884 | 1885 | 1887 |
|---|---|---|---|
| E Staniland | W S Unwin | W S Unwin | G Nickalls |
| Beat E L Puxley, Brasenose by 3 lengths | Beat T A Brassey, Balliol by 2 lengths | Beat S R Fothergill, New College 'Easily' | Beat S R Fothergill, New College by 50 yards |

| 1891 | 1898 | 1920 | 1921 |
|---|---|---|---|
| V Nickalls | C D Burnell | S Earl | S Earl |
| Beat H S Hawes, Hertford by 2 lengths | Beat J A Tinné, Univ. by half a second | | |

| 1922 | 1934 | 1935 | 1940 |
|---|---|---|---|
| S Earl | J M McC Fisher | J D Sturrock | L G Thirkell |

| 1950 |
|---|
| H J Renton |

# *The Wingfield Sculls*

| 1866 | 1872 | 1884 | 1885 |
|------|------|------|------|
| E B Michell | C C Knollys | W S Unwin | W S Unwin |
| Won by 40 yards in 27 min. 36 sec. | Won by 300 yards in 27 min. 30 sec. | Won by 6 lengths in 24 min. 12 sec. | |

| 1887 | 1888 | 1889 | 1891 |
|------|------|------|------|
| G Nickalls | G Nickalls | G Nickalls | G Nickalls |
| Won by 35 sec. in 25 min. 23 sec. | Won by 10 lengths in 23 min. 36 sec. | Rowed Over | Rowed Over |

| 1892 | 1894 | 1895 | 1946 |
|------|------|------|------|
| V Nickalls | V Nickalls | V Nickalls | R D Burnell |
| by 3&1/2 length, 23 min. 40 sec | | Won in 25 min. 6 sec. | Won by 4 lengths in 22 min.46 sec. |

# Henley Royal Regatta

## The Diamond Challenge Sculls

| 1846 | 1865 | 1866 | 1872 |
|---|---|---|---|
| E G Moon | E B Michell | E B Michell | C C Knollys |
| Beat T H Fellows, Leander Club, 'Easily' | Beat C B Lawes, Third Trinity B C, by 4 lengths, 9 min. 11 sec. | Beat W B Woodgate, Kingston R C, by 2&1/2 lengths, 9 min. 55 sec. | Beat C H Lawton of York by '8 or 10 lengths', 10 min. 48 sec. |

| 1884 | 1885 | 1888 | 1889 |
|---|---|---|---|
| W S Unwin | W S Unwin | G Nickalls | G Nickalls |
| Beat R H Smith, Thames R C, by about a length, 9 min. 44 sec | Beat F I Pitman, Third Trinity B C, Easily, 9 min. 22 sec. | Beat W Sweetman, Ryde R C, Easily, 10 min. 23 sec | Beat C J Psotta, New York Athletic Club, by 100 yards, 8 min. 56 sec. |

| 1890 | 1891 | 1893 | |
|---|---|---|---|
| G Nickalls | V Nickalls | G Nickalls | |
| Beat G E B Kennedy, Kingston R C, 1/2 length, 8 min. 57.5 sec | Sculled Over, his brother having withdrawn | Beat G E B Kennedy, Kingston R C, by3 lengths, 9 min. 12 sec. | |

## The Silver Goblets and Nickalls' Challenge Cup

| | 1920 | 1922 | 1960 |
|---|---|---|---|
| Bow | G O Nickalls (steers) | G O Nickalls (steers) | I L Elliott (Keble) |
| Stroke | R S C Lucas | R S C Lucas | D C Rutherford (steers) |
| | Beat S I Fairbairn & B Logan, Thames R C 'Easily' in 8 min. 53 sec | Beat H E West & K Vernon, Thames R C 'Easily' in 9min. 19 sec. | Beat R J Nicholson & C L Marshall, Nottingham Britannia R C, by 2/3 of a length, 7min. 58sec. |

## The Wyfold Challenge Cup

| | 1907 |
|---|---|
| **Bow** | C R Cudmore |
| **2** | J A Gillan |
| **3** | D Mackinnon |
| **Stroke** | J R Somers-Smith (steers) |

Beat London R C 'by a long distance', 8 min 49 sec

## The Visitors' Challenge Cup

| | 1907 | 1923 | 1948 |
|---|---|---|---|
| **Bow** | C R Cudmore | C Horsfall (steers) | R J Kinsman (steers) |
| **2** | J A Gillan | E C Garton | J M G Andrews |
| **3** | D Mackinnon | G K Hampshire | J M Clay |
| **Stroke** | J R Somers-Smith (steers) | Hon B L Bathurst | A J M Cavenagh |
| | Beat First Trinity B C by 2&1/4 lengths, 8 min. 7 sec. | Beat Trinity College, Oxford by 1&3/4 length, 7min. 44 sec. | Beat New College by 1&1/2 lengths, 7min. 51 sec. |

| | 1953 |
|---|---|
| **Bow** | P G P D Fullerton (steers) |
| **2** | D P Wells |
| **3** | J A Gobbo |
| **Stroke** | J H Richards |

Beat King's College, Cambridge by 3&1/2 lengths, 7min. 29 sec.

## Grand Challenge Cup

| | 1910 | 1911 | 1920 | 1921 |
|---|---|---|---|---|
| **Bow** | M M Cudmore | Burgess | H C Irvine | H C Irvine |
| **2** | L G Wormald | C L Baillieu | Hon B L Bathurst | R Armstrong-Jones |
| **3** | E Millington-Drake | L G Wormald | S Earl | S Earl |
| **4** | W D Nicholson | J A Gillan | A T M Durand | A T M Durand |
| **5** | D Mackinnon | D Mackinnon | W E C James | W E C James |
| **6** | A S Garton | A S Garton | R S C Lucas | R S C Lucas |
| **7** | R E Burgess | A G Kirby | G O Nickalls | G O Nickalls |
| **Stroke** | P Fleming | P Fleming | E D Horsfall | E D Horsfall |
| **Cox** | A W F Donkin | H B Wells | W H Porritt | W H Porritt |
| | Beat Jesus College, Cambridge by 2 lengths, 7min. 19 sec.E R | Beat Jesus College, Cambridge by 2&1/4 lengths, 7min. 2 sec. | Beat Leander Club by 2 lengths, 7min. 24 sec. | Beat Jesus College, Cambridge by 1 length, 6min. 54 sec. |

# The Stewards' Challenge Cup

|  | 1893 | 1899 | 1907 |
|---|---|---|---|
| **Bow** | H B Cotton (steers) | M C McC Thornhill | Hon R P Stanhope |
| **2** | W M Poole | R Carr | E H L Southwell |
| **3** | V Nickalls | C D Burnell | A G Kirby |
| **Stroke** | G Nickalls | H G Gold (steers) | G Nickalls (steers) |
|  | Beat Thames R C by 3/4 length, 7min. 45 sec. | Beat Favorite Hammonia R C, Hamburg by 5 lengths, 7 min. 51 sec. | Beat Leander Club by 3 lengths in 8min. 42 sec. |

|  | 1908 | 1920 | 1921 |
|---|---|---|---|
| **Bow** | C R Cudmore | S. Earl (steers) | S. Earl (steers) |
| **2** | J A Gillan | A T M Durand | A T M Durand |
| **3** | D Mackinnon | W E C James | W E C James |
| **Stroke** | J R Somers-Smith (steers) | E D Horsfall | E D Horsfall |
|  | Beat London R C by 1&1/2 lengths, 7 min. 40 sec. | Beat Thames R C 'Easily', 8min. 41sec. | Beat Leander Club by 3 lengths, 7min. 32 sec. |

# The Ladies' Challenge Plate

|  | 1903 |  |
|---|---|---|
| **Bow** | J D Stobart |  |
| **2** | E L Coles |  |
| **3** | J H Morrell |  |
| **4** | C P Ackers |  |
| **5** | V Fleming |  |
| **6** | G C James |  |
| **7** | C A Willis | Beat Eton College by '3 feet |
| **Stroke** | H G StC Rose | over a length' in 7min. 33 |
| **Cox** | C E Seymour | sec. |

# Olympic Games Medals

| 1908 LONDON | 1912 STOKHOLM | 1920 ANTWERP |
|---|---|---|
| Fours (Gold) | Eights (Gold) | Eights (Silver) |
| C R Cudmore (bow) | E R Burgess (bow) | S Earl (3) |
| J A Gillan (2) | L G Wormald (3) | W E C James (5) |
| D Mackinnon (3) | E D Horsfall (4) | R S C Lucas (6) |
| J R Somers-Smith (stroke, steers) | J A Gillan (5) | G O Nickalls (7) |
| | A S Garton (6) | E D Horsfall (stroke) |
| Eights (Gold) | A G Kirby (7) | |
| G Nickalls (4) | P Fleming (stroke) | |
| C D Burnell (5) | H B Wells (cox) | |
| G S Maclagan (cox) | | |

| 1928 AMSTERDAM | 1936 BERLIN | 1948 LONDON |
|---|---|---|
| Eights (Silver) | Fours (Silver) | Double Sculls (Gold) |
| G O Nickalls (7) | J D Sturrock (stroke) | R D Burnell (stroke) |

# British Empire Games

| 1938 SYDNEY | 1950 AUKLAND |
|---|---|
| Eights (Gold) | Eights (Bronze) |
| J D Sturrock (6) | R D Burnell (5) (capt.) |

# FISA World Championships

| 1981 MUNICH |
|---|
| Eights (Silver) |
| M D Andrews (bow) |

# Glossary

This book will be read mainly by those who have been to Oxford or who enjoy and know the sport of rowing. Nonetheless many readers may not be familiar with all the terms and proper names; it is hoped this glossary will answer the immediate query raised behind such words and prevent the enquirer from being at sea in jargon.

**Blade(s)** the spoon of an oar, also the title given to the winning of an oar through achieving a bump on each day of Torpids or Summer Eights.

**Demyship** a Magdalen Scholarship. The title is derived from *demi-socii* or *half-fellows*. Magdalen's founder, William of Waynflete, originally provided them for the College. Recipients (known as Demies) are still admitted to the College's Foundation.

**Eights** apart from being the title for boats of eight oars, it is also the title for the bumps races held in fifth week of Trinity Term, the senior event of the inter-collegiate rowing calendar. Also known as Eights Week or Summer Eights.

**Head** a procession race in the form of a time trial, held during the autumn and winter months. Also the title for the crew that is fastest in its category at such an event. At Oxford (and Cambridge) the crew that is top of the first division in bumping races.

**Hilary Term** middle term of the year from January to March.

**The House** the name by which Christ Church is often known, from its Latin title, *Aedis Christi*, House of God.

**Isis** the name for the River Thames between Folly Bridge and Iffley Lock.

**Lit. Hum.** Literae Humaniores, the Oxford Classics degree also known as **'Greats'**.

**J.C.R.** Junior Common Room, the body of undergraduates in the College and the rooms they occupy for socialising.

**M.C.R.** Middle Common Room, the body of graduate students in the College and the rooms they occupy for socialising.

**Michaelmas Term** the first term of the academic year, from October to December.

**Mods.** Honour Moderations, the first year examinations (or in the case of Classics, second year), they are awarded in classifications of First, Second etc. Not all students take Mods, some take Prelims. Depending on the subject.

**Prelims.** Preliminary examinations are first year examinations and are not classified into Firsts, Seconds etc. These are only awarded on a Pass/Fail/Distinction basis.

**President** the Head of House of Magdalen, other colleges may use other titles such as Master, Warden or Provost.

**S.C.R.** The Senior Common Room, both the body of Fellows of a College and the rooms that body occupies for eating, socialising and entertaining.

**Schools** are the title given to final public examinations in Oxford, properly 'Final Honours Schools', the word is used here to indicate those rowing who are not participating in the full activities of the Club owing to the proximity of racing to the exams.

**Torpids** the Hilary Term inter collegiate bumps races. The name Torpids derives from the event's origins as a race for the second boats of the colleges, which were naturally slower than the first boats. Now for as many boats as a college wishes to put out.

**Trinity Term** the last term of the year, from April to June.

**Tubbed** the verb from **'Tub'** in the context of a **'Tub Pair'**, a wide stable boat used to teach two people the basics of rowing, usually steered by the person coaching. Largely out of fashion now.

## PUTNEY TO MORTLAKE

Also known as the Boat Race course and the Championship course, the stretch of the tideway between Putney and Mortlake is 4 miles 374 yards long, marked by a stone on the embankment at each end. The course is a huge S-bend. The Boat Race normally runs from Putney to Mortlake on the incoming tide, and the Head of the River Race normally runs from Mortlake to Putney on the outgoing tide. The key markers are the mile post (one mile above the Putney stone), Hammersmith bridge, Chiswick steps and Barnes bridge.

## ROWING INSTITUTIONS

ARA: the Amateur Rowing Association (1882) is the governing body of rowing for Great Britain and England. Scotland, Wales and Ireland have their own governing bodies.

FISA: the Fédération Internationale des Sociétés d'Aviron (1892) is the governing body for international rowing, and the oldest international sports federation. FISA events, including world championships and world cup regattas and regattas run under FISA rules such as the Olympic Games, use multi-lane courses of 2000 metres.

Olympic games: rowing is a founding sport of the modern Olympic games, first held in 1896.

World rowing championships: the world rowing championships began in 1893 as the European championships, and are run by FISA, the international rowing federation.

British Empire and Commonwealth games: rowing was an official sport in the Empire and Commonwealth games until 1986. Since then Commonwealth championships have been held during the same years as the Commonwealth games.

## CONVERSION TABLES

Imperial to metric

| 1 mile | 1760 yards | 1.6093 kilometres |
|---|---|---|
| 1 nautical mile | 6080 feet | 1.852 kilometres |
| 1 knot | 1 nautical mile per hour | 0.914 metres |
| 1 yard | 3 feet | 0.914 metres |
| 1 foot | 12 inches | 0.3046 metres |
| 1 inch | 2.54 centimetres | |

Metric to imperial

| 1 kilometre | 1000 metres | 0.62137 mile | 1093.6 yards |
|---|---|---|---|
| 1 metre | 100 centimetres | 1.0936 yards | 3.281 feet |
| 1 centimetre | 10 millimetres | 0.3937 inch | |

Weights

| 1 cwt | | 50.8 kilograms |
|---|---|---|
| 1 stone | 14 pounds (lb) | 6.3504 kilograms |
| 1 pound (lb) | 16 ounces (oz) | 0.4536 kilogrammes |
| 1 kilogramme | 2.20462 (lb) | |

Old money

| £1 | 20 shillings (s) | 240 pence (d) |
|---|---|---|
| 1 shilling (s) | | 12 pence (d) |
| 1 guinea | £1: 1s | 252 pence (d) |
| New £1 | 100 pence | |

## HENLEY ROYAL REGATTA

**Grand Challenge Cup** (1839): top ranking eight-oared open event.

**Ladies' Challenge Plate** (1845): second ranking eight-oared event, opened to clubs in 1985.

**Thames Challenge Cup** (1868): eight-oared event for club crews.

**Temple Challenge Cup** (1992): eight-oared event for student crews.

**Stewards' Challenge Cup** (1841): top ranking four-oared open event.

**Visitors' Challenge Cup** (1847): four-oared event with same qualification rules as Ladies' Plate, opened to clubs in 2001.

**Wyfold Challenge Cup** (1847): four-oared event from 1855; same qualification rules as the Thames Cup from 1996.

**Silver Goblets and Nickalls' Challenge Cup** (1845): open event for pair-oars.

**Diamond Challenge Sculls** (1844): open event for single sculls.

# Bibliography

## Magdalen College Boat Club

Captain's and Secretary's Books from 1887

Magdalen College Archive MC: O4 (Boat Club); MC: PR/2 (President's Notebooks); MS 1004, 1106 (M.C.B.C. material from various sources); MC: P2 (the Dodds-Parker papers); GPD/8 (the Porritt papers); GPD/20 Sully Unwin papers); GPD/24, GPD/38, GPD/41, GPD/71 (various papers and medals); MC:P131 (material from Peter Fullerton); MC:P136 (press cuttings on Magdalen rowing); MC:P145 (Charles Cozens papers); MC:P163 (letters from Edward VIII to Henry Bensley Wells); MC:P182 (Philip Quixano Henriques Simon papers)

Roger Hutchins, Well Rowed Magdalen!, Magdalen College Boat Club 1993

Henley Royal Regatta records, 1839 to 2004

## Rowing

R.D. Burnell, Swing Together, Oxford University Press 1952

R.D. Burnell, The Oxford and Cambridge Boat Race 1829-1953, Oxford University Press 1954

R.D. Burnell, Henley Regatta: A History, Oxford University Press 1957

Richard Burnell, Henley Royal Regatta, A Celebration of 150 Years, William Heinemann 1989

Richard Burnell and Geoffrey Page, The Brilliants, A History of the Leander Club, Leander Club 1977

L.S.R. Byrne and E.L. Churchill, The Eton Book of the River, Spottiswoode, Ballantyne and Co. 1935

Sir Theodore Cook, Henley Races, Oxford University Press 1919

Christopher Dodd, The Oxford and Cambridge Boat Race, Stanley Paul 1983

Christopher Dodd and John Marks, Battle of the Blues, P to M 2004

Christopher Dodd, The Story of World Rowing, Stanley Paul 1992

G.C. Drinkwater and T.R.B. Sanders, The University Boat Race, Official Centenary History 1829-1929, Cassell & Co. 1929

H.R.A. Edwards, The Way of the man with a Blade, Routledge & Kegan 1963

Eric Halladay, Rowing in England: A Social History: The Amateur Debate, Manchester University Press 1990

R.C. Lehmann, The Complete Oarsman, Methuen 1924

W.F. Macmichael, The Oxford and Cambridge Boat Races 1829-1869, Deighton, Bell & Co. 1870

Dr John E. Morgan, University Oars: being a Critical Enquiry into the after health of the men who rowed in the Boat Race, Macmillan & Co 1873

G.O. Nickalls, A Rainbow in the Sky, Chatto and Windus 1974

G.O. Nickalls and Dr P.C. Mallam, Rowing, Pitman 1939

Guy Nickalls, Life's a Pudding, Faber and Faber 1939

Iris Winifred Preston, From Newnham College Boat Club to C.U.W.B.C., 1992

Ogier Rysden, The Book of the Blues, F.E. Robinson 1900

The Rev W.E. Sherwood, Oxford Rowing: A History of Boat-Racing at Oxford from the Earliest Times, Henry Frowde 1900

Geo G.T. Treherne, Record of the University Boat Race 1829-1883, Bickers & Son 1884

Neil Wigglesworth, The Social History of English Rowing, Frank Cass 1992

## General

Janie Hampton, The Austerity Olympics: When the Games came to London in 1948, Aurum Press 2008

David Kynaston, The City of London, A World Of Its Own 1815-1890, Pimlico 1994

David Miller, Athens to Athens: The Official History of the Olympic Games and the I.O.C. 1894-2004, Mainstream Publishing 2003

Kenneth Nicholls Palmer, Ceremonial Barges on the River Thames: A History of the Barges of the City of London Livery, Unicorn Press 1997

Clare Sherriff, The Oxford College Barges their History and Architecture, Unicorn Press 2003

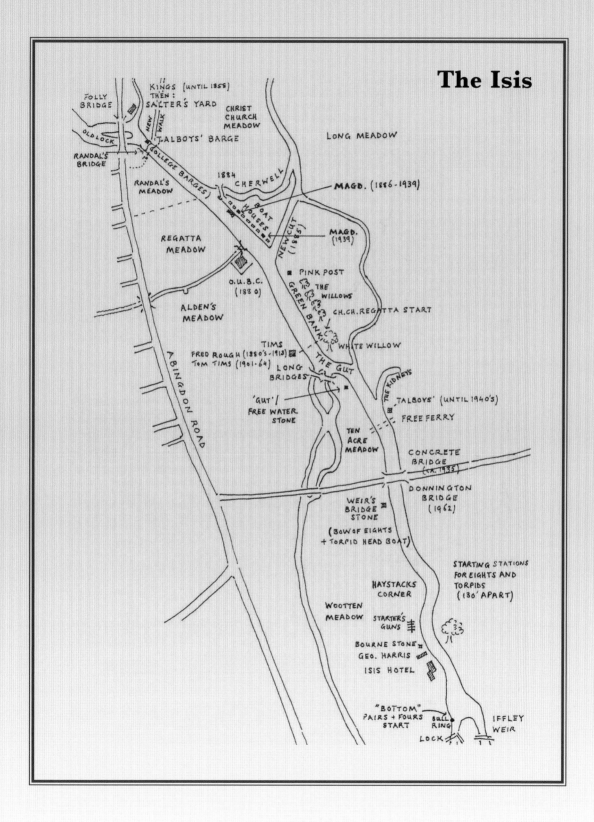

# The Isis

FOLLY BRIDGE

KINGS (UNTIL 1858) THEN: SALTER'S YARD

CHRIST CHURCH MEADOW

LONG MEADOW

NEW WALK

OLD LOCK

RANDAL'S BRIDGE

TALBOYS' BARGE

COLLEGE BARGES

RANDAL'S MEADOW

1884

CHERWELL

MAGD. (1886-1939)

BOAT HOUSES

REGATTA MEADOW

NEWCUT (1885)

MAGD. (1939)

O.U.B.C. (1880)

GREEN BANK

PINK POST

THE WILLOWS

CH. CH. REGATTA START

ALDEN'S MEADOW

TIMS

FRED ROUGH (1880's-1913)

TOM TIMS (1901-64)

THE GUT

WHITE WILLOW

LONG BRIDGES

THE KIDNEYS

'GUT' / FREE WATER STONE

TALBOYS' (UNTIL 1940's)

FREE FERRY

ABINGDON ROAD

TEN ACRE MEADOW

CONCRETE BRIDGE (CA. 1935)

DONNINGTON BRIDGE (1962)

WEIR'S BRIDGE STONE

(BOW OF EIGHTS + TORPID HEAD BOAT)

STARTING STATIONS FOR EIGHTS AND TORPIDS (130' APART)

HAYSTACKS CORNER

WOOTTEN MEADOW

STARTER'S GUNS

BOURNE STONE

GEO. HARRIS

ISIS HOTEL

"BOTTOM" PAIRS + FOURS START

BULL RING

LOCK

IFFLEY WEIR

## Photograph Acknowledgements

The author is very grateful to the following for the use of their images:

Peter Burnell p154
The Revd Jock Fletcher-Campbell p145
Heather Clary p247
Robin Dunbar p199
John Friend p45
Lizz Fullerton (née Stevens) p120-121, 128-129
Peter Fullerton p174
Andrew Gillan p94, 95, 107
Gathorne Girdlestone p47, 122, 130-131, 134
Henley Rowing Club p71
Henley Royal Regatta p55
Eric Houston p98
Imperial War Museum p110

Leander Club p89, 127, 151, 153
Magdalen College School p44, 45, 46, 69
Jock Mullard p250
Mark Nelson-Griffiths p117
Stella Newton p309
Peter Nordberg p 245
Oxford Mail p180
River and Rowing Museum p23
David Rutherford p170, 182, 185
Sanders of Oxford p30-31
Mark Simon p215
Alastair Stewart p276, 281
Chlöe Strevens p13, 250
The Times p32, 104
Vincent's Club p114
George Young p13